The Missionary Enterprise

THE MISSIONARY ENTERPRISE
Classic 19th Century Discourses
On the Conquering Power
Of the Gospel

Edited by
BARON STOW

Solid Ground Christian Books
Birmingham, Alabama USA

Solid Ground Christian Books
2090 Columbiana Rd, Suite 2000
Birmingham, AL 35216
205-443-0311
sgcb@charter.net
http://solid-ground-books.com

The Missionary Enterprise
CLASSIC DISCOURSES ON THE CONQUERING POWER OF THE GOSPEL

Edited by Baron Stow (1801-1869)

Taken from 1846 edition by Gould, Kendall and Lincoln, Boston, MA

Solid Ground Classic Reprints

First printing of new edition September 2005

Cover work by Borgo Design, Tuscaloosa, AL
Contact them at nelbrown@comcast.net

Special thanks to Ric Ergenbright for permission to use the image on the cover. Visit him at ricergenbright.org

ISBN: 1-59925-017-9

PREFACE.

The preparation of this volume was undertaken at the suggestion of others, whose opinions, ever entitled to respect, seemed to present a demand for service, which the Editor did not consider himself as at liberty to disregard. This claim he was the more happy to honor, as it afforded an opportunity, through the medium of secular enterprise, to promote an interest which he has long regarded as of primary and paramount importance. Whatever may be the measure of profit from the pecuniary investment, the hope is fondly cherished, both by the Publishers and the Editor, that large benefits, of a much higher order, will accrue to that noble Cause which it is especially intended to advance.

The task of selection has been, in some instances, peculiarly difficult. Several discourses, of great excellence, have been omitted, which, perhaps, would have been included, had not circumstances appeared to encourage the expectation, that a second series might be demanded. Should this volume be favorably received, another may succeed, comprising not only sermons, but a rich variety of addresses, essays, and eloquent appeals, all pertaining to the same great subject — Christian Missions. Many of this class of productions are too valuable to be left scattered in ephemeral forms, and should be gathered up, and added to the increasing stock of our Missionary literature, and thus made to extend and perpetuate their salutary efficiency.

Corrections and additions have been made, by some of the authors, with special reference to this publication. Marginal notes and references, not necessary to be retained, have been omitted; and, in a few instances, the text has been slightly abridged. Two of the sermons are original, having been printed from the authors' manuscripts. Obligations are due to the proprietors of Dr. Mason's Works, for permission to transfer into this compilation the valuable sermon, entitled "Messiah's Throne."

The reader of these Discourses will perhaps discover, that the authors differ in their exhibitions of statistical facts. These apparent discrepancies will be sufficiently explained, by a reference to so much of the history of the respective productions, as may be found in the table of contents. They were delivered, not only by different men, but also at different periods, and before the public bodies of various Christian denominations; and therefore must be, in some respects, modified by the diversity of circumstances in which they had their origin.

One fact, it is confidently believed, will fix the admiration of every candid reader; and that is, the extraordinary *harmony* of both spirit and sentiment which appears throughout the volume. Each performer executes his own chosen part in the chorus, thus avoiding the monotony of *unison*, and yet the nicest ear will seldom detect a discordant note.

The spirit of Missions is the spirit of Concord. The key-note was struck on the plains of Bethlehem; and all who have sympathy with the angelic announcement, are sure to think, feel, utter, and act in concert, both with the heavenly host, and with one another.

Bowdoin Street, May, 1846.

CONTENTS.

I.

THE MORAL DIGNITY OF THE MISSIONARY ENTERPRISE.

BY REV. FRANCIS WAYLAND, D. D.,

PRESIDENT OF BROWN UNIVERSITY, PROVIDENCE, R. I.

Delivered before the Boston Baptist Foreign Mission Society, October 26, 1823. - 1

II.

ARGUMENTS FOR MISSIONS.

BY REV. EDWARD D. GRIFFIN, D. D.,

LATE PRESIDENT OF WILLIAMS COLLEGE, WILLIAMSTOWN, MASS.

Delivered before the American Board of Commissioners for Foreign Missions, at Middletown, Conn., September 14, 1826. - - - - - - - 22

III.

THE THEORY OF MISSIONS TO THE HEATHEN.

BY REV. RUFUS ANDERSON, D. D.,

ONE OF THE SECRETARIES OF THE AMERICAN BOARD OF COMMISSIONERS FOR FOREIGN MISSIONS.

Delivered in Ware, Mass., at the ordination of Mr. Edward Webb, as a Missionary to the heathen, October 23, 1845. - - - - - - - 37

CONTENTS.

IV.

JESUS THE GREAT MISSIONARY.

BY REV. EDWARD N. KIRK,

PASTOR OF THE MOUNT VERNON CHURCH, BOSTON.

Delivered in Boston, at the ordination of Mr. Samuel Wolcott, as a Foreign Missionary, Nov. 3, 1839. - - - - - - - - - - - 55

V.

CHRIST, A HOME MISSIONARY.

BY REV. WILLIAM R. WILLIAMS, D. D.,

PASTOR OF AMITY STREET BAPTIST CHURCH, NEW YORK.

Delivered in Philadelphia, before the American Baptist Home Mission Society, June 7, 1836. - - - - - - - - - - - - 78

VI.

EFFICIENCY OF PRIMITIVE MISSIONS.

BY REV. BARON STOW,

PASTOR OF BALDWIN PLACE CHURCH, BOSTON.

Delivered in New York, before the General Convention of the Baptist Denomination in the United States, April 25, 1838. - - - - - - - 99

VII.

RESOURCES OF THE ADVERSARY, AND MEANS OF THEIR DESTRUCTION.

BY REV. LYMAN BEECHER, D. D.,

PRESIDENT OF LANE SEMINARY, CINCINNATI, OHIO.

Delivered in New York, before the American Board of Commissioners for Foreign Missions, October 12, 1827. - - - - - - - - - - 121

VIII.

THE EARTH FILLED WITH THE GLORY OF GOD.

BY REV. SAMUEL MILLER, D. D.,

PROFESSOR IN THE THEOLOGICAL SEMINARY, PRINCETON, N. J.

Delivered in Baltimore, before the American Board of Commissioners for Foreign Missions, September 9, 1835. - - - - - - - - - 143

IX.

INCREASE OF FAITH NECESSARY TO THE SUCCESS OF CHRISTIAN MISSIONS.

BY REV. WILLIAM R. WILLIAMS, D. D.,

PASTOR OF AMITY STREET BAPTIST CHURCH, NEW YORK.

Delivered in New York, at the Annual Meeting of the Board of Managers of the Baptist General Convention, April 30, 1834. - - - - - - 164

X.

THE CROSS.

BY REV. RICHARD FULLER, D. D.,

PASTOR OF THE BAPTIST CHURCH, BEAUFORT, S. C.

Delivered in Baltimore, before the General Convention of the Baptist Denomination in the United States, April 28, 1841. - - - - - - - 187

XI.

THE GOSPEL ADAPTED TO THE WANTS OF THE WORLD.

BY REV. NATHAN S. S. BEMAN, D. D.,

PASTOR OF THE FIRST PRESBYTERIAN CHURCH, TROY, N. Y.

Delivered in Providence, R. I., before the American Board of Commissioners for Foreign Missions, September 9, 1840. - - - - - - - - 208

XII.

THE MORAL ELEVATION OF THE CHURCH ESSENTIAL TO MISSIONARY SUCCESS.

BY REV. GEORGE B. IDE,

PASTOR OF THE FIRST BAPTIST CHURCH, PHILADELPHIA.

Delivered in Providence, R. I., at the Annual Meeting of the Board of Managers of the Baptist General Convention, April 30, 1845. - - - - - 225

XIII.

THE BEARINGS OF MODERN COMMERCE ON THE PROGRESS OF MODERN MISSIONS.

BY REV. JOHN S. STONE, D. D.,

RECTOR OF CHRIST CHURCH, BROOKLYN, N. Y.

Delivered in New Haven, Conn., before the Board of Missions of the Protestant Episcopal Church in the United States, June 19, 1839. - - - - 247

XIV.

MESSIAH'S THRONE.

BY REV. JOHN M. MASON, D. D.,

LATE PASTOR OF THE CEDAR STREET CHURCH, NEW YORK.

Delivered in London, before the London Missionary Society, May 13, 1802. - 272

XV.

MISSIONARY POWER.

BY REV. BARON STOW,

PASTOR OF BALDWIN PLACE CHURCH, BOSTON.

Delivered before the Society for Missionary Inquiry, in the Literary and Theological Institution, Hamilton, New York, August 17, 1842. - - - - 289

THE MISSIONARY ENTERPRISE.

THE MORAL DIGNITY OF THE MISSIONARY ENTERPRISE.

BY

REV. FRANCIS WAYLAND, D. D.

The field is the world.—MATTHEW 13: 38.

PHILOSOPHERS have speculated much concerning a process of sensation, which has commonly been denominated the emotion of sublimity. Aware that, like any other simple feeling, it must be incapable of definition, they have seldom attempted to define it; but, content with remarking the occasions on which it is excited, have told us that it arises in general from the contemplation of whatever is vast in nature, splendid in intellect, or lofty in morals. Or, to express the same idea somewhat varied, in the language of a critic of antiquity,* "that alone is truly sublime, of which the conception is vast, the effect irresistible, and the remembrance scarcely if ever to be erased."

But although philosophers alone have written about this emotion, they are far from being the only men who have felt it. The untutored peasant, when he has seen the autumnal tempest collecting between the hills, and, as it advanced, enveloping in misty obscurity, village and hamlet, forest and meadow, has tasted the sublime in all its reality; and, whilst the thunder has rolled and the lightning flashed around him, has exulted in the view of nature moving forth in her majesty. The untaught sailor-boy, listlessly hearkening to the

---

* Longinus, Sect. VII.

idle ripple of the midnight wave, when on a sudden he has thought upon the unfathomable abyss beneath him, and the wide waste of waters around him, and the infinite expanse above him, has enjoyed to the full the emotion of sublimity, whilst his inmost soul has trembled at the vastness of its own conceptions. But why need I multiply illustrations from nature? Who does not recollect the emotion he has felt whilst surveying aught in the material world of terror or of vastness?

And this sensation is not produced by grandeur in material objects alone. It is also excited on most of those occasions in which we see man tasking to the uttermost the energies of his intellectual or moral nature. Through the long lapse of centuries, who without emotion has read of Leonidas and his three hundred throwing themselves as a barrier before the myriads of Xerxes, and contending unto death for the liberties of Greece!

But we need not turn to classic story to find all that is great in human action; we find it in our own times and in the history of our own country. Who is there of us that even in the nursery has not felt his spirit stir within him, when with childlike wonder he has listened to the story of Washington? And although the terms of the narrative were scarcely intelligible, yet the young soul kindled at the thought of one man's working out the deliverance of a nation. And as our understanding, strengthened by age, was at last able to grasp the detail of this transaction, we saw that our infantile conceptions had fallen far short of its grandeur. Oh! if an American citizen ever exults in the contemplation of all that is sublime in human enterprise, it is when, bringing to mind the men who first conceived the idea of this nation's independence, he beholds them estimating the power of her oppressor, the resources of her citizens, deciding in their collected might that this nation should be free, and through the long years of trial that ensued, never blenching from their purpose, but freely redeeming the pledge they had given, to consecrate to it, "their lives, their fortunes, and their sacred honor."

> "Patriots have toiled, and in their country's cause
> Bled nobly, and their deeds, as they deserve,
> Receive proud recompense. We give in charge
> Their names to the sweet lyre. The historic muse,
> Proud of her treasure, marches with it down
> To latest times; and sculpture in her turn
> Gives bond, in stone and ever-during brass,
> To guard them and immortalize her trust."

It is not in the field of patriotism alone that deeds have been achieved to which history has awarded the palm of moral sublimity. There have lived men, in whom the name of patriot has been merged in that of philanthropist; who, looking with an eye of compassion over the face of the earth, have felt for the miseries of our race, and have put forth their calm might to wipe off one blot from the marred and stained escutcheon of human nature, to strike off one form of suffering from the catalogue of human wo. Such a man was Howard. Surveying our world like a spirit of the blessed, he beheld the misery of the captive, he heard the groaning of the prisoner. His determination was fixed. He resolved single-handed to gauge and to measure one form of unpitied, unheeded wretchedness, and, bringing it out to the sunshine of public observation, to work its utter extermination. And he well knew what this undertaking would cost him. He knew what he had to hazard from the infection of dungeons, to endure from the fatigues of inhospitable travel, and to brook from the insolence of legalized oppression. He knew that he was devoting himself upon the altar of philanthropy, and he willingly devoted himself. He had marked out his destiny, and he hastened forward to its accomplishment, with an intensity "which the nature of the human mind forbade to be more, and the character of the individual forbade to be less."* Thus he commenced a new era in the history of benevolence. And hence the name of Howard will be associated with all that is sublime in mercy, until the final consummation of all things.

Such a man is Clarkson, who, looking abroad, beheld the sufferings of Africa, and looking at home, saw his country stained with her blood. We have seen him, laying aside the vestments of the priesthood, consecrate himself to the holy purpose of rescuing a continent from rapine and murder, and of erasing this one sin from the book of his nation's iniquities. We have seen him and his fellow philanthropists for twenty years never waver from their purpose. We have seen them persevere amidst neglect and obloquy and contempt and persecution, until the cry of the oppressed having roused the sensibilities of the nation, the "Island Empress" rose in her might, and said to this foul traffic in human flesh, Thus far shalt thou go, and no farther.

---

* Foster's Essay.

It will not be doubted that in such actions as these, there is much which may truly be called the moral sublime. If, then, we should attentively consider them, we might perhaps ascertain what must be the elements of that enterprise, which may lay claim to this high appellation. It cannot be expected that on this occasion we should analyze them critically. It will, however, we think, be found, upon examination, that to that enterprise alone has been awarded the meed of sublimity, of which the conception was vast, the execution arduous, and the means to be employed simple but efficient. Were not the object vast, it could not arrest our attention. Were not its accomplishment arduous, none of the nobler energies of man being tasked in its execution, we should see nothing to admire. Were not the means to that accomplishment simple, our whole conception being vague, the impression would be feeble. Were they not efficient, the intensest exertion could only terminate in failure and disgrace.

And here we may remark, that wherever these elements have combined in any undertaking, public sentiment has generally united in pronouncing it sublime, and history has recorded its achievements among the noblest proofs of the dignity of man. Malice may for a while have frowned, and interest opposed; men who could neither grasp what was vast, nor feel what was morally great, may have ridiculed. But all this has soon passed away. Human nature is not to be changed by the opposition of interest or the laugh of folly. There is still enough of dignity in man to respect what is great, and to venerate what is benevolent. The cause of man has at last gained the suffrages of man. It has advanced steadily onward, and left ridicule to wonder at the impotence of its shaft, and malice to weep over the inefficacy of its hate.

And we bless God that it is so. It is cheering to observe, that amidst so much that is debasing, there is still something that is ennobling in the character of man. It is delightful to know that there are times when his morally bedimmed eye "beams keen with honor;" that there is yet a redeeming spirit within him, which exults in enterprises of great pith and moment. We love our race the better for every such fact we discover concerning it, and bow with more reverence to the dignity of human nature. We rejoice that, shattered as has been the edifice, there yet may be discovered now and then a massive pillar, and here and there a well turned arch, which remind us of the symmetry of its former proportions, and the perfection of its original structure.

Having paid this our honest tribute to the dignity of man, we must pause, and shed a tear over somewhat which reminds us of any thing other than his dignity. Whilst the general assertion is true, that he is awake to all that is sublime in nature, and much that is sublime in morals, there is reason to believe that there is a single class of objects, whose contemplation thrills all heaven with rapture, at which he can gaze unmelted and unmoved. The pen of inspiration has recorded, that the cross of Christ, whose mysteries the angels desire to look into, was to the tasteful and erudite Greek, foolishness. And we fear that cases very analogous to this may be witnessed at the present day. But why, my hearers, should it be so? Why should so vast a dissimilarity of moral taste exist between seraphs who bow before the throne, and men who dwell upon the footstool? Why is it that the man, whose soul swells with ecstasy whilst viewing the innumerable suns of midnight, feels no emotion of sublimity when thinking of their Creator? Why is it that an enterprise of patriotism presents itself to his imagination beaming with celestial beauty, whilst the enterprise of redeeming love is without form or comeliness? Why should the noblest undertaking of mercy, if it only combine among its essential elements the distinctive principles of the gospel, become at once stale, flat, and unprofitable? When there is joy in heaven over one sinner that repenteth, why is it that the enterprise of proclaiming peace on earth, and good will to man, fraught, as it would seem, with more than angelic benignity, should to many of our fellow men appear worthy of nothing better than neglect or obloquy?

The reason for all this we shall not on this occasion pretend to assign. We have only time to express our regret that such should be the fact. Confining ourselves therefore to the bearing which this moral bias has upon the missionary cause, it is with pain we are obliged to believe, that there is a large and most respectable portion of our fellow citizens, for many of whom we entertain every sentiment of personal esteem, and to whose opinions on most other subjects we bow with unfeigned deference, who look with perfect apathy upon the present system of exertions for evangelizing the heathen; and we have been greatly misinformed, if there be not another, though a very different class, who consider these

1*

exertions a subject for ridicule. Perhaps it may tend somewhat to arouse the apathy of the one party, as well as to moderate the contempt of the other, if we can show that this very missionary cause combines within itself the elements of all that is sublime in human purpose, nay, combines them in a loftier perfection than any other enterprise, which was ever linked with the destinies of man. To show this will be our design; and in prosecuting it, we shall direct your attention to the grandeur of the object; the arduousness of its execution; and the nature of the means on which we rely for success.

I. THE GRANDEUR OF THE OBJECT. In the most enlarged sense of the terms, *The field is the World.* Our design is radically to affect the temporal and eternal interests of the whole race of man. We have surveyed this field *statistically*, and find, that of the eight hundred millions who inhabit our globe, but two hundred millions have any knowledge of the religion of Jesus Christ. Of these we are willing to allow that but one half are his real disciples, and that therefore there are seven of the eight hundred millions to whom the gospel must be sent.

We have surveyed this field *geographically*. We have looked upon our own continent, and have seen that, with the exception of a narrow strip of thinly settled country, from the Gulf of St. Lawrence to the mouth of the Mississippi, the whole of this new world lieth in wickedness. Hordes of ruthless savages roam the wilderness of the West, and men almost as ignorant of the spirit of the gospel, are struggling for independence in the South.

We have looked over Europe, and beheld there one nation putting forth her energies in the cause of evangelizing the world. We have looked for another such nation; but it is not to be found. A few others are beginning to awake. Most of them, however, yet slumber. Many are themselves in need of missionaries. Nay, we know not but the movement of the cause of man in Europe is at present retrograde. There seems too evidently a coalition formed of the powers that be, to check the progress of moral and intellectual improvement, and to rivet again on the human mind the manacles of papal superstition. God only knows how soon the reaction will commence, which shall shake the continent to its centre, scatter thrones and sceptres and all the insignia of prescriptive authority, like the dust of the summer threshing floor, and establish throughout the Christian world representative governments, on the broad basis of common sense and inalienable right.

We have looked over Africa, and have seen that upon one little portion, reclaimed from brutal idolatry by missionaries, the Sun of Righteousness has shined. It is a land of Goshen, where they have light in their dwellings. Upon all the remainder of this vast continent, there broods a moral darkness, impervious as that which once veiled her own Egypt, on that prolonged and fearful night when no man knew his brother.

We have looked upon Asia, and have seen its northern nations, though under the government of a Christian prince, scarcely nominally Christian. On the West, it is spell-bound by Mohammedan delusion. To the south, from the Persian gulf, to the sea of Kamtschatka, including also its numberless islands, except where here and there a Syrian church, or a missionary station twinkles amidst the gloom; the whole of this immense portion of the human race is sitting in the region and shadow of death. Such then is the field for our exertion. It encircles the whole family of man, it includes every unevangelized being of the species to which we belong. We have thus surveyed the missionary field, that we may know how great is the undertaking to which we stand committed.

We have also made an estimate of the *miseries* of this world. We have seen how in many places the human mind, shackled by ignorance and enfeebled by vice, has dwindled almost to the standard of a brute. Our indignation has kindled at hearing of men immortal as ourselves, bowing down and worshipping a wandering beggar, or paying adoration to reptiles and to stones.

Not only is intellect, everywhere under the dominion of idolatry, prostrated; beyond the boundaries of Christendom, on every side the dark places of the earth are filled with the habitations of cruelty. We have mourned over the savage ferocity of the Indians of our western wilderness. We have turned to Africa, and seen almost the whole continent a prey to lawless banditti, or else bowing down in the most revolting idolatry. We have descended along her coast, and beheld villages burnt or depopulated, fields laid waste, and her people, who have escaped destruction, naked and famishing, flee to their forests at the sight of a stranger. We have asked, What fearful visitation of Heaven has laid these settlements in ruins? What destroying pestilence has swept over this land, consigning to oblivion almost its entire population? What mean the smoking ruins of so many habitations? And why is yon fresh sod crimsoned and slippery with the traces of recent murder? We have been pointed to the dark slave-ship hovering over her coast, and have been told that two hundred thousand defenceless beings are annually stolen away, to be murdered on their passage, or consigned for life to a captivity more terrible than death!

We have turned to Asia, and beheld how the demon of her idolatry has worse than debased, has brutalized the mind of man. Everywhere his despotism has been grievous; here, with merciless tyranny, he has exulted in the misery of his victims. He has rent from the human heart all that was endearing in the charities of life. He has taught the mother to tear away the infant as it smiled in her bosom, and cast it, the shrieking prey, to contending alligators. He has taught the son to light the funeral pile, and to witness, unmoved, the dying agonies of his widowed, murdered mother!

We have looked upon all this; and our object is, to purify the whole earth from these abominations. Our object will not have been accomplished till the tomahawk shall be buried forever, and the tree of peace spread its broad branches from the Atlantic to the Pacific; until a thousand smiling villages shall be reflected from the waves of the Missouri, and the distant valleys of the West echo with the song of the reaper; till the wilderness and the solitary place shall have been glad for us, and the desert has rejoiced and blossomed as the rose.

Our labors are not to cease, until the last slave-ship shall have visited the coast of Africa, and, the nations of Europe and America having long since redressed her aggravated wrongs, Ethiopia, from the Mediterranean to the Cape, shall have stretched forth her hand unto God.

How changed will then be the face of Asia! Brahmins and sooders and castes and shasters will have passed away, like the mist which rolls up the mountain's side before the rising glories of a summer morning, while the land on which it rested, shining forth in all its loveliness, shall, from its numberless habitations, send forth the high praises of God and the Lamb. The Hindoo mother will gaze upon her infant with the same tenderness which throbs in the breast of any one of you who now hears me, and the Hindoo son will pour into the wounded bosom of his widowed parent, the oil of peace and consolation.

In a word, point us to the loveliest village that smiles upon a Scottish or New England landscape, and compare it with the filthiness and brutality of a Caffrarian kraal, and we tell you that our object is to render that Caffrarian kraal as happy and gladsome as that Scottish or New England village. Point us to the spot on the face of the earth where liberty is best understood and most perfectly enjoyed, where intellect shoots forth in its richest luxuriance, and where all the kindlier feelings of the heart are constantly seen in their most graceful exercise; point us to the loveliest and happiest neighborhood in the world on which we dwell; and we tell you that our object is to render this whole earth, with all its nations and kindreds and tongues and people, as happy, nay, happier than that neighborhood.

We have considered these beings as immortal, and candidates for an eternity of happiness or misery. And we cannot avoid the belief that they are exposed to eternal misery. Here you will observe the question with us is not, whether a heathen, unlearned in the gospel, can be saved. We are willing to admit that he may. But if he be saved, he must possess holiness of heart; for without holiness no man shall see the Lord. And where shall we find holy heathen? Where is there the vestige of purity of heart among unevangelized nations? It is in vain to talk about the innocence of these children of nature. It is in vain to tell us of their graceful mythology. Their gods are such as lust makes welcome. Of their very religious services, it is a shame even to speak. To settle the question concerning their future destiny, it would only seem necessary to ask, What would be the character of that future state, in which those principles of heart which the whole history of the heathen world develops, were suffered to operate in their unrestrained malignity?

No! solemn as is the thought, we do believe, that dying in their present state, they will be exposed to all that is awful in the wrath of Almighty God. And we do believe that God so loved the world, that he gave his only begotten Son, that whosoever believeth on him should not perish, but have everlasting life. Our object is to convey to those who are perishing the news of this salvation. It is to furnish every family upon the face of the whole earth with the word of God written in its own language, and to send to every neighborhood a preacher of the cross of Christ. Our object will not be accomplished until every idol temple shall have been utterly abolished, and a temple to Jehovah erected in its room; until this earth, instead of being a theatre on which immortal beings are preparing by crime for eternal condemnation, shall become one universal temple, in which the children of men are learning the anthems of the blessed above, and becoming meet to join the general assembly and church of the first-born, whose names are written in heaven. Our design will not be completed until

> "One song employs all nations, and all cry
> Worthy the Lamb, for he was slain for us;
> The dwellers in the vales, and on the rocks
> Shout to each other, and the mountain tops
> From distant mountains catch the flying joy;
> Till, nation after nation taught the strain,
> Earth rolls the rapturous hosanna round."

The object of the missionary enterprise embraces every child of Adam. It is vast as the race to whom its operations are of necessity limited. It would confer upon every individual on earth, all that intellectual and moral cultivation can bestow. It would rescue a world from the indignation and wrath, tribulation and anguish, reserved for every son of man that doeth evil, and give it a title to glory, honor, and immortality. You see, then, that our object is, not only to affect every individual of the species, but to affect him in the momentous extremes of infinite happiness and infinite wo. And now we ask, What object ever undertaken by man can compare with this same design of evangelizing the world? Patriotism itself fades away before it, and acknowledges the supremacy of an enterprise, which seizes, with so strong a grasp, upon both the temporal and eternal destinies of the whole family of man.

But all this is not to be accomplished without laborious exertion. Hence we remark,

II. THE MISSIONARY UNDERTAKING IS ARDUOUS ENOUGH TO CALL INTO ACTION THE NOBLEST ENERGIES OF MAN.

Its arduousness is explained in one word, our *Field is the World*. Our object is to effect an entire moral revolution in the whole human race. Its arduousness then results of necessity from its magnitude.

I need not say to an audience acquainted with the nature of the human mind, that a large moral mass is not easily and permanently affected. A little leaven does not soon leaven the whole lump. To produce a change even of speculative opinion upon a single nation, is an undertaking not easily accomplished. In the case before us, not a nation, but a world is to be *regenerated:* therefore the change which we would effect is far from being merely speculative. If any man be in Christ, he is a new creature. Nothing short of this new creation will answer our purpose. We go forth, not to persuade men to turn from one idol to another, but to turn universally from idols to serve the living God. We call upon those who are earthly, sensual, devilish, to set their affections on things above. We go forth exhorting men to forsake every cherished lust, and present themselves a living sacrifice, holy and acceptable unto God. And this mighty moral revolution is to be effected, not in a family, a tribe, or a nation, but in a world which lieth in wickedness.

We have to operate upon a race divided into different nations, speaking a thousand different languages, under every different form of government from absolute inertness to unbridled tyranny, and inhabiting every district of country, salubrious or deadly, from the equator to the poles. To all these nations must the gospel be sent, into all these languages must the Bible be translated, to all these climes, salubrious or deadly, must the missionary penetrate, and under all these forms of government, mild or despotic, must he preach Christ and him crucified.

Besides, we shall frequently interfere with the more sordid interests of men; and we expect them to increase the difficulties of our undertaking. If we can turn the heathen to God, many a source of unholy traffick will be dried up, and many a convenience of unhallowed gratification taken away. And hence we may expect that the traffickers in human flesh, the disciples of mammon, and the devotees of pleasure, will be against us. From the heathen themselves we have the blackest darkness of ignorance to dispel. We have to assault systems venerable for their antiquity, and interwoven with everything that is proud in a nation's history. Above all, we have to oppose the depravity of the human heart, grown still more inveterate by ages of continuance in unrestrained iniquity. In a word, we go forth to urge upon a world dead in trespasses and sins, a thorough renewal of heart, and an universal reformation of practice.

Brief as is this view of the difficulties which surround us, and time will not allow us to state them more in detail, you see that our undertaking is, as we said, arduous enough to task to the uttermost the noblest energies of man.

This enterprise requires consummate wisdom in the missionary who goes abroad, as well as in those who manage the concerns of a society at home. He who goes forth unprotected, to preach Christ to despotic or badly governed nations, must be wise as a serpent, and harmless as a dove. With undeviating firmness upon everything essential, he must combine the most yielding facility upon all that is unimportant. And thus while he goes forth in the spirit and power of Elias, he must at the same time become all things to all men, that by all means he may gain some. Great abilities are also required in him who conducts the mission at home. He must awaken, animate, and direct the sentiments of a very large portion of the community in which he resides, whilst at the same time, through a hundred different agents, he is exerting a powerful influence upon half as many nations a thousand or ten thousand miles off. Indeed it is hazarding nothing to predict, that if efforts for the extension of the gospel continue to multiply with their present ratio of increase, as great abilities will, in a few years, be required for transacting the business of a missionary society, as for conducting the affairs of a political cabinet.

The missionary undertaking calls for perseverance; a perseverance of that character, which, having once formed its purpose, never wavers from it till death. And if ever this attribute has been so exhibited as to challenge the respect of every man of feeling, it has been in such instances as are recorded in the history of the missions to Greenland and to the South Sea Islands, where we beheld men, for fifteen or twenty years, suffer everything but martyrdom, and then, seeing no fruit from their labor, resolve to labor on till death, if so be they might at last save one benighted heathen from the error of his ways.

This undertaking calls for self-denial of the highest and holiest character. He who engages in it must, at the very outset, dismiss every wish to stipulate for anything but the mere favor of God. His first act is a voluntary exile from all that a refined education loves; and every other act must be in unison with this. The salvation of the heathen is the object for which he sacrifices, and is willing to sacrifice, every thing that the heart clings to on earth. For this object he would live; for this he would die; nay, he would live any where, and die any how, if so be he might rescue one soul from everlasting wo.

Hence you see that this undertaking requires courage. It is not the courage which, wrought up by the stimulus of popular applause, can rush now and then upon the cannon's mouth; it is the courage which, alone and unapplauded, will, year after year, look death, every moment, in the face, and never shrink from its purpose. It is a principle which will "make a man intrepidly dare every thing which can attack or oppose him within the whole sphere of mortality, retain his purpose unshaken amidst the ruins of the world, and press toward his object while death is impending over him." * Such was the spirit which spake by the mouth of an Apostle when he said, And now I go bound in the spirit unto Jerusalem, not knowing the things which shall befall me there; save that the Holy Ghost witnesseth in every city, saying that bonds and afflictions abide me. Yet none of these things move me; neither count I my life dear unto myself, so that I may finish my course with joy, and the ministry which I have received of the Lord Jesus.

But above all, the missionary undertaking requires faith, in its holiest and sublimest exercise. And let it not be supposed that we speak at random, when we mention the sublimity of faith. "Whatever," says the British moralist, "withdraws us from the power of the senses; whatever makes the past, the distant, or the future predominate over the present, advances us in the dignity of thinking beings." † And when we speak of faith, we refer to a principle which gives substance to things hoped for, and evidence to things not seen; which, bending her keen glance on the eternal weight of glory, makes it a constant motive to holy enterprise; which, fixing her eagle eye upon the infinite of future, makes it bear right well upon the purposes of to-day; a principle which enables a poor feeble tenant of the dust to take strong hold upon the perfections of Jehovah; and, fastening his hopes to the very throne of the Eternal, "bid earth roll, nor feel its idle whirl." This principle is the unfailing support of the missionary through the long years of his toilsome pilgrimage; and, when he is compared with the heroes of this world, it is peculiar to him. By as much

---

* Foster. † Tour to the Hebrides, Iona.

then as the Christian enterprise calls into being this one principle, the noblest that can attach to the character of a creature, by so much does its execution surpass in sublimity every other.

III. Let us consider THE MEANS BY WHICH THIS MORAL REVOLUTION IS TO BE EFFECTED. It is, in a word, by the preaching of Jesus Christ and him crucified. It is by going forth and telling the lost children of men, that God so loved the world, that he gave his only begotten Son to die for them; and by all the eloquence of such an appeal to entreat them, for Christ's sake, to be reconciled unto God. This is the lever by which, we believe, the moral universe is to be raised; this is the instrument by which a sinful world is to be regenerated.

And consider the commanding simplicity of this means, devised by Omniscience to effect a purpose so glorious. This world is to be restored to more than it lost by the fall, by the simple annunciation of the love of God in Christ Jesus. Here we behold means apparently the weakest, employed to effect the most magnificent of purposes. And how plainly does this bespeak the agency of the omnipotent God! The means which effect his greatest purposes in the kingdom of nature, are simple and unostentatious; while those which man employs are complicated and tumultuous. How many intellects are tasked, how many hands are wearied, how many arts exhausted in preparing for the event of a single battle; and how great is the tumult of the moment of decision! In all this, man only imitates the inferior agents of nature. The autumnal tempest, whose sphere of action is limited to a little spot upon our little world, comes forth attended by the roar of thunder and the flash of lightning; while the attraction of gravitation, that stupendous force which binds together the mighty masses of the material universe, acts silently. In the sublimest of natural transactions, the greatest result is ascribed to the simplest, the most unique of causes. He spake and it was done; he commanded and it stood fast.

Contemplate the benevolence of these means. In practice, the precepts of the gospel may be summed up in the single command, Thou shalt love the Lord thy God with all thy heart, and thy neighbor as thyself. We expect to teach one man obedience to this command, and that he will feel obliged to teach his neighbor, who will feel obliged to teach others, who are again to become teachers, until the whole world shall be peopled with one family of brethren. Animosity is to be done away by inculcating universally the obligation of love. In this manner we expect to teach rulers justice, and subjects submission; to open the heart of the miser, and unloose the grasp of the oppressor. It is thus we expect the time to be hastened onward when men shall beat their swords into ploughshares, and their spears into pruning-hooks; when nations shall no more lift up sword against nation, neither shall they learn war any more.

With this process, compare the means by which men, on the principles of this world, effect a melioration in the condition of their species. Their almost universal agent is, threatened or inflicted misery. And, from the nature of the case, it cannot be otherwise. Without altering the disposition of the heart, they only attempt to control its exercise. And they must control it by showing their power to make the indulgence of that disposition the source of more misery than happiness. Hence when men confer a benefit upon a portion of their brethren, it is generally preceded by a protracted struggle to decide which can inflict most, or which can suffer longest. Hence the arm of the patriot is generally and of necessity bathed in blood. Hence with the shouts of victory from the nation he has delivered, there arise also the sigh of the widow, and the weeping of the orphan. Man produces good by the apprehension or the infliction of evil. The gospel produces good by the universal diffusion of the principles of benevolence. In the former case, one party must generally suffer; in the latter, all parties are certainly more happy. The one, like the mountain torrent, may fertilize now and then a valley beneath, but not until it has wildly swept away the forest above, and disfigured the lovely landscape with many an unseemly scar. Not so the other;

> "It droppeth as the gentle dew from heaven
> Upon the place beneath; it is twice blessed;
> It blesseth him that gives, and him that takes."

Consider the efficacy of these means. The reasons which teach us to rely upon them with confidence may be thus briefly stated.

1. We see that all which is really terrific in the misery of man results from the disease of his moral nature. If this can

be healed, man may be restored to happiness. Now the gospel of Jesus Christ is the remedy devised by Omniscience specifically for this purpose, and therefore we do certainly know that it will inevitably succeed.

2. It is easy to be seen, that universal obedience to the command, Thou shalt love the Lord thy God with all thy heart, and thy neighbor as thyself, would make this world a heaven. But nothing other than the gospel of Christ can persuade men to this obedience. Reason cannot do it; philosophy cannot do it; civilization cannot do it. The cross of Christ alone has power to bend the stubborn will to obedience, and melt the frozen heart to love. For, said one who had experienced its efficacy, the love of Christ constraineth us, because we thus judge, that if one died for all, then were all dead; and that he died for all, that they which live should not live to themselves, but unto Him who died for them, and rose again.

3. The preaching of the cross of Christ is a remedy for the miseries of the fall which has been tested by the experience of eighteen hundred years, and has never in a single instance failed. Its efficacy has been proved by human beings of all ages, from the lisping infant to the sinner an hundred years old. All climates have witnessed its power. From the ice-bound cliffs of Greenland to the banks of the voluptuous Ganges, the simple story of Christ crucified has turned men from darkness to light, and from the power of Satan unto God. Its effect has been the same with men of the most dissimilar conditions; from the abandoned inhabitant of Newgate, to the dweller in the palaces of kings. It has been equally sovereign amidst the scattered inhabitants of the forest and the crowded population of the densest metropolis. Every where and at all times it has been the power of God unto salvation to every one that believeth.

4. And lastly, we know from the word of the living God, that it will be successful, until this whole world has been redeemed from the effects of man's first disobedience. As truly as I live, saith Jehovah, all the earth shall be filled with the glory of the Lord. Ask of me, saith he to his Son, and I will give thee the heathen for thine inheritance, and the uttermost parts of the earth for thy possession. In the Revelation which he gave to his servant John of things which should shortly come to pass; I heard, said the Apostle, great voices in heaven, saying, The kingdoms of this world

are become the kingdoms of our Lord, and of his Christ, and he shall reign forever and ever. Here then is the ground of our unwavering confidence. Heaven and earth shall pass away, but one jot or one tittle shall in no wise pass from the word of God, until all be fulfilled. Such, then, are the means on which we rely for the accomplishment of our object, and such the grounds upon which we rest our confidence of success.

And now, my hearers, deliberately consider the nature of the missionary enterprise. Reflect upon the dignity of its object; the high moral and intellectual powers which are to be called forth in its execution; the simplicity, benevolence, and efficacy of the means by which all this is to be achieved; and we ask you, Does not every other enterprise to which man ever put forth his strength dwindle into insignificance, before that of preaching Christ crucified to a lost and perishing world?

Engaged in such an object, and supported by such assurances, you may readily suppose, we can very well bear the contempt of those who would point at us the finger of scorn. It is written, In the last days there shall be scoffers. We regret that it should be so. We regret that men should oppose an enterprise, of which the chief object is, to turn sinners unto holiness. We pity them, and we will pray for them; for we consider their situation far other than enviable. We recollect that it was once said by the Divine Missionary, to the first band which he commissioned, He that despiseth you, despiseth me, and he that despiseth me, despiseth him that sent me. So that this very contempt may at last involve them in a controversy infinitely more serious than they at present anticipate. The reviler of missions, and the missionary of the cross, must both stand before the judgment-seat of Him who said, Go ye into all the world, and preach the gospel to every creature. It is affecting to think, that whilst the one, surrounded by the nation, who, through his instrumentality, have been rescued from everlasting death, shall receive the plaudit, Well done, good and faithful servant; the other may be numbered with those despisers who wonder and perish. O that they might know, even in this their day, the things which belong to their peace, before they are hidden from their eyes!

You can also easily perceive how it is that we are not soon disheartened by those who tell us of the difficulties, nay, the hopelessness, of our undertaking. They may point us to countries once the seat of the church, now overspread with Mahommedan delusion; or, bidding us look at nations who once believed as we do, now contending for what we consider fatal error, they may assure us that our cause is declining. To all this we have two answers. First, the assumption that our cause is declining, is utterly gratuitous. We think it not difficult to prove, that the distinctive principles we so much venerate, never swayed so powerful an influence over the destinies of the human race as at this very moment. Point us to those nations of the earth to whom moral and intellectual cultivation, inexhaustible resources, progress in arts, and sagacity in council, have assigned the highest rank in political importance, and you point us to nations whose religious opinions are most closely allied to those we cherish. Besides, when was there a period, since the days of the apostles, in which so many converts have been made to these principles, as have been made, both from Christian and Pagan nations, within the last five and twenty years? Never did the people of the saints of the Most High look so much like going forth in serious earnest, to take possession of the kingdom and dominion, and the greatness of the kingdom under the whole heaven, as at this very day. We see, then, nothing in the signs of the times which forebodes a failure, but every thing which promises that our undertaking will prosper. But, secondly, suppose the cause did seem declining; we should see no reason to relax our exertions, for Jesus Christ has said, Preach the gospel to every creature. Appearances, whether prosperous or adverse, alter not the obligation to obey a positive command of Almighty God.

Again, suppose all that is affirmed were true. If it must be, let it be. Let the dark cloud of infidelity overspread Europe, cross the ocean, and cover our own beloved land. Let nation after nation swerve from the faith. Let iniquity abound, and the love of many wax cold, even until there is on the face of this earth, but one pure church of our Lord and Saviour Jesus Christ. All we ask is, that we may be members of that one church. God grant that we may throw ourselves into this Thermopylæ of the moral universe.

But even then, we should have no fear that the church of God would be exterminated. We would call to remembrance the years of the right hand of the Most High. We would recollect there was once a time, when the whole church of

Christ, not only could be, but actually was, gathered with one accord in one place. It was then that that place was shaken as with a rushing mighty wind, and they were all filled with the Holy Ghost. That same day, three thousand were added to the Lord. Soon, we hear, they have filled Jerusalem with their doctrine. The church has commenced her march. Samaria has with one accord believed the gospel. Antioch has become obedient to the faith. The name of Christ has been proclaimed throughout Asia Minor. The temples of the gods, as though smitten by an invisible hand, are deserted. The citizens of Ephesus cry out in despair, Great is Diana of the Ephesians! Licentious Corinth is purified by the preaching of Christ crucified. Persecution puts forth her arm to arrest the spreading "superstition." But the progress of the faith cannot be stayed. The church of God advances unhurt, amidst racks and dungeons, persecutions and death; yea, "smiles at the drawn dagger, and defies its point." She has entered Italy, and appears before the walls of the eternal city. Idolatry falls prostrate at her approach. Her ensign floats in triumph over the capitol. She has placed upon her brow the diadem of the Cæsars!

After having witnessed such successes, and under such circumstances, we are not to be moved by discouragements. To all of them we answer, *Our Field is the World.* The more arduous the undertaking, the greater will be the glory. And that glory will be ours; for God Almighty is with us.

This enterprise of mercy the Son of God came down from heaven to commence, and in commencing it, he laid down his life. To us has he granted the high privilege of carrying it forward. The legacy which he left us, as he was ascending to his Father and our Father, to his God and to our God, was, Go ye into all the world, and preach the gospel to every creature; and, lo, I am with you always, even unto the end of the world. With such an object before us, under such a leader, and supported by such promises, other motives to exertion are unnecessary. Each one of you will anxiously inquire, how he may become a co-worker with the Son of God, in the glorious design of rescuing a world from the miseries of the fall!

Blessed be God, this is a work in which every one of us is permitted to do something. None so poor, none so weak, none so insignificant, but a place of action is assigned him; and the cause expects every man to do his duty. We answer, then,

1. You may assist in it by your prayers. After all that we have said about means, we know that every thing will be in vain without the influences of the Holy Spirit. Paul may plant, and Apollos water, but it is God who giveth the increase. And these influences are promised, and promised alone, in answer to prayer. Ye then who love the Lord, keep not silence, and give him no rest, until he establish and make Jerusalem a praise in the whole earth.

2. You may assist by your personal exertions. This cause requires a vigorous, persevering, universal, and systematic effort. It requires that a spirit should pervade every one of us, which shall prompt him to ask himself every morning, What can I do for Christ to-day? and which should make him feel humbled and ashamed, if at evening, he were obliged to confess he had done nothing. Each one of us is as much obligated as the missionaries themselves, to do all in his power to advance the common cause of Christianity. We, equally with them, have embraced that gospel, of which the fundamental principle is, *None of us liveth to himself.* And not only is every one bound to exert himself to the uttermost, the same obligation rests upon us so to direct our exertions, that each of them may produce the greatest effect. Each one of us may influence others to embark in the undertaking. Each one whom we have influenced, may be induced to enlist that circle of which he is the centre, until a self-extending system of intense and reverberated action shall embody into one invincible phalanx, "the sacramental host of God's elect." Awake, then, brethren, from your slumbers. Seek first the kingdom of God and his righteousness. And recollect that what you would do, must be done quickly. The day is far spent; the night is at hand. Whatsoever thy hand findeth to do, do it with thy might; for there is no work, nor device, nor knowledge, nor wisdom, in the grave whither thou goest.

3. You may assist by your pecuniary contributions. An opportunity of this kind will now be presented. And here, I trust, it is unnecessary to say that in such a cause we consider it a privilege to give. How so worthily can you appropriate a portion of that substance which Providence has given you, as in sending to your fellow-men, who sit in the region and shadow of death, a knowledge of the God who made them, and of Jesus Christ whom he hath sent? We pray you, so use the mammon of unrighteousness, that when ye fail, they may receive you into everlasting habitations.

But I doubt not you already burn with desire to testify your love to the crucified Redeemer. Enthroned in the high and holy place, he looks down at this moment upon the heart of every one of us, and will accept of your offering, though it be but the widow's mite, if it be given with the widow's feeling. In the last day of solemn account, he will acknowledge it before an assembled universe, saying, Inasmuch as ye did it unto one of the least of these my brethren, ye did it unto me!

May God of his grace enable us so to act, that on that day we may meet with joy the record of the doings of this hour; and to his name shall be the glory in Christ. AMEN.

ARGUMENTS FOR MISSIONS.

BY

REV. EDWARD D. GRIFFIN, D. D.

And Jesus came and spake unto them, saying, All power is given unto me in heaven and in earth. Go ye therefore and teach all nations, baptizing them in the name of the Father, and of the Son, and of the Holy Ghost; teaching them to observe all things whatsoever I have commanded you. And lo, I am with you alway, even unto the end of the world. — MATTHEW 28 : 18, 19, 20.

I RISE to advocate the cause of missions to the heathen and to plead for a dying world. My sole object is to enforce the claims of five hundred millions of perishing men by some plain and simple arguments which have affected my own mind. And I have chosen this text because it contains some of the arguments and suggests the rest. Both the authority of Christ and his personal reward are here distinctly brought to bear on the subject. For his obedience " unto death " he received the inheritance, including " the heathen " and " the uttermost parts of the earth," with authority to manage the whole estate. This authority he employed in sending forth missionaries to disciple all nations and to bring to him the unnumbered millions promised for his seed.

My first argument, then, is founded upon the authority of Christ. The injunction in the text was not addressed to the eleven exclusively, but to them as depositaries of the divine commands, and through them to the whole body of ministers in every age. This appears from the promise subjoined, " Lo I am with you alway, *even unto the end of the world.*" Indeed the eleven were expressly commanded to transmit to their successors all the injunctions which they themselves received, one of which was to disciple all nations. " Go ye — and *disciple all nations,* — teaching them to observe *all things whatsoever I have commanded you."* This command then is now sounding in the ears of the ministers and churches of the nineteenth century.

And yet some when called upon for their aid are heard to say, I do not approve of such things: just as though they had a right to place themselves on the seat of judgment and decide for themselves what they will approve and what not, when the command of God is in their ear and his sword at their breast. Hark! did you not hear that thunder? " Curse ye Meroz;— curse ye bitterly the inhabitants thereof; because they came not up to the help of the Lord, to the help of the Lord against the mighty."

My second argument is grounded on the example of Christ and his apostles. The Saviour of the world sent out a band of missionaries and charged them to "preach the Gospel to every creature;" "and they went forth and preached every where" "that men should repent." No one objection can be raised against missions at the present day which will not equally lie against Christ and his apostles. The attempt is no more presumptuous now than then; the prospect is no more discouraging; the difficulties are no greater; the power that is engaged to give success is the same, for the promise remains unchanged, " Lo, I am with you alway, even unto the end of the world."

My third argument is founded on what we owe to the heathen. Is the Gospel no blessing to you? And would it not be an equal blessing to them? And are we not bound to extend to others all the happiness in our power? To say that pagans can be as happy without the Gospel as with it, is to say that the Gospel is no blessing to men; and then you do not believe that it came from God. If the Gospel would be no blessing to the heathen, why do you preach or support it at home? Are you universalists? But still you find motives enough to preach or support what you call the Gospel at home. Why then not send it to other nations? If all mankind are to be saved, — and mercy requires that the tidings be circulated with sectarian zeal through Christendom, to dispel the gloomy fears of former generations, — why not send the glorious news to Asia? If things are so, let armies of missionaries be collected to stop those bloody rites which guilt and fear have invented to atone for sin and prevent future punishment. Let them hasten to stop the self-torturing pilgrimages, to take down the wretch who hangs voluntarily suspended by a hook thrust through his side, to drag the infatuated victim from under the car of Juggernaut, and the widow from the funeral pile, and terminate forever the destruction of infants in the Ganges. Let them pour upon the ravished ear of Asia the tidings that all guilt was expiated on Calvary; that they have no need of their bloody rites, nor even of a reformation of manners; that they may live in pleasure here without apprehension, and enter on eternal pleasure hereafter.

Let it be true that all men will be saved, or even that men are as likely to be saved without the Gospel as with it, — is the Gospel of no service in the present life, as a foundation of hope, as a purifier of manners, as a tamer of the passions, as a means of civilization, as a handmaid to science? What nation since the commencement of the Christian era ever arose from savage to civilized without Christianity? If you are the friends of the human family, I call upon you to weep over the degraded and comfortless condition of five hundred millions of people destitute of the light of science, and the pleasures of refined society, subject, in a large proportion of cases, to all the hardships of the savage state, and in every instance to the horrors of a gloomy superstition.

But what believer in revelation except a universalist, will say that men are as likely to be saved without the Gospel as with it? Be it so that *good* heathen will be saved, — but the mass of the heathen are not good. They are sunk in the grossest vice. All the passions, and all the crimes, that ever degraded man, there rage with little restraint. Owing to some defect which nothing but revelation can explain, man is universally inclined to evil. This truth, which every page of history attests, which a thousand poets have mournfully sung, which all the statutes of legislators have acknowledged, is confirmed by every day's experience. It is equally certain to every believer in Christianity, that the grand means to reform the world is the Gospel of Christ. Let nations with all these native passions run wild without this means of reformation, and what can you expect but that they will sink into the lowest depths of vice? Tell me not that their ignorance excuses them. Whence, then, that resentment with which you contemplate savages breaking into a village at night, burning houses, murdering infants in their mothers' arms, — dragging their prisoners to the slow tortures of the stake, and rioting on their groans? Does ignorance excuse all the infernal passions and crimes of the heathen world? They will not plead this themselves. If they are conscious of no fault in these things, whence their resentment against each other? When they take revenge, do they not give judgment that pagans may sin? Do they not this when they execute their laws on criminals? "their conscience ... bearing witness, and their thoughts the mean while accusing ... one another." But if any doubt remains, read the Epistle to the Romans; contemplate the picture of the heathen world sketched in the first chapter, and the inference drawn in the third. And what said the charitable John? "We know that we are of God, and the whole world lieth in wickedness." The only means to reclaim the world is the Gospel of Christ. What nation since the world began was ever reclaimed without the Scriptures? Talk as you will of the salvation of pious heathen; let it be admitted, if you please, that now and then a pagan becomes a good man; yet the mass of the heathen are grossly wicked, and will always remain so till reformed by the Gospel of Christ.

But I go further. Show me one instance in which God has ever saved or enlightened an adult without his word and ordinances. But his word and ordinances cannot travel to the heathen alone, and there explain themselves. The living preacher must go with them. Even in the days of miracles you never hear of a Bible carried through the air to a distant land, and there expounding itself, nor of a pagan taught to read without a human teacher. In the highest reign of miracles and inspiration, prophets and apostles must carry to men the word and ordinances of God, or no salvation was accomplished. You may take your opinions from yourself if you will; I will take mine from the word of God. And what does that teach? "The Scripture saith, — Whosoever shall call upon the name of the Lord shall be saved. How then shall they call on him in whom they have not believed? and how shall they believe in him of whom they have not heard? and how shall they hear without a preacher? and how shall they preach except they be sent?" If this does not absolutely prove that no adult heathen can be saved, it proves at least that no salvation can come to him in the known and ordinary way. Every imagination, then, that the heathen will come in of themselves, if let alone, — is a bewildering fancy.

My fourth argument is drawn from the sacrifices of the missionaries themselves, and the debt of gratitude which we owe them. To see these interesting youth, with the spirit of martyrs, offering themselves to die under an Indian or an African sun; for the love of Christ tearing themselves from parents, and brothers, and sisters, to see them no more; taking an eternal leave of the scenes and companions of their youth; abandoning their native shore and their native tongue, to bear the tidings of a precious Saviour to distant nations; to see delicate young females, who have been dandled in the lap of parental tenderness, with a heroism which nothing but Christian principles could support, tearing themselves for the last time from the arms of trembling mothers and speechless sisters, to encounter the dangers of the seas and the still greater dangers of a torrid clime, in order to support their husbands by their smiles and prayers in a foreign land, among sooty pagans; this is a scene which makes selfishness blush and hang its head; which shames all the ordinary piety that is couched in ease at home, trembling at self-denials. I beseech you to follow these precious youth with your prayers and your tenderest concern. They have gone in the service of our Father's family. They sacrifice all for us. Shall we not follow them with the interest of brothers and sisters through the groves of India and the forests of America? And when we hear of their trials, their dangers, their escapes, their successes, shall we not feel as though we were receiving accounts from our near kindred? When they tell us of the triumphs of Hindoo converts, or send to our ears the young hosannas of Syrian or Sandwich children, shall we not mingle our souls with theirs, and join in the joy as though they were bone of our bone and flesh of our flesh? Yes, dear missionaries, we will remember you and all the sacrifices you have made, till these hearts shall cease to beat. God Almighty go with you and keep you in the hollow of his hand till we meet in heaven.

Sometimes, in restrained and modest terms, these beloved men hint to us their wants. I fear they do not tell all. I fear they may yet suffer in a foreign land for want of a little more of that wealth which is heaped up in America. Much has, indeed, been given; and I thank you and the American churches in the name of all the poor pagans of the wilderness. I thank you in the name of those blessed men who have forsaken all for Christ. When they lay their heads down far from mother and sister, your charity will spread their couch and cover them from the cold; your charity will furnish their table and refresh them when they are weary. I wish I could present to your view a thousand pagan children clothed in the garments which you have furnished, and learning to utter the praises of God out of the books which you have given. But many of you, I trust, will have greater joy at last. You will see them clad in brighter robes; you will see them touch the golden harp, and hear them say, But for your instrumentality we had not come to this. Then, I know, your reward will be full.

I can only say, if you have anything more to spare we shall gladly receive it. And what you give will cheer the interesting wanderer on the plains of Ceylon and the shores of Owyhee, who have left all for Christ, and whose sacrifices and prayers, I hope, will prove the salvation of our children.

My fifth argument is, that foreign missions are likely to prove the most glorious means of grace to us at home. While you are feeling for pagan souls and sending your sons to them, I firmly believe that your prayers and bounty will return unto your own bosom. Such confidence I have in God, for I have heard him say, "He that watereth shall be watered also himself." I believe that while you are anxious to raise heathen nations from death, you will be enabled to shake off your grave clothes yourselves; that while you are seeking to draw forth Indian children from their sepulchres and present them alive to their rejoicing parents, your own children will start into life by your side; that while the love of distant nations glows in our hearts, it will melt us all down into love to each other, and burn up all our jealousies and strifes. Some of these effects I seem already to discern. God grant that they may increase, until the joy of America shall respond to that of Asia and in one burst of praise rise united to heaven. May your charities return into your own bosom and that of your children for days and years and an eternity to come.

My sixth argument is, that all the wealth of the world was given to Christ as a recompense for redeeming our souls: and shall the ingratitude of man withhold from him his hire? It will not always be thus. The time will come when "*Holiness to the Lord*" shall be written on all the possessions of men, — on the very "bells of the horses;" and when "the pots in the Lord's house," (those used for culinary purposes in the families of the priests,) shall, in point of holiness, be "like the bowls before the altar," which received the blood of the victims until it was sprinkled; and when " every pot in Jerusalem and in Judah shall be holiness unto the Lord of hosts." The common vessels used to dress our food, instead of being regarded as instruments of luxury or display, like our Bibles and psalm-books shall be all for God. Men will write *Holiness to the Lord* on every dollar and on every foot of ground. They will no longer labor to hoard but to do good.

That will be such a generation as has not yet appeared. A few scattered individuals have approached towards this character, but the mass of mankind in every age have held their property as their own, and not as a sacred deposit. With multitudes the thought of giving to God never entered their minds. Go to them for their proportion to support the Gospel at home, and they will turn you away, or deal out a paltry pittance that makes you ashamed. Go to them in behalf of the heathen, and they have nothing to spare. Though their poorer neighbors are giving by handfuls, they have nothing to spare. They are so in debt for new lands and tenements, that they cannot give a cent to save a world from death. It is not more evident than Lucifer himself has a separate interest from Christ, than that these men have. Wrapped up in themselves, they mean that the universe shall take care of itself. It is not for them to go abroad to inquire how it fares with other nations; their business is at home. In their own little sordid selves they lie buried, and not a meaner object is to be seen in the universe of God.

There is another class, including by far the greater part of the better sort, who are willing to give to Christ something like one or two per cent. of their income, but hold the rest with an unyielding grasp. It will be otherwise in that coming day. I say not what they will give, for God has not fixed the limit for obvious reasons. In the first place, the wants of men in different countries and ages call for different degrees of charity. In the second place, had God prescribed the exact amount, the contribution would have been no more an index of the heart than the payment of any other tax. As by this part of human conduct he specially intended to draw forth the dispositions of men, he left the proportion to be fixed by themselves, after giving them some general intimations of his will. The only intimations of the kind were contained in the Hebrew law; and even there he left much to the spontaneous motion of the heart. Enough however was fixed to serve as a general guide to the conscience. In the first place, they were to devote the first fruits of their fields and of their flocks: in the second place, they were to give to the Levites a tenth of all the products of both: in the third place, they were to consume another tenth in charity feasts with the Levites and the poor: in the fourth place, they were to offer many expensive sacrifices, some fixed by law and others voluntary. These four items cannot be reckoned at less than three tenths of their income. In the fifth place, the many contributions demanded for the poor, (some fixed by law and others voluntary,) together with all that was required for hospitality, are moderately estimated at another tenth. Indeed under the pressure of all these laws, a conscientious and liberal Hebrew would hardly get through the year without parting with one half of his income. This page God wrote and hung out of heaven and retired, leaving men to follow their own judgment and inclination to the end of the world. In the day when *Holiness to the Lord* shall be written on all the possessions of men, this page will be read and better understood. Then a law which has slept through so many selfish ages will be revived again, and holy men will feel it a privilege to give something like four tenths or one half of their income to God. And then they will look back on the contracted ages gone by, with much the same surprise as that with which we review the slave trade or the superstitions of the tenth century.

And all these increased contributions will be wanted. A little calculation would surprise you here. The single work of furnishing the people of the United States with Bibles for a century to come, almost exceeds belief. If we increase in numbers as we have done, before this century runs out, more than six millions of Bibles must be annually issued to supply our own population. To raise up ministers, too, for the unnumbered thousands that will inhabit these states, will require perhaps a still greater tax. And among other cares, poor, forsaken Africa must not be neglected. Her crime of having a sable skin must not exclude her from the kingdom of heaven. Great will be the expense of training up her sons to serve at her altars; and this charge must fall chiefly on America. Here, as in no other civilized nation on earth, materials may be selected from a million and a half of her race. Nor are Bibles and ministers all. Expensive missions, for a great many years to come, must be supported in every part of the pagan and Mohammedan world. And this expense must fall chiefly on Christians at home. Missionaries cannot be fed by ravens, nor will the heathen themselves support them. All the disposable wealth of Christendom will be put in requisition. Those hundreds of thousands which are now rusting in the coffers of the rich must be brought forth. Those mighty sums which support wars and theatres must be consecrated to God. No longer must wealth enough sleep in a single commercial city to convert a nation. No longer must any Ananias and Sapphira keep back a part of what they have professedly devoted to the Lord. Let all professors of religion hear this.

Already this reviving spirit of liberality has begun to appear. Princely fortunes have been given by some; thousands and tens of thousands by others. The poor laborer has divided with God his hard-earned gains. Women have given up their ornaments. Children have thrust forward their little hands, to drop their all into the missionary box. The world is fast waking up to the conviction, that the silver and the gold are the Lord's.

My seventh argument is, that these exertions are necessary to bring to Christ the seed and the kingdom, the victory and the triumph, promised him as his reward. This world belongs to Christ. No other being has a right to erect an interest on this ground. And yet, after the lapse of eighteen centuries, two thirds of the earth remain in pagan or Mohammedan darkness. Ought so great a part of a world which Christ has redeemed and owns, to continue in the hands of his enemy? If the suffrages of nations were to be collected, what would a redeemed race say? To whom would they assign a world given to Christ for redeeming them? Would they resign it to his enemy, who has despoiled it of its Eden, and covered it with briers and thorns, and turned it into a great charnel-house? or would they give it to him who came to rescue it from the hands of destroying devils, and died to save their souls? What is the vote of a redeemed race on this subject? If human instrumentality is wanted to drive the usurper from his seat, shall not a whole race rise up to the effort? Christ could have conquered his enemy without instruments; but he chose to bring in the nations in a way suited to moral agents, — by instructions, so conveyed as to favor calm reflection, that is, through human organs; and he chose to employ men as co-workers with him, that he might train them to benevolent action. He is not dependent on us for his happiness. It is the height of benevolence, that he is willing to consider the rescued nations as his reward. It is like one who in the division of spoils selects a captive for his portion, and makes the release of that unhappy one the gain most welcome to his heart. And vast indeed must be the good that can satisfy the benevolence of the Son of God, and be an adequate reward for his wonderful obedience "unto death." Let him have the infinite joy. And if human instrumentality is wanted, let the whole mass of Christendom rise up to the work. Is there a wretch so withered and debased, that he will not do all in his power to push things forward to this glorious issue?

The Redeemer began his triumph when he ascended from Olivet. At the moment of parting from his disciples, he was surrounded by no outward lustre. Perhaps the bright cloud which received him contained the habiliments of glory with which he was ever afterwards to be arrayed. Decked thus in his regal robes, he began his triumphant march; returning in state, like a glorious conqueror to his royal city. I see him attended with "thousands of angels," and "twenty thousand" "chariots of God," leading "captivity captive," with death and hell chained to his chariot wheels. I hear them shout, "Lift up your heads, O ye gates, and be ye lifted up, ye everlasting doors, and the King of glory shall come in. Who is this King of glory? The Lord strong and mighty, the Lord mighty in battle. [The Lord who has returned with glorious scars, a Conqueror from his wars.] Lift up your heads, O ye gates, even lift them up, ye everlasting doors, and the King of glory shall come in."

Early, too, he commenced his triumph on earth. In the wonderful campaign, he went forth single-handed against two worlds. He girded his sword upon his thigh, and marched directly into the heart of Satan's kingdom. Wherever he went, he conquered. At his approach, temples and altars fell; oracles grew dumb; the Roman empire, the chief seat of Satan's visible kingdom, shook to its centre, and afterwards opened to the Conqueror and fell prostrate at his feet. He marched through the nations, breaking down the prisons which Satan had reared to confine his wretched captives. Millions who had been immured in dungeons from their birth, were brought forth to the joyous light. Wherever he came, freedom and joy sprung up around him. His trophies were not wasted provinces, but souls delivered from the destroyer.

The high-minded spirit of chivalry celebrated the feats of disinterested knights, who roamed the kingdoms, as imagination feigned, to deliver oppressed females from enchanted castles, or from the grasp of giants and genii; but how much more benignant a deliverer is here; marching through the nations, and rescuing those who had no helper from the tyranny of Satan. God speed thee, thou glorious Conqueror! Go on and prosper; and may the blessing of millions ready to perish come upon thee. We will follow the wheels of his triumphal chariot, and shout as we go, "Hosanna to the Son of David: blessed is he that cometh in the name of the Lord: hosanna in the highest!"

His triumphant kingdom commenced among the Jews at Pentecost, and among the Gentiles at the baptism of Cornelius. From that time it spread like lightning through all the countries from Spain to India, and from Scythia to Ethiopia, until in three centuries it mounted the throne of the Cesars. But after it had breasted an embattled race for three hundred years, and had placed its foot on the neck of a subjugated world, it fell by luxury and pride, — by an assumption of lordly dominion, and by engrafting upon the simple institutions of Christ the pomp and pageantry of pagan rituals; until in punishment one half of the dominions which had been rescued from the prince of darkness was given back into the hands of the Mohammedans, and the rest sunk under the tyranny and mummeries of Rome, until it lay conquered and besotted at the feet of the man of sin.

But this and every other enemy shall be destroyed. To complete the triumph of the Redeemer on earth, Satan must not only be again expelled from the Roman empire, but be bound "a thousand years," that he "deceive the nations no more till the thousand years be fulfilled."

And when all his elect are brought home and displayed in one happy family around the throne, with what infinite joy will he bend over his redeemed Church and contemplate their blessedness and hear their praise. And what glory and honor and blessing will their bursting hearts forever ascribe to him. John had a vision of this scene and makes the following report. "After this I beheld, and lo, a great multitude which no man could number, of all nations and kindreds and people and tongues, stood before the throne and before the Lamb, clothed with white robes and palms in their hands; and cried with a loud voice, saying, Salvation to our God which sitteth upon the throne and to the Lamb. And all the angels stood round about the throne and about the elders and the four living creatures, and fell before the throne on their faces and worshipped God, saying, Amen: blessing and glory and wisdom and thanksgiving and honor and power and might be unto our God for ever and ever. Amen." At another time he saw a grand jubilee held in heaven in honor of the Lamb; the redeemed first beginning the song, the angels then striking in, and before it was done the whole creation employed in the bursting praise. "And when he had taken the book the four living creatures and four and twenty elders, [the representatives of the whole Church,] fell down before the Lamb, having every one of them harps and golden vials full of odors, which are the prayers of saints. And they sung a new song, saying, Thou art worthy to take the book and to open the seals thereof; for thou wast slain and hast redeemed us to God by thy blood out of every kindred and tongue and people and nation, and hast made us unto our God kings and priests, and we shall reign on the earth. And I beheld and I heard the voice of many angels round about the throne and [about] the living creatures and the elders; (and the number of them was ten thousand times ten thousand and thousands of thousands;) saying with a loud voice, Worthy is the Lamb that was slain to receive power and riches and wisdom and strength and honor and glory and blessing. And every creature which is in heaven and on the earth and under the earth, and such as are in the sea, and all that are in them, heard I saying, Blessing and honor and glory and power be unto him that sitteth upon the throne, and unto the Lamb for ever and ever. And the four living creatures said, Amen; and the four and twenty elders fell down and worshipped him that liveth for ever and ever."

How delightful to contemplate the honors which encircle the Lamb in the midst of his Father's throne. After wandering an exile from heaven for more than thirty years for our revolt, how joyous to know that he has found a home. After the crown of thorns, we are happy to see him wear the diadem of the universe. After depending for bread on the charity of his female followers, we are glad to see him the Heir of all things, and able, in his turn, to impart to others. After being so long neglected and despised by men, we rejoice that he has found those who know how to honor his worth; we exult to hear the shout of all heaven in his praise. After the agonies of the garden and the cross, we sing and shout for joy that he has found infinite and eternal delight in the glory of his Father and the salvation of his Church. Let him have his happiness and his honors. Amidst all the sufferings of life it shall be our solace that the despised Nazarene has found his throne, — that the man of sorrows is happy at last. Of all the luxuries that ever feasted the human soul, the sweetest is to see the Lamb that was slain in the midst of his Father's throne. We will embalm his name in our grateful hearts. We will embalm it by our praise, which shall live while we have breath and sink away upon our dying lips. And we will embalm it among the songs of the upper world. If we are permitted to come and stand where the elders bow, how will *we* bow and sing. When we shall look down to hell and see our old companions there, and then back to Calvary, and then look up and read the touching traces of love in those melting eyes and among the prints of the nails and the thorns, we *will* embalm his name, if love and songs can do it. We will tell all heaven of his love. If ever new inhabitants should come in from other worlds, they shall hear the story of Calvary. If commissioned in remote ages of eternity to visit other systems, we will carry the amazing tidings to them. We will tell them to all we meet. We will erect monuments of the wonderful facts on every plain of heaven, and inscribe them all over with the story of the manger, the garden, and the cross. While gratitude and truth remain, the name and the love of Jesus shall never be forgotten.

And now, my beloved brethren, I invite you to go with me and look for a moment over the interesting scene which is opening on earth. For many years the Christian world had been sunk in a profound slumber in regard to this duty; but for the last four and thirty years they have been waking up. He who has engraven Zion on the palms of his hands, — who never wants means to fulfil his promises, — has sent his heavenly influence to rouse the Christian world. He beheld the desolations of Zion and has come to rebuild her ruined walls. He heard the groans of his people as with harps on the willows they were weeping "by the rivers of Babylon," and has come to bring them again "to Zion with songs and everlasting joy upon their heads." Eternal thanks to God for what our eyes have seen and our ears have heard for the last four and thirty years. Eternal thanks to God for the increasing wonders which are rapidly opening on the world. And O, can we restrain the bursting emotion? for ever blessed be his great and glorious name for what we have begun to see in our own land. It is more than thirty years since the Christians in Great Britain awoke; and they have been holding on their way with increasing majesty and glory, until that little island bestows annually more than a million of dollars upon strangers. It is fourteen years since New England broke her slumbers, and now the mass of her population seems drenched in the missionary spirit. I saw the day cover the plains of Europe. I saw the westward-travelling light spread itself over these eastern states. Nine years ago I saw the rays of the morning tip our Presbyterian horizon. I saw the dawn blush deeper and deeper. I knew it would not all return again to midnight. I knew the sun would rise. At length I saw his golden limb above the eastern woods; and from the course of day I knew that soon the heavenly flood would cover all the plains to Arkansas and the Pacific. Already the influence of heaven has dropped upon the wilderness, and the yell of the war whoop is changed to notes of praise. We must not stop till every Indian tongue has joined the general song. We must not stop till our influence has cheered the whole extent of South America. And then we must go forth to the islands, and hold on our way till we meet our brethren in other fields and unite with them in completing the harvest of the world.

We owe the sincerest gratitude to God for giving us our existence in such a day as this. Many prophets and kings desired to see this day and saw it not. One spirit has seized the Christian world to send the Gospel, with a great company of its publishers, to all the nations of the earth. Missionary and Bible Societies, those stupendous monuments of Christian charity, have risen so rapidly and in so great numbers throughout Europe and America, that in contemplating them we are "like them that dream." These societies have already accomplished wonders, and are constantly stretching forward to future achievements beyond the reach of imagination. On the burning sands of Africa, where Christian feet never before trod, there is the holy band of missionaries, struggling, amidst dangers and deaths, to lead the sable tribes of Ethiopia to stretch forth their hands to God. On the plains of Hindostan, a "consecrated host" are translating the Scriptures into more than thirty different languages, spoken by a population greater than that of all Europe. On the borders of China they have produced a version which will give the oracles of God to one quarter of the population of the globe,

In the southern islands a nation is born in a day. From the hill of Zion, — from the top of Calvary, — they are freighting every caravan of pilgrims with Bibles for all the countries of the east. Certainly the angel has begun his flight through the midst of heaven, "having the everlasting Gospel to preach — to every nation, and kindred, and tongue, and people."

My soul is enlarged and stands erect as I look down the declivity of years and see the changes which these young Davids, under God, will make in all the earth. Countless millions are shortly to awake from the sleep and darkness of a hundred ages to hail the day that will never go down. I see the darkness rolling upon itself and passing away from a thousand lands. I see a cloudless day following and laying itself over all the earth. I see the nations coming up from the neighborhood of the brutes to the dignity of the sons of God, — from the stye in which they had wallowed, to the purity of the divine image. I see the meekness of the Gospel assuaging their ferocious passions, melting down a million contending units into one, silencing the clangor of arms, and swelling into life a thousand budding charities which had died under the long winter. I hear the voice of their joy. It swells from the valleys and echoes from the hills. I already hear on the eastern breeze the songs of new-born nations. I already catch from the western gale the praise of a thousand islands. I ascend the Alps and see the darkness retiring from the papal world. I ascend the Andes and see South America and all the islands of the Pacific one altar. I ascend the mountains of Thibet, and hear from the plains of China and from every jungle and pagoda of Hindostan the praises of the living God. I see all Asia bowing before him who eighteen centuries ago hung in the midst of them on Calvary. I traverse oceans and hear from every floating Bethel the songs of the redeemed.

> "The dwellers in the vales and on the rocks
> Shout to each other; and the mountain tops,
> From distant mountains, catch the flying joy;
> Till, nation after nation taught the strain,
> Earth rolls the rapturous hosanna round."

Come that blessed day. Let my eyes once behold the sight, and then give this worthless body to the worms.

THE THEORY OF MISSIONS TO THE HEATHEN.

BY

REV. RUFUS ANDERSON, D. D.

Now then we are ambassadors for Christ; as though God did beseech you by us, we pray you in Christ's stead, be ye reconciled to God. — 2 CORINTHIANS 5: 20.

COMPARING the present period of the church with the apostolical, we come to two very different results respecting our own age. One is, that the facilities enjoyed by us for propagating the gospel throughout the world, are vastly greater than those enjoyed by the apostles. The other is, that it is far more difficult now, than it was then, to impart a purely spiritual character to missions among the heathen.

As to facilities, we have the advantage of the apostles in all respects, except the gift of tongues. The world, as a whole, was never so open to the preacher of the gospel since the introduction of the Christian dispensation. The civilization, too, that is connected with modern science, is all connected also with Christianity in some of its forms. I should add, that the civilization which the gospel has conferred upon our own New England is the highest and best, in a religious point of view, the world has yet seen.

But on the other hand, this very perfection of our own social religious state becomes a formidable hindrance to establishing such purely spiritual missions among heathen nations, as were those of the apostolical times. Not that this is the only hindrance to this result; there are many others, but this is an important one. For, the Christian religion is identified, in all our conceptions of it from our earliest years, with the almost universal diffusion among its professors of the blessings of education, industry, civil liberty, family government, social order, the means of a respectable livelihood, and a well-ordered community. Hence *our* idea of piety in converts among the heathen very generally involves the acquisition and possession, to a great extent, of these blessings; and *our* idea of the propagation of the gospel by means of missions is, to an equal extent, *the creation among heathen tribes and nations of a highly improved state of society, such as we ourselves enjoy.* And for this vast intellectual, moral, and social transformation we allow but a short time. We expect the first generation of converts to Christianity, even among savages, to come into all our fundamental ideas of morals, manners, political economy, social organization, right, justice, equity; although many of these are ideas which our own community has been ages in acquiring. If we discover that converts under the torrid zone go but half clothed, that they are idle on a soil where a small amount of labor will supply their wants, that they sometimes forget the apostle's cautions to his converts, not to lie one to another, and to steal no more, in communities where the grossest vice scarcely affects the reputation, and that they are slow to adopt our ideas of the rights of man; we at once doubt the genuineness of their conversion, and the faithfulness of their missionary instructors. Nor is it surprising that this feeling is strongest, as it appears to be, in the most enlightened and favored portions of our country; since it is among those whose privilege it is to dwell upon the heights of Zion, that we have the most reason to expect this feeling, until they shall have reflected maturely on the difference there is between their own circumstances and states of mind, and those of a heathen and barbarous people.

Now the prevalence of these sentiments at home has exerted an influence on all the missions. Nor is the influence new. You see it in the extent to which farmers and mechanics — pious but secular men — were sent, many years ago, along with the missionaries, to assist in reclaiming the savages of the wilderness from the chase, and settling them in communities like our own — a practice now nearly discontinued, except where the expense is borne by the national government.

Unless this influence is guarded against by missionaries and their directors, the result is that the missions have a *two-fold object of pursuit;* the one, that simple and sublime spiritual object of the ambassador for Christ mentioned in the text, "persuading men to be reconciled to God;" the other, the re-organizing, by various direct means, of the structure of that social system, of which the converts form a part. Thus the object of the missions becomes more or less complicated, leading to a complicated, burdensome, and perhaps, expensive course of measures for its attainment.

I may be allowed, therefore, to invite attention to what is conceived to be *our true and only office and work in missions to the heathen.* "Now then we are ambassadors for Christ; as though God did beseech you by us, we pray you in Christ's stead, be ye reconciled to God.' The ambassadors here spoken of were missionaries — misionaries to the heathen, for such were Paul and his associates; sent, instead of Christ the Mediator, on a ministry withheld from angels, to plead with rebellious men to become reconciled to God. They are ambassadors sent on the same general errand that brought the Lord Jesus from heaven, and their commission is to proclaim abroad the fact, history, design and effect of his atonement, and bring its renovating power to bear as widely as possible upon the human race.

It will be necessary to dwell a short time on the leading aspects of this enterprise. And,

1. The vocation of the missionary who is sent to the heathen, is not the same with that of the settled pastor.

The work of human salvation is one of vast extent, whether we regard the time it is to occupy, the objects upon which it operates, the agents it employs, or the results which are to be accomplished. And it is performed with that regard for order and gradual development, which generally characterizes the works of God. Upon the Lord Jesus it devolved to make the atonement, thus preparing the way, as none else could do, for reconciling man to his Maker; and then He returned to the heaven whence he came. Upon his immediate disciples it then devolved to make proclamation of the atonement, and its kindred and dependent doctrines, throughout the world, the whole of which world, excepting Judea, was then heathen. This they were to do as his representatives and ambassadors; and to expedite the work, they were furnished with the gift of tongues, and an extraordinary divine influence attended their preaching. Their commission embraced only the proclamation of the gospel and planting its institutions. As soon as the gospel by their means had gained a footing in any one district of country, they left the work in charge to others, called elders and also bishops or overseers of the flock and church of God, whom they ordained for the purpose. Sometimes they did not remain even long enough to provide spiritual guides for the churches they had planted. "For this cause," says Paul to Titus, "left I thee in Crete, that thou shouldest set in order the things that are wanting, and ordain elders in every city, as I had appointed thee." The elders were the pastors of the new churches. Elsewhere the apostle speaks of different departments of labor and influence assigned to the ministers of Christ. He says that when Christ ascended up on high, he gave gifts unto men; to some apostles, to some prophets, to some evangelists, to some pastors and teachers. Whatever was the peculiar office of "prophets" and "teachers," none can doubt that "evangelists" were fellow-laborers of the apostles in the missionary work, and that "pastors" had the stated care and instruction of particular churches. Now missionaries are the true and proper successors of the apostles and evangelists, and their sphere of duty is not the same with that of pastors, who are successors, in their sacred functions, not so much of the apostles and evangelists, as of the elders and bishops. It enters into the nature of the pastor's relation, that he remain or be intended to remain long the spiritual instructor of some one people. It is indeed as really his business to call sinners to repentance, as it is that of the missionary; but, owing to his more permanent relations, and to the fact that he is constituted the religious guide and instructor of his converts during the whole period of their earthly pilgrimage, his range of duty in respect to them is more comprehensive than that of the missionary in respect to his converts. The pastor is charged, in common with the missionary, with reconciling men to God; and he has also an additional charge, arising from the peculiar circumstances of his relation, with respect to their growth in grace and sanctification. But the missionary's *great* business in his personal labors, is with the unconverted. His embassy is to the rebellious, to beseech them, in Christ's stead, to be reconciled to God. His vocation, as a soldier of the cross, is to make conquests, and to go on, in the name of his divine Master, "conquering and to conquer;" committing the security and permanency of his conquests to another class of men created expressly for the purpose. The idea of *continued conquest* is fundamental in missions to the heathen, and is vital to their spiritual life and efficiency. It will doubtless be found on inquiry, that missions among the heathen have always ceased to be healthful and efficient, have ceased to evince the true missionary spirit in its strength, whenever they have ceased to be actively aggressive upon the kingdom of darkness.

In a word, the missionary prepares new fields for pastors; and when they are thus prepared, and competent pastors are upon the ground, he ought himself to move onward, — the pioneer in effect of a Christian civilization — but in office, work and spirit, an ambassador for Christ, to preach the gospel where it has not been preached. And, whatever may be said with respect to pastors, it is true of the missionary, that he is to keep himself as free as possible from entanglements with literature, science and commerce, and with questions of church government, politics and social order. For,

2. The object and work of the missionary are preëminently spiritual.

His embassy and message are as really from the other world, as if he were an angel from heaven. He who devotes himself to the work of foreign missions, comes thereby under peculiar engagements and obligations. His situation is in some important respects peculiar, compared with that of all others. His sphere of action lies beyond the bounds of his native land, beyond the bounds of Christendom, where society and the family and human nature lie all in ruins. As the great Originator and Lord of the enterprise came from the realms of heavenly blessedness to this world when it was one universal moral waste, so his representatives and ambassadors have now to go from those portions of the earth that have been illuminated by his gospel to regions that are as yet unvisited by these benign influences. They are therefore required preëminently to renounce the world. From the nature of the case, they make a greater sacrifice of worldly blessings, than their brethren at home can do, however much disposed. They forsake their native land and the loved scenes of their youthful days. Oceans separate them from their relatives and friends. They encounter torrid heats and strange diseases. They traverse pathless wilds, and are exposed to burning suns and chilling night-damps, to rain or snow. Yet these things, when in their most repulsive forms, are reckoned by missionaries as the least of the trials appertaining to their vocation. The foreign missionary's greatest sacrifices and trials are *social* and *religious*. It is here that he has a severity of trial, which even the domestic missionary ordinarily cannot have. Whatever the devoted servant of Christ upon the frontiers may endure for the present, he sees the waves of a Christian civilization not far distant rolling onward, and knows that there will soon be all around him gospel institutions and a Christian community. But it is not so with the foreign missionary. It requires great strength of faith in Christ for him to look at his rising family, and then with unruffled feelings towards the future. True, he sees the gospel taking hold of minds and hearts in consequence of his ministry, and souls converted and reconciled to God; he gathers churches; he sees around him the germs of a future Christian civilization. But then, owing to the imperfect and disordered state of society in heathen communities, he dares not anticipate so much social advancement for two or three generations to come, as would make it pleasant to think of leaving his children among the people for whose spiritual well-being he delights to spend his own strength and years. And then his heart yearns ofttimes to be braced and cheered by social Christian fellowship of a higher order than he finds among his converts from heathenism. It is not the "flesh-pots of Egypt" he looks back upon, nor any of the pleasant things that used to gratify his *senses* in his native land; but he does sometimes think of the kindred spirits he would find in that land, and of the high intellectual and spiritual fellowship he would enjoy in their society, and how it would refresh and strengthen his own mind and heart. Often there is a feeling of weakness and faintness arising from the want of such fellowship, which is the most painful part of his sufferings. The foreign missionary is obliged, indeed, to act preëminently upon the doctrine of a future life, and of God's supreme and universal government, and to make a deliberate sacrifice of time for eternity, and of earth for heaven. And this he does as an act of duty to his Redeemer, for the sake of extending the influence of his redemption, and bringing its reconciling and saving power to bear upon the myriads of immortal souls dwelling beyond the utmost verge of the Christian church.

And thus the foreign missionary is driven, as it were, by the very circumstances of his position, as well as led by his commission and his convictions of duty, to concentrate his attention and energies upon the SOUL, ruined though immortal. And truly it is a vast and mighty ruin he beholds— more affecting to look upon in the light of its own proper eternity, than would be the desolation of all the cities in the world. It is too vast a ruin for a feeble band to attempt the restoration of every part at once. As Nehemiah concentrated his energies upon rebuilding the walls of the city of his fathers, rightly concluding that if the walls were rebuilt and threw their encouraging protection around, the other portions of the city would rise of course; so the missionary, as a thoughtful and wise man, sets himself to reconcile the alienated heart to God, believing that that point being gained, and the principle of obedience implanted, and a highly spiritual religion introduced, a social renovation will be sure to follow. He considers not, therefore, so much the relations of man to man, as of man to God; not so much the relations and interests of time, as those of eternity; not so much the intellectual and social degradation and debasement, the result of barbarism or of iron-handed oppression, as the alienation and estrangement of the heart of man from his Maker, and the deadly influence of hateful and destroying passions upon his soul. As when a house is burning in the dead of night, our first and great concern is not for the house, but for the sleeping dwellers within; so the missionary's first and great concern is for the *soul*, to save it from impending wrath.

And the *means* he employs in this ministry of reconciliation, are as single and spiritual as the end he has in view.

He *preaches the cross of Christ*. The apostle Paul declares that this was his grand theme. And it is remarkable how experience is bringing modern missionaries to the same result. Their grand agent is oral instruction; their grand theme is the cross. And now, perhaps, not less than in the days of the apostles, the Holy Spirit appears to restrict his *converting* influences among the heathen chiefly to this species of agency, and to this grand theme. Excepting in the schools, the usefulness of books is chiefly with those whose hearts have been in some measure moved and roused by the preached word. It appears to be the will of the great Redeemer, who came in person to begin the work, that his salvation shall every where be proclaimed in person by his ambassadors, and that his message of grace shall have all the impressiveness of look, and voice, and manner, which they are able to give it. After the manner of their illustrious predecessor, they must teach publicly, and from house to house, and warn every one night and day with tears. The necessity of this, in order to reconcile rebellious men to God, has not been diminished by the multiplication of books through the press. Well-authenticated cases of *conversion* among pagans, by means of books alone, — not excepting even the Scriptures, — are exceedingly rare. By the divine appointment, there must also be the living preacher; and his preaching must not be " with the wisdom of words, lest the cross of Christ should be made of none effect."

You see, then, brethren, the high spiritual calling of the missionary. At the very threshold of his work, he is required, in a preëminent degree, to renounce the world. His message, wherein lies his duty and all his hope of success, is concerning the cross of Christ; and the object of it is to restore the lost spiritual relation between man and God. The impression he is designing to make is directly upon the soul. And his work lies so altogether out of the common range of worldly ideas, and even of the ideas of many professed Christians, that multitudes have no faith in it; it is to them like a root out of a dry ground, and they see no form nor comeliness in it, and nothing that should lead them to desire it. Nor is it until the civilizing results come out, that these unsanctified, or very partially sanctified persons can give the missionary work any degree of their respect.

The necessity of connecting a system of *education* with modern missions, is not inconsistent with the view we have taken of the true theory of missions to the heathen. The apostles had greatly the advantage of us in procuring elders, or pastors for their churches. In their day the most civilized portions of the world were heathen — as if to show the weakness of mere human learning and wisdom; and the missionary labors of the apostles and their associates, — so far as we have authentic accounts of them, — were in the best educated, and in some respects highly educated portions of the earth. Wherever they went, therefore, they found mind in comparatively an erect, intelligent, reasoning posture; and it would seem that men could easily have been found among their converts, who, with some special but brief instruction concerning the gospel, would be fitted to take the pastoral care of churches. But it appears, that, until schools expressly for training pastors were in operation, — as ere long they were at Alexandria, Cæsarea, Antioch, Edessa, and elsewhere, — it pleased God essentially to aid in qualifying men for the office of pastors by a miraculous agency; the Holy Ghost exerting upon them a supernatural influence, by which their understandings were strengthened and spiritually illuminated, and they gifted with powers of utterance.

But, at the present time, the whole civilized world is at least nominally Christian, and modern missions must be prosecuted among uncivilized, or at least partially civilized tribes and nations, from which useful ideas have in great measure perished. Even in those heathen nations which make the greatest pretensions to learning, as in India, we find but little truth existing on any subject. Their history, chronology, geography, astronomy, — their notions of matter and mind, and their views of creation and providence, religion and morals, — are exceedingly destitute of truth. And yet it is not so much a *vacuity* of mind here that we have to contend with, as it is *plenitude of error* — the unrestrained accumulations and perversions of depraved intellect for three thousand years. But among savage heathens, it is *vacuity* of mind, and not a *plenitude*, we have to operate upon. For, the savage has few ideas, sees only the objects just about him, perceives nothing of the relations of things, and occupies his thoughts only about his physical experiences and wants. He knows nothing of geography, astronomy, history, — nothing of his own spiritual nature and destiny, and nothing of God.

In these circumstances, and without the power of conferring miraculous gifts, modern missionaries are constrained to resort to education, in order to procure pastors for their churches. They select the most promising candidates, and take the usual methods to train them to stand alone and firm in the gospel ministry, and to be competent spiritual guides to others. This creates, it will be perceived, a necessity for a system of education of greater or less extent in each of the missions, embracing even a considerable number of elementary schools. The whole is designed to secure, through the divine blessing, a competent native ministry, who shall aid missionaries in their work, and at length take their places. The schools, moreover, of every grade, are, or ought to be so many preaching places, so many congregations of youth, to whom, often with parents and friends attending, the gospel is more or less formally proclaimed.

I have thus endeavored, my brethren, to set before you the foreign missionary enterprise, in what I conceive to be its true scriptural character; as an enterprise, the object of which, and the sole object, is the reconciling of rebellious men in heathen lands to God.

And what is true of the individual missionary, is of course equally true of the Missionary Society, which directs his labors, and is the medium of his support. The Society sends forth men to be evangelists, rather than permanent pastors; and when pastors are required by the progress and success of the work, it seeks them among native converts on the ground. And herein it differs from the appropriate usages of the Home Missionary Society, which, operating on feeble churches within Christian communities, or in districts that are soon to be covered with a Christian civilization of some sort, sends forth its preachers, all to become settled pastors as soon as possible. The foreign missionary work is, in fact, a vast *evangelism;* with conquest, in order to extend the bounds of the Redeemer's kingdom, for its object; having as little to do with the relations of this life, and the things of the world and sense, and as few relations to the kingdoms of this world, as is consistent with the successful prosecution of its one grand object — the restoring, in the immortal soul of man, of that blessed attraction to the Centre of the Spiritual Universe which was lost at the fall.

This method of conducting foreign missions, beside its evident conformity to Scripture, is supported by various weighty considerations.

1. It is the only method that, as a system of measures, will commend itself strongly to the consciences and respect of mankind.

The first mission sent forth under the care of the American Board, was such a mission. And it was sent to the subjects of a nation, with which our country was then unhappily at war. But the missionaries were regarded on all hands as belonging preëminently to a kingdom not of this world, and having an object of a purely spiritual nature. And when, notwithstanding this, the policy of the East Indian government would have sent them away, it was this that gave convincing and overwhelming force to the following appeal made by our brethren to the Governor of Bombay:

"We entreat you by the spiritual miseries of the heathen, who are daily perishing before your eyes, and under your Excellency's government, not to prevent us from preaching Christ to them. We entreat you by the blood of Jesus which he shed to redeem them, — as ministers of Him, who has all power in heaven and earth, and who with his farewell and ascending voice commanded his ministers to go and teach all nations, we entreat you not to prohibit us from teaching these heathen. By all the principles of our holy religion, by which you hope to be saved, we entreat you not to hinder us from preaching the same religion to these perishing idolaters. By all the solemnities of the judgment day, when your Excellency must meet your heathen subjects before God's tribunal, we entreat you not to hinder us from preaching to them that gospel, which is able to prepare them, as well as you, for that awful day."

Nothing but a consciousness of the high spirituality of their object, and the impossibility of connecting it with questions of a secular nature, imparted boldness to our brethren to make this appeal, and gave it favor and efficacy in the high places of power. And it is this, which lately preserved our brethren on Mount Lebanon harmless amid the fury and carnage of a civil war. And this it is that imparts a degree of inviolability to the persons and efforts of Protestant heralds of the cross among all the nations which respect their religion. It is the grand predominance of the *spiritual* in their characters and pursuits, showing that they really do belong to a kingdom not of this world, and are not to be involved in the conflicting relations and interests of earthly communities. English statesmen in India acknowledge, that the general prevalance of Christianity in that country would at length make it impossible for their nation to hold the country in subjection, and yet they encourage the labors of the missionary. This they do because the missionary's *object*, — whatever be the known *tendency* of his labors, — is not to change the civil relations of the people, but to give them the gospel and save their souls; and because these statesmen are convinced in their consciences, that this is an object of unquestionable benevolence and obligation, for which Christ died, for which the ministry was instituted, — which at this day is to be countenanced and encouraged, at all events, by every man claiming the name of a Christian; and which, — however humbling it shall prove in its results to avaricious and ambitious nations, — cannot be otherwise than beneficial on the broad scale of the world, and to the great family of man.

2. This method of conducting missions is the only one, on

which missionaries can be obtained in large numbers, and kept cheerfully in the field.

For objects that are not spiritual and eternal, men will seldom renounce the world for themselves and their families, as missionaries must do. Mere philosophers have never gone as missionaries; and seldom do mere philanthropists go into the heathen world, nor would they remain long, should they happen to go. Nor will a merely impulsive, unreflective piety ever bring about a steady, persevering, laborious, self-denying mission. It generally gives out before the day for embarkation, or retires from the field before the language is acquired, and the battle fairly commenced. Nothing but the grand object of reconciling men to God, with a view to their eternal salvation, and the happiness and glory thus resulting to Christ's kingdom, will call any considerable number of missionaries into the foreign field, and keep them cheerfully there. And it is necessary that this object be made to stand out alone, in its greatness and majesty, towering above all other objects, as the hoary-headed monarch of the Alps towers above the inferior mountains around him. It is not fine conceptions of the beautiful and orderly in human society that will fire the zeal of a missionary; it is not rich and glowing conceptions of the life and duties of a pastor; it is not broad and elevated views of theological truth, nor precise and comprehensive views of the relations of that truth to moral subjects. It is something more than all this, often the result of a different cast of mind and combination of ideas. The true missionary character indeed is based upon a single sublime conception — that of *reconciling immortal souls to God*. To gain this with an effective practical power, the missionary needs himself to have passed from death unto life, and to have had deep experience of his own enmity to God and hell-desert, and of the the vast transforming agency of the reconciling grace of God in Christ. As this conception has more of moral greatness and sublimity in it than any other that ever entered the mind of man, no missionary can attain to the highest elevation and dignity of his calling, unless he have strong mental power and a taste for the morally sublime. This the apostle Paul had. What conceptions of his office, and work, and of spiritual things animated the great soul of that apostle! "Now, then, we are ambassadors for Christ; as though God did beseech you by us, we pray you in Christ's stead, be ye reconciled to God." "Eye hath not seen, nor ear heard, neither have entered into the heart of man the things which God hath prepared for them that love him." "O, the depth of the riches both of the wisdom and knowledge of God." "Able to comprehend with all saints what is the breadth, and length, and depth, and height, and to know the love of Christ, which passeth knowledge."

To make persevering and useful missionaries, however, it is not necessary that the power of thought and of spiritual apprehension should come nearly up to that of the apostle Paul. But there should be a similar cast of mind, similar views and feelings, and a similar character. There should be a steady and sober, but real enthusiasm, sustained by a strongly spiritualized doctrinal experience, and by the " powers of the world to come," intent upon reconciling men to God from a conviction of its transcendent importance.

Such men must compose the great body of every mission, or it will not be worth supporting in the field; and the only way such men can be induced to engage in the work, is by having the idea of spiritual conquest, through the cross of Christ, the predominant and characteristic idea of the enterprise. That will attract their attention while they are preparing for the ministry; that will enlist their consciences and draw their hearts; that will constrain them to refuse every call to settle at home, however inviting; and if they have learning and eloquence, that will lead them the more to desire to go where Christ has not been preached, where useful talent of every kind will find the widest scope for exercise.

Nor will any other scheme of missions, that was ever devised, keep missionaries cheerfully in the field. It is only by having the eye intent on the relations the heathen sustain to God, and on their reconciliation to him, and by cultivating the spirit of dependence on God and the habit of looking to him for success, that the piety of a mission can be kept flourishing, its bond of union perfect, its active powers all in full, harmonious and happy exercise. And unless these results are secured, missionaries, like the soldiers of a disorganized army, will lose their courage, their energy and zeal, their serenity and health, and will leave the field. Alas for a mission, where the absorbing object of attention with any of its members is anything else, than how Christ crucified shall be preached to the heathen so as most effectually to persuade them to be reconciled to God.

3. This method of conducting missions is the only one, that will subjugate the heathen world to God.

No other will be found mighty to pull down the strong holds of the god of this world. The weapons of our warfare must be spiritual. The enemy will laugh at the shaking of a spear, at diplomatic skill, at commerce, learning, philanthropy, and every scheme of social order and refinement. He stands in fear of nothing but the cross of Christ, and therefore we must rely on nothing else. With that we may boldly pass all his outworks and entrenchments, and assail his very citadel. So did Philip, when he preached Jesus as the way of reconciliation to the eunuch; so did Peter, when preaching to the centurion; so did Apollos, when preaching to the Greeks; so did Paul, through his whole missionary career. It is wonderful what faith those ancient worthies had in the power of a simple statement of the doctrine of salvation through the blood of Christ. But they had felt its power in their own hearts, they saw it on the hearts of others, and they found reason to rely on nothing else. And the experience of modern missions has done much to teach the inefficacy of all things else, separate from this. Who does not know, that the only cure for the deep-seated disorders of mankind must be wrought in the heart, and that nothing operates there like the doctrine of salvation by the cross of Christ? This is true in the most highly civilized communities; but perhaps it is specially true among benighted heathens. In their deplorable moral degradation, they need just such an argument, striking even the very senses, and convincing of sin, of their own lost state, and of the love of God. Nothing else will be found like that to bridge the mighty gulf which separates their thoughts from God and the spiritual world. Nothing else will concentrate, like that, the rays of divine truth and grace upon their frozen affections. With the truth, that God so loved the world as to give his only begotten Son that whosoever believeth on him should not perish but have everlasting life, we go forth through the heathen world; and, with any thing like the faith in its efficacy through the Holy Spirit which the apostles had, we shall be blessed with much of their success. Yes, my brethren, this is the only effectual way of prosecuting missions among the heathen — *holding up* CHRIST AS THE ONLY SAVIOUR OF LOST SINNERS. It requires the fewest men, the least expense, the shortest time. It makes the least demand for learning in the great body of the laborers. It involves the least complication in means and measures. It is the only course that has the absolute promise of the presence of Christ, or that may certainly look for the aid of the Holy Spirit. It keeps Christ constantly before the missionary's own soul, as an object of intensest interest and desire, with a vast sanctifying, sustaining, animating influence on his own mind and preaching. It furnishes him with a power transcending all that human wisdom ever contrived, for rousing and elevating the soul of man and drawing it heavenward — the idea of LOVE, infinite and infinitely disinterested, personified in the Lord Jesus, and suffering to the death to save rebellious and ruined man! And if the doctrine comes glowing from our own experience, we shall not fail to get the attention of the heathen, and our success among them will far exceed what we might expect among gospel-hardened sinners here at home. I might dwell long on the history of missions, ancient and modern, in the most satisfactory illustration of this point, did the time permit; but it is not necessary.

Let me add, that there is no way so direct and effectual as this, to remove the social disorders and evils that afflict the heathen world; indeed, there is no other way. Every specific evil and sin does not need and cannot have a separate remedy, for they are all streams from one fountain, having a common origin in a depraved and rebellious heart. Urge home, then, the divinely-appointed remedy for a wicked heart; purify the fountain; let love to God and man fill the soul; and soon its influence will appear in every department and relation of life. If reforms in religion and morals are not laid deep in the heart, they will be deceptive, and at all events transient. The evil spirit will return in some form, and with seven-fold power. New England owes her strong repugnance to slavery, and her universal rejection of that monstrous evil, to the highly evangelical nature of her preaching. And were the whole southern section of our own land, or even a considerable portion of it, favored with such highly evangelical preaching, slavery could not there long exist. But in heathen lands especially, an effective public sentiment against sin, in any of its outward forms, can be created no where, except in the church; and it can be there created only by preaching Christ in his offices and works of love and mercy, with the aid of the ordinances he has given for the benefit of his disciples, especially the sacrament of his supper.

Thus at length, even in barbarous heathen lands, the force of piety in the hearts of the individual members of the church will be raised above that of ignorance, prejudice, the power of custom and usage, the blinding influence of self-interest falsely apprehended, and the ridicule and frowns of an ungodly and perverse world. Indeed, if we would make any thing of converts in pagan lands, we must bring them to the ordinances of the gospel, and into the church, as soon as they give satisfactory evidence of regeneration; for they are too child-like, too weak, too ignorant to be left exposed to the dangers that exist out of the fold, even until they shall have learned all fundamental truths. And besides, the school of Christ for young converts from heathenism, *stands within the fold*, and *there*, certainly, the compassionate Saviour would have them all gathered, and carried in the arms, and cherished "even as a nurse cherisheth her children."

Finally; This method of conducting missions is the only one, that will unite in this work the energies of the churches at home.

Well understood, this will unite the energies of the churches — so far as Christians can be induced to prosecute missions for the purpose of reconciling men to God. Making this the grand aim of missions, and pressing the love of Christ home upon the hearts and consciences of men, as the grand means of effecting this, will certainly commend itself to the understandings and feelings of all intelligent Christians. Not only will a large number of good and faithful missionaries be obtained, but they will be supported, and prayed for, and made the objects of daily interest and concern. And how delightful it is to think, that the Head of the church has been pleased to make the object and work of missions so entirely simple, so spiritual, and so beyond the possibility of exception, that evangelical Christians of every nation and name can unite in its promotion. But if we change the form of the work, and extend the range of its objects of direct pursuit, and of course multiply the measures and influences by which it is to be advanced, we then open the door for honest and invincible diversities of opinion among the best of men, and render it impossible that there should be united effort, on a scale at all commensurate with the work, and for a long period. The church militant becomes divided and weak, and is easily paralyzed and thwarted in its movements by the combined and united legions of the Prince of darkness.

It would seem, therefore, that missions to the heathen must have a highly spiritual nature and developement, or prove utterly impracticable and abortive. Such, it is believed, are the convictions of all who have had much experience in such enterprises. Unless missions have this nature and developement in a very high degree, they will not commend themselves strongly to the consciences and respect of mankind; they will neither command the requisite number of laborers, nor keep them cheerfully in the field; they will prove inadequate to the subjugation of the heathen world to God; nor will they unite in this great enterprize the energies and prayers of the churches. In a word, they will not continue long to exist, unless Christ the Lamb of God be in them, reconciling the world unto himself, and causing his servants to make the salvation of the souls of men their all-commanding end and aim. Men may *resolve* that it shall be otherwise; but their purposes, however decided, will be in vain against the unalterable laws, which God has given the work of missions to the heathen.

BELOVED BROTHER,— In the system of missions, with which you are soon to be connected, the aim has been, and is more and more, as experience is acquired, to prosecute the work on the principles advocated in this discourse. So far as your own influence is concerned, see that the system be rendered still more spiritual in its temper, objects, and measures. See, too, that your own renunciation of the world is entire before you enter upon your self-denying work, and that it be your determination to know nothing among the heathen but Christ and him crucified. Only by looking constantly unto Jesus, will you be able to run with patience the race set before you. As an ambassador of Christ, sent to plead with men in his stead to be reconciled to God, see that you are true to your vocation, and faithful to your trust, and that you never descend from the elevated ground you occupy. Whatever oscillations in public sentiment there may be from time to time in the Christian mind at home, you need not fear, if your character, preaching, and influence are formed on the New Testament, that you will be forgotten in the contributions and prayers of God's people. At all events, be faithful unto death, and whatever be your lot here below, the result in eternity will be more blessed to you, than it is possible for your mind now to conceive, or your heart to desire.

FATHERS AND BRETHREN, — Let it be our prayer, that

God will be pleased to strengthen our own faith in the realities of the unseen world. Then shall we be better able to pray as we ought for our missionary brethren, that they may be intent on their single but great object of winning souls to Christ, and be so imbued with the spirit of Christ, that his image shall be fully stamped on all their converts. Let us urge upon our brethren among the heathen the imperative duty of making full proof of their ministry as *missionaries*, rather than as *pastors;* and let us lay upon them "no greater burden," than the "necessary things" appertaining to their high and peculiar vocation. We must indeed hold them to the principle, that they shall treat those only as loyal subjects of our infinite Sovereign, who give evidence of hearty submission and reconciliation; but we will leave it to their better-informed judgments to determine, — in the remote, vast, and varied, and to us almost unknown fields of their labors, — what is and what ought to be satisfactory evidence of actual reconciliation. Then will our brethren rejoice in having a simple, well-sustained, and glorious enterprise before them, and also "for the consolation" of the liberty conceded to them by the "elders" and the "whole church." In this good old way, marked with the footsteps of the apostles, there is hope for the world, for the whole world, that it may be reconciled to God. And when the principles of love and obedience are once restored to men, and men are at peace with God, and united to Him, then will they be at peace with one another. Then wars will cease, and all oppression. Then the crooked in human affairs shall be made straight and the rough places plain, the valleys shall be exalted and the mountains and hills made low, and the glory of the Lord shall be revealed, and all flesh see it together.

> "In one sweet symphony of praise,
>   Gentile and Jew shall then unite;
> And Infidelity, ashamed,
>   Sink in the abyss of endless night.
>
> " Soon Afric's long-enslaved sons
>   Shall join with Europe's polished race,
> To celebrate, in different tongues,
>   The glories of redeeming grace.
>
> " From east to west, from north to south,
>   Emanuel's kingdom shall extend;
> And every man, in every face,
>   Shall meet a brother and a friend."

JESUS THE GREAT MISSIONARY.

BY

REV. EDWARD N. KIRK.

For the Son of man is come to seek and to save that which was lost.—LUKE 19: 10.

THE meaning of that word — *lost*, is the separating-point from which diverge the most important sentiments, that divide the nominally Christian world. It affects essentially all our religious opinions, character, and career. If one sees in it but a flourish of rhetoric, or an oriental exaggeration; then his conscience slumbers; then his sympathies feel no deep appeal from man's condition and prospects; and then his heart lies chilled beneath the cold moon-beams of the gospel. For, to him that gospel opens on the one hand, no thrilling scene of spirits fallen, defiled, benighted and accursed; and on the other, no enrapturing display of love, of condescension lower than angels had dared anticipate, of mercy's immeasurable sacrifice made despite of base ingratitude and of parricidal rebellion. To him the gospel is a description of goodness similar to, but no greater than that displayed in the ordinary gifts of Providence. Such is the theory and such are the fruits of the skeptical and semi-skeptical philosophy. Wherever it is accepted, the distinction between man's native powers and sensibilities and his actual character as a subject of God's government, is lost sight of; human nature is admired almost to adoration; repentance, as that deep emotion which breaks the heart and bruises the spirit, is despised. Thus, whatever other "sacrifices" are offered to God, among them is not found a "broken heart and a bruised spirit." Thus it acts on the personal piety of the individual, and thus it affects his influence on others. In himself he finds more to admire than to condemn; when he discovers wrong, he considers it superficial; no deep and painful sense of spiritual necessity corresponding to descriptions in the Bible, is felt by him. Calm self-complacency is indeed the very feeling which he seeks to derive from religion. And if he sees anything else and opposite in others, it causes only contempt or pity. He approves not their deep and pungent convictions of guilt and misery, nor comprehends how the atoning sacrifice of the Lamb of God is needed for his guilt, and the regenerating power of the Holy Ghost for his depravity.

Their fundamental error is on two points, and respects two aspects of human nature — man as the subject of law; and man in his capacity for a spiritual life.

Their views of man's guilt and ill-desert are comparatively slight. They allow him to be satisfied with the contemplation of his own excellence, his intellectual qualities, his social feelings, his moral sensibilities. They hold in abhorrence only certain crimes against civil laws and social order. They excite and they allow no deep and heart-breaking convictions for spiritual offences; they arouse no fears of endless punishment. They go to the neglecter of religion, and persuade him to become more attentive to religious truths and duties. They go to the Pagan, and urge him to embrace a purer rite, a more rational theology. Their appeals are not made to the conscience, to start it from deep slumbers, and make it echo the thunders of coming judgment. And when they find it awakened, they proclaim to it no peace-speaking sacrifice for sin; in fact, they censure this very alarm, and attribute it to ignorance and error. Hence they find nothing in man's prospects to enlist deeply their own solicitude. Hence they accord not with us in our endeavors to awaken a slumbering world by strong appeals to make it hear — amid what they call its innocent amusements and occupations — the voice of an insulted Deity, of an outraged Father, of the threatening majesty of Heaven.

Thus we differ from them in our estimate of the extent and purity of the precepts of the divine law. We consider all the world as its guilty violators; we consider all human virtue in man's unconverted state, as truly sin; and the more sinful, the more it becomes an object of admiration to its possessor, and an occasion of undervaluing the mediation and propitiatory sacrifice of the Son of God.

Equally antipathetic are our views of man's spiritual

character. Of the dignity of his original character and position, of the noble character of some of the sentiments of a few, we have as high an estimate as any. But we believe that the spiritual image of God is effaced from the human soul; man is fallen, terribly, desperately fallen; the gold has lost its lustre. His virtues are to us the white exteriors and the gilded ornaments of the sepulchre. His smiles are to us the more painful, as they convince us that he is, or tries to be contented with his state of spiritual poverty, guilt, and degradation. In a word, we consider man as alienated from God; intellectually and physically alive, spiritually dead. And therefore we cannot content ourselves by endeavoring to refine and elevate a few of the most highly favored of our race; we must reach all men. They are all wanderers from the home of the soul, the bosom of God; and they must all be persuaded to return. The malady of sin lies deeply fixed in the immortal part, the soul; and therefore intellectual elevation and social refinement do not remove it, and have no tendency to remove it. We regard the gospel applied by God's spirit as the sole remedy. Christ is their life; Christ, the lamb of God that taketh away the sin of the world; Christ, the ever-living intercessor; Christ, the medium and fountain of the life-giving Spirit. The world — all the world, high and low, princes and peasants, learned and ignorant, virtuous and vicious, idolaters, infidels and nominal Christians — must believe in Christ, or "be damned;" damned at that tribunal where the believers shall be pardoned; damned by the malediction of the Holy One who appears "in the glory of his Father, taking vengeance on them that obey not the gospel."

From these different estimates of man arise, what should not arise, hostile feelings; but hence arise also necessarily, our different courses with regard to man. With our views, we shall never be satisfied without the most strenuous efforts to bring all mankind to repentance and faith in Christ. With their views, they naturally look with indifference on the earnestness and self-denial of missionary life, and the success of missionary enterprise, so far as the work of the Spirit of God upon the heart is concerned.

It behooves us then to review our premises. The sincere mind is ever ready to ask — Am I right? We are willing to ask and wait candidly for the reply to these questions; — How must I regard human nature, myself and my fellow-men? What is my highest duty with respect to my immortal self, and what with respect to my fellow men?

Nay; we are not taking up this subject for the first time. We have already decided and felt and acted upon it. We who have embarked in the missionary enterprise, are a small minority of the civilized world, perhaps a minority even of the religious world. We have spent large sums of money, yea squandered wealth, if we are wrong; we are still doing it, and we are arousing the churches to intenser feeling and more liberal effort. We desire to consecrate our very selves to this enterprise. Life is rapidly passing away, and we are devoting its best hours and energies to this work. Some of our number have severed every tie of home and nation, have adopted a life of exile and privation; wisely, if our views of man are truth; madly and miserably, if they are error. We are now assembled to sympathize with another who has ventured his temporal all upon the truth of our sentiments. We together look upon the situation of mankind apart from the provisions of the gospel, and away from under its influences, as inconceivably dreadful and desperate. Our souls are moved with deep compassion, our hearts are oppressed, as we contemplate his present state and his prospects beyond this life. We want to rush to his rescue. Are we right or are we wrong? Are these emotions excited in view of truth and stern reality, or by a delusion of our own imaginations? Have we yielded to the influence of an unenlightened education; or is it in view of facts that we are impelled and that we act? We desire truth and only truth. We desire to see things now, as far as practicable, as we shall see them, when the illusions of time shall have given place to the light of eternity. We have also a desire to vindicate our course to an intelligent world; and if we are right, to become in our turn the reprovers of its unbelieving indifference. And we may by divine blessing accomplish one other good by our meditations upon this subject; even that of guarding our hearts against the chills of unbelief, and of quickening in them a deeper sympathy, stronger zeal and holier purposes.

Brethren, we spend this tender and sacred hour in contemplating, devoutly, JESUS, THE GREAT MISSIONARY. He is the Judge that ends the strife. He is the Logos, the Truth. All his views were truth, all his sentiments righteousness. There was, even in his finite human nature, no error in theory, no misapprehension of facts, no exaggerated impulse, no passion. He says he came to seek and to save that which is lost. That looks to us like calling him the Great Missionary, the Pattern of all Missionaries, the Founder of our missionary institutions. We go forth to seek and to save that which is lost; and we believe that our views and our course are an imitation of his, and an obedience to his last command, " Go ye into all the world, and preach the gospel to every creature."

We propose then to examine the meaning of the term "lost," as here employed, by the views which Jesus entertained of men, and by his conduct toward them. By,

I. HIS ESTIMATE OF MAN. What extent of meaning did he attach to the term " lost " ?

1. He regarded man as a depraved and apostate spirit. Depraved and apostate are relative terms, referring to a certain standard of perfection and excellence. Man was made for great moral purposes, to conform to a type of perfect excellence, to attain great heights of moral elevation. Such was in fact the original, native tendency of his constitution. And there is his dignity. Now if the Saviour considered the present state of man as conformed to that type, then he did not regard him as depraved and apostate. And happily we are left to no conjectures here. We have something better too, than dry and uncertain etymologies. Whenever we can ascertain what Jesus considered holiness and the spiritual life to be, then we can tell from our own knowledge of man, what he considered to be his actual state. And yet better, — we may know directly what opinions he had on this subject. His ideas of holiness are seen in his own character and actions, — of which it might be enough here to say, that all men consider them perfect, and yet totally unlike those of any other man. One has well said of him; " To God, as the source of his spiritual life, was his soul ever turned ; and this direction of his mind was a matter of indispensable necessity to him. It was his meat and his drink to do the will of his Father. Without uniting himself wholly to God, consecrating himself to God unreservedly, feeling himself to be perfectly one with God, he could not have lived, he could not have been at peace in his spirit a single instant. By this means the morality of Jesus became perfectly religious; it was not merely something which flowed from a sense of duty, it was a holy sentiment of the heart." Now whom did Jesus regard as possessing that spiritual life which consists in rising above created good to live in God, to feast on his smile and breathe the atmosphere of his love ? Was it the poor

idolater of the surrounding pagan tribes; was it the proud, sanctimonious Pharisee, inwardly full of putrefaction as the grave; was it the infidel, sensual Sadducee, who ridiculed all pretensions to spiritual communion; was it the crowd who followed him, not for truth and spiritual aliment, but for bread; was it the rich young ruler, so amiable, so pure, so sincere, who went away sorrowful when he learned that God and mammon cannot be loved and served together; nay, was it the half-converted Peter, whom he rebuked as fearing, in the spirit of Satan, the sacrifice of self; or John and James who then looked, in serving God, for the honors of a temporal kingdom; was it, in a word, the being, of whom it is recorded, that Jesus "knew what was in man," and therefore trusted not himself to him? Oh no! the Son of God walked like a living man among the tombs; and the silence of the second death had reigned there forever, if his own omnipotent voice had not cried — " Lazarus, come forth."

We have another exhibition of the Saviour's views of what constitutes the spiritual life, in his benedictions. "Blessed are the poor in spirit, the pure in heart, the peace-makers, they who hunger and thirst after righteousness, they who love him more than parents and possessions; nay, that forsake all things, even life itself, for His sake and the gospel's." Now, can we believe that he considered mankind generally in his day or that he considers the men of this or any other period, as pure in heart, peace-makers, seeking spiritual good with an eagerness like that of the corporeal appetites; seeking their rest in God, as the weary body seeks its couch; longing for God, as the hunted hart pants for the water brook, or as the shipwrecked mariner longs for morning light? Can mankind generally say sincerely, "My heart and my flesh crieth out for the living God?" Impossible.

Our Saviour again presents the standard of human excellence; "Thou shalt love the Lord thy God with all thy heart, soul, mind and strength, and thy neighbor as thyself." And did he think that idolaters, the profane, the neglecters of God's service, those who love pleasure more than God, the proud, the covetous, the sensual, — did he believe that they were good, when compared with that standard — thou shalt love God supremely and perfectly? Or the envious, ambitious, fraudulent, cruel, tyrannical, impure slanderers; do they love others as themselves? Do they in India, Africa, Europe, America? Did they in any part or age of the world?

Ask history. It is indeed too generally the record of the powerful. But it shows what all would do if their circumstances permitted. And have the powerful been good? Have their lives been examples of piety; have their energies been consecrated to the public welfare? There have been a Cyrus, an Aristides, a Joshua, a St. Louis, an Alfred. But they are the exceptions. The history of kingdoms is a record of wars and their horrors, of frauds and oppressions. What says the social state of mankind? Let the condition of woman speak in all the lands where human nature has acted out its unobstructed tendencies. What is a Turkish wife, an Indian mother, a Hindoo widow? Come home then to the criminal codes and criminal courts and criminal establishments of Christian America. Leave the poetry of the parlor; lay down that enchanting book which enraptures you with its visions of human dignity and loveliness; leave that circle of refinement, where a favored few have separated themselves from the vulgar, to enjoy a higher intellectual and social life; and come with me out among the mass of this moving population. Let us go into the lanes and alleys, the alms-houses, the hospitals, the prisons. Shrink not, admirer of human nature! this is man, godlike man. Do you know that thousands of the very children of this city are liars, thieves, impure, profane? And what of the pagan world! Oh! let the missionary tell you, who, having gone out to make common interest with the heathen, has examined deeply into his character. Here are nearly five hundred millions; and yet the portrait in the first chapter of the epistle to the Romans remains fearfully accurate. And does this being, man, remain as he was, when, coming pure and perfect from his Creator's hands, he was pronounced very good? And what commission have diseases and death in this fair world? Who opened the door by which they rushed in upon their prey? Did God make man for this? *You* must say, Yes. The Bible says, "by *sin*, death entered into the world; and so death passed upon all men, for that *all* have sinned." Each breath you draw marks the death of three of your race. The first may be the lovely bride, decked for the altar; the next the father of a dependent family; the next the sovereign, who has been the father of his people. No place is so exalted, none so sacred, that disease cannot invade it. No tie is so tender and so precious that death will spare it. And when you visit the burial-yard; ask whether man is as God made him? Was he made to be the slave of Satan; the sport of tempests and the prey of death; was he made for poverty and filth, for rags and wo? Oh no! he is fallen. The race is fallen. If we want another test, we have it in the pure worship which Jesus rendered the Father. Place this by the side of human religions. The greater part of them are bloody, and seem to have preserved the tradition, that "without shedding of blood, is no remission" of sins. But they are also impure, and thus declare the deep apostacy of man, when his very religions remove him farther from God and holiness. If he makes a Jupiter, he is a monster of lust; a Mars, he drives his chariot over the dying; a Mercury, he is chief of robbers; a Juggernaut, he feasts on mangled human limbs. And when a pure revelation is given to him, first in a single nation, he turns backward ever toward idolatry; and when Christianity is given to the nations, they pervert and pervert it, until, of the two hundred and fifty millions who possess it, one hundred and ninety millions are sunk in superstition and idolatry little better than paganism itself. The moral condition of France and Spain and Italy, the history of religious persecutions conducted in the name of Jesus Christ, and as the expansion of his spirit and as obedience to his precepts, appear to us sad confirmations of the truth of our view, that man is lost, because he is a depraved and apostate creature.

We learn again our Saviour's estimate of men, in the direct expression of his views. And here we are at a loss to select; for the full exhibition of all that is contained in the Evangelists on this point, would be but piling passage on passage. He describes the condition and prospects of man in parables and in simple historic language in ways that appear to us impossible to misapprehend. If man is an apostate and depraved creature, then we shall expect to hear that the way to heaven is of difficult attainment, and entered by but few. If man is not an apostate, but an innocent, upright, pure being, then he has only to obey his instincts, to cultivate his noble nature, and he is holy and happy. It surely connot be difficult to decide what Jesus thought on that point. "Broad is the road that leadeth to destruction, and *many* go in thereat, while narrow is the way that leadeth to life, and *few* there be that find it. If any man will come after me, let him" what? cultivate his good heart? — no; "deny himself." And in how many ways does he describe us as poor and miserable and blind, and sick and weary, burdened, imprisoned, enslaved, dead, exposed to endless destruction. If not sick, we have no need of him; if not sinners, he has no message to us, for "they that are whole need not a physician, but they that are sick." In his conversation with Nicodemus, he says that we must be regenerated, and that whoever is not, cannot be saved. And mark his emphatic reason: "that which is born of the flesh, is flesh." By our natural birth, we inherit only that which cannot inherit heaven. In the natural birth, there is a terrible entailment of degeneracy; and so there needs a supernatural birth, a birth of the Spirit. With all this in view, it is impossible to believe that Jesus regarded man as a refined, noble, elevated being, — as in his present state, the type of perfection. He never says it, he never intimates it. We look in vain for passages in all his addresses, as well as in all the writings of his disciples, to find a language or a sentiment like that which we constantly hear about the purity and nobleness and virtue of individual men.

But in this connection we cannot pass by the portrait of man given in the story of the prodigal son. Its very object was to reprove the self-righteous men who thought they had done no wrong, and had not wandered from their father's house. We cite this here particularly, because the very term whose meaning we seek, is the hinge of the story. Here was one *lost* to his father. There is something in the word — *lost*, which falls on our ear like a death-knell. It presents to us the twofold idea contained in this story, and in the two in its context, — that of disappointment to God's affectionate interest for us, and to our own hopes of blessedness. Observe the word *lost* illustrated here three times. The shepherd has lost his sheep, than which nothing is dearer to him; the woman her means of living; the father his son. Observe this picture of man; a wanderer — a wanderer from home, from God, from heaven and infinite love. The son of a kind and wealthy man feels the temptings of ambitious independence, and yields to their influence. He leaves the paternal roof to escape the paternal eye. He gathers all, and goes into a far country, to find his happiness. But it was there "he began to be in want." It was there he plunged from depth to deeper depths of misery. Poor young man! we pity him; we blame him too. But alas! we are speaking of ourselves. This is the portrait of the race. Fellow-men, we are in that far country; we are lost to God and to ourselves. Yes, he says it; — for behold yon shepherd; what does he in the wild and desert place, exposing himself to pains and dangers? Oh, he comes to seek and to save that which is lost. Yes, we are lost to God; — for, behold that aged and injured father running to meet the wandering boy when yet a great way off; falling on his neck; embracing, kissing him, exclaiming "This, my son, was dead and is alive again, was *lost*, and is found;" — lost to the angels; for there is joy in heaven over one repenting sinner. Our noble faculties, our affections are lost to God; for we love him not, praise nor serve him; and in place of preparing to dwell in his blessed family, we force him to pronounce and execute upon us the fearful sentence of his law. That young man returned; but not until he was convinced of his guilt and folly, not until he felt that he was in want. Had any one met him there, and convinced him that he had not wandered — then he had never returned. That young man returned; and heaven is to be re-peopled by these returning, repenting prodigals; — and will there be there any elder sons of Adam's family, who have never wandered? We believe not. That man is a depraved and apostate creature, is written on every line of the Saviour's biography and on every syllable of his instructions. But,

2. He regarded man also as a condemned criminal. According to his saying to Nicodemus, "He that believeth not, is condemned already." This was said in connection with a comparison of man's moral condition to the physical state of the Israelites who were bitten by the fiery serpents. They, says the Saviour, were to be healed by looking at the uplifted symbol of God's righteous judgments against their sins; so we, who are dying beneath the righteous anger of God, are to be healed by believing on Him who was lifted up for us on the accursed tree. But whoever believes not, remains in his state of condemnation. This condemnation includes two facts — that of transgression, and that of punishment. — Jesus did regard men as sinners. But our ideas of sin are superficial and unimpressive; those of Jesus were deep and awful. He traced each outward sin to the heart, the fountain of spiritual death; and he detected sin in the heart, where no outward sign was given to man. And he showed that it were better to lose limb and life, reputation and each dear interest of earth, rather than to remain a sinner; for sin is

the transgression of the law, of God's holy law. It is a terrible thing to infringe the laws that control the material world. For, says a French preacher, "though the sea should burst its limits, and cover the earth with a new deluge; though its furious waves should overturn and sweep away every thing in their passage; though they should roll down with their fracas the rocks rent from the mountains, the uprooted trees, the dead bodies of men and animals, and should make of our globe only a watery waste,— the disorder thus produced would not deserve to be named by the side of that which sin produces. Though the world should totter on its ancient base, and reel from its foundations; though the stars and their systems should rush into wild disorder, and dash against each other; and the universe revert to a more frightful chaos than that from which God brought it at the beginning; this disorder, this overturning of all material things, would not deserve to be compared with the disorder that sin produces." And this, because the one is the disorder of ignoble and perishable matter; the other is the ruin of mind. And not only has sin taken possession of the heart of man,— but without supernatural aid, that possession must be indefinitely permanent. There is no tendency in human depravity towards self-recovery and perfection. In all that we have known of it, its course is ever downward, downward, and forever downward! Sin never yet exhausted itself in this world, nor in one heart. Every instance of recovery from its dominion is called by Jesus the conquest of a strong man armed by a stronger than he. And while man is thus a sinner, a transgressor of law, he is exposed to eternal death. If the warnings and expostulations of Christ do not teach that, then they are to us without meaning. "Wo unto thee, Chorazin, and to thee, Bethsaida; for it shall be more tolerable for Tyre and Sidon, Sodom and Gomorrah, than for you! And thou Capernaum! exalted to heaven, shalt be thrust down to hell. What is a man profited, if he shalt gain the whole world, and lose his own soul? Or what shall a man give in exchange for his soul? There shall be weeping and wailing and gnashing of teeth. Dives after death lifted up his eyes in hell, being tormented." The net and fishes, the wise and foolish virgins, the wheat and tares, the separation of the sheep and goats, the treatment of the unfaithful steward, all tell us what he believes concerning man's eternal destiny. But nothing he uttered is more terrible than the declaration, that he himself will say at last to the wicked, "Depart, ye cursed, into everlasting fire, prepared for the devil and his angels." Men may close their ears, and shut their eyes to this; but it is the word of God. Men may refuse to hear it; but there it stands, a yet unfulfilled prophecy, made if possible more certain to us, by the past fulfilment of the others which surround it. Yes, as certain as was the destruction of Babylon and Tyre, the deluge of water and the flood of fire on a guilty world; as certain and as terrible as was the destruction of Jerusalem, will be the utterance and execution of those terrific words. And as idle and impotent will be the scoffs and self-reasonings of this day, as were those of that day, to arrest the judgments of God. But who can measure their meaning? "*Cursed!*" it is terrible to be cursed by a man, a wicked man, without cause; but to be cursed by a Father, by a being who never errs in judgment, a being who never condemns unjustly, a being who suffered to save us, a being who has long expostulated in view of this very judgment, a being who commands the elements of the universe to execute his purposes, a being who ranks his glorious perfections to flash conviction to the centre of my guilty conscience! You say, this is extravagant; but it is scriptural. You say, it is cruel; but whether is it cruelty to flatter and deceive and hide impending danger, or to expose it fully and earnestly? Men are to be cursed. What *is* this curse? A charge to the universe to dry up each fountain of delight, and open on my guilty soul its avenging streams. What *does* this curse? "It strips the world, external and internal, of love and sympathy for my poor heart, nature of its charms, earth of its fruit, the heavens of their blessings, existence of its joys, and dries up the last drop of happiness in the last fold of my heart;" seals up the door of heaven against my spirit, and blots out the star of hope. When this terrific word falls from the lips of the blessed Jesus, it forbids an angel wing ever to flit by my drear abode; "it withers up my soul to its root, like that unfortunate tree, which the breath of the Lord cursed, and of which an Apostle said the next day in astonishment — Lord, the fig-tree that thou cursedst, is *withered* away." What must this curse, this banishment be? No tongue can tell — no imagination now conceive it. Christ has warned us with a solemnity that may well intimidate and arouse. We can conceive of it as nothing less than eternal banishment from light and life and hope, to regions prepared for the devil and his angels, where the soul "shall be enveloped and penetrated with a misery immense, infinite; where it shall find nothing more in all beings, but an universal hell,—a hell within, a hell without, a hell in God himself."

The Son of man came to seek and to save that which is lost—lost to God, to itself, to heaven, to hope, to purity and peace and love—lost forever! One Scripture phrase concentrates the whole truth; man lives $ἄθεος$, without God. He was made in the image of God, made for him; made holy and perfect, filled with light and pure affection. Then his eye beheld the glory of God. Then he groped not in that darkness which now surrounds him, then he pined not beneath the maladies and miseries and mortality which now afflict him. I have said we have more exalted views of man than either the skeptic or semi-skeptic philosophy contains. We have. We believe in his original dignity; and we have such views of that, that man in his present state is a source of constant distress to us; and we desire perpetually to be proclaiming in his hearing, the dignity he has lost. We would say perpetually to him, as we should to the degenerate descendant of a noble family, still wearing their name and title, and even imitating their lofty bearing,—"Shame, shame on thee! Thy name, thy palace, thy lordly mien are all thy reproach." We have such exalted views also of the perfectibility of man, that we cannot endure to see the world contenting itself with anything short of the image of God, and of perfect communion with him. Man was a noble being when God said of him—he is good. But he aspired too high; he tried to become a centre of light and strength and happiness to himself, and to be independent of God. He withdrew from God's spiritual dominion, and God abandoned his spiritual nature to itself, and made him in his wretchedness a spectacle to himself and to the universe. The brute creation have fled him, for he has become their enemy; the very earth has felt the blighting curse that lighted on him. He was chased from Eden's happy garden, and the cherub-sentry with flaming sword still stands to bar his return. Happy Eden! scene of our sweet communion with God; happy Eden, witness of our dignity and of our blessedness; thou art lost to us and we to thee! My brethren, we are strong and high believers in the dignity of human nature. No man shall deprive us of this our boasting; yet, not in human nature as it is, but as it was, and as by grace it may become. But as he is, man is lost. And we want to sit down by the side of every brother of the human race, and weep with him for the crown which is fallen from our brow, the home and the heaven which we have lost. We want to undo the deceiving of his pride, and sigh and pray with him for the recovery of our birthright.

But are the heathen, who have not our light, exposed to perdition? A careless world, unwilling to make thorough inquiry into the condition and prospects of other men, complacently wraps itself in the mantle of an imagined charity, and says, "The mercy of God will never consign them to endless punishment, when they have sincerely done their best according to the light they enjoy." And there, indeed, we are agreed with the world; but we are forced to stop there; for we have too many proofs that there are few of them who will have that plea. We find also a part of the church, though unable to hope much for the pagan world, yet unwilling to adopt the harsh conclusion, that these hundreds of millions are rushing blindly to endless ruin; and preferring to rest in a vague hope that it will not be so, rather than to search the Scriptures to ascertain if God has given us any instruction on the subject, and imposed upon us any responsibility in the matter. Here we shall fail of time for a solemn topic. The sneers of the world terrify us not in such a matter. The charge of cruelty troubles not our conscience, while we seek not to make their destruction a fact, but to ascertain whether they are really exposed to destruction, in order that we may aid them to escape it. Indeed, if we were not distrustful of our own imperfect motives, we should say that ours is the true charity, which welcomes evidence, though it bring us to the results of distressing sympathy and of self-denying labor. We are inclined to suspect the depth of that charity which, to save its possessor pain, and spare him labor, settles a great principle of the divine government, a great future fact, not by examining God's testimony, but by appealing to a mere human sensibility. If we consult our sympathies, we say, "The poor pagans will not go to a miserable eternity; but where they will go we know not." But when we ask, "What has God asserted on this subject?" we rise from the answer with heavy hearts. The cry of the perishing then swells on our ear — "Come over and help us," — until we wish for a thousand tongues to proclaim to them the way of life. An outline of God's testimony is all we can here present. If we examine their lives, considered in the light of a disciplinary, probationary or preparatory state, we cannot believe that they go to heaven. They, as well as we, must be regenerated, and that in this world. But we find them as in Paul's day, infanticides, liars, adulterers, covenant-breakers, bestial, sensual, devilish, murderers of mothers. All this seems to us a preparation not for heaven, but for perdition. We find them too, just what the Canaanites were, whom God in his anger swept from the earth, but surely not into heaven. They are idolaters if there ever were any, and God declares that such cannot enter the kingdom of heaven. Again, to believe that they are in the way to heaven, is to regard all the apostles' anxieties and labor for their salvation as unfounded, extravagant and useless. And again; the apostle has fully reasoned out the case in two places. In the one he shows that they sin against their light as we do against ours. In the other, this is his missionary argument — "For whosoever shall call on the name of the Lord, shall be saved. But how shall they call on him in whom they have not believed; and how believe in him of whom they have not heard; and how hear, without preachers; and how preach, unless *sent?*" No, my brethren, it may be natural sympathy, or it may be distrust of God's testimony, which says, "Let the heathen alone;" but it is not enlightened piety. Then we are right in our estimate of man; then we should not be dazzled by his external appendages, his intellectual and social traits. Then we may say to the higher and lower Deistic philosophies, — Your boast is vain, when you claim the exclusive admiration of human nature; for we have higher views than either of you. You would satisfy man with certain social excellences, certain pagan virtues, certain moral sentiments, which have little or no reference to God; but we believe that man was made to live in God, and to reflect his image to the universe. You are teaching him to aspire to an intellectual millennium; we are aiming to prepare the world to return to the love of God and a spiritual life. We hold, too, the key that unlocks the deep mystery of man's present condition. A French writer of your school says — "I resemble, O Lord! the night-globe, which, in the obscure path where thy finger leads it, reflects from the one side, eternal light, and on the other is plunged in mortal shades." "How abject, how august," says one of another school, "how complicate, how wonderful is man!" There is something great in man, and something abject. To us, the mystery is solved. Man was great, good, godlike in his powers and in his character; but he is fallen in character, and in that fall has dragged down his powers and native sentiments; leaving, like a volcanic rupture, fragments of an Eden, scattered flowers that live here an exotic life.

We shall now consider, much more briefly, Jesus as our pattern.

II. IN HIS TREATMENT OF MEN.

We see in what light he regarded man, and how his holy soul was moved with compassion towards him. We now demand, What did his compassion lead him to do? If to make great sacrifices, then his views of man's lost estate must have been very strong; for although it may be love, it is also foolish love that makes a greater sacrifice and effort for another, than his necessities demand. But when a being of infinite intelligence makes great sacrifices, greater than we are capable of estimating, the evidence is complete, that the misery threatening or actually affecting those whom he aids, is equally immeasurable by us. On the subject of the condescension and sacrifices of the Lord Jesus Christ, the language of the Bible is deep, mystic, suggestive. He had a glory with the Father before the world was, but he *left* it. What was that glory? we would ask — where, and how did he leave it in becoming a man? The veil of flesh hides it from our sight. He was rich; when, where, in what? The clouds and darkness of an infinite majesty rest around his person, and hide from feeble mortals the splendors of his primitive empire. But he became poor. He took on him or was invested with flesh. Then he was, before he was flesh; he was before Abraham; he was David's root and lord, before he was his offspring and successor. Mysterious language! He took on him, at the very instant when angels were adoring him as the only-begotten of the Father, the form of a servant, and came to be despised and rejected, to hear hisses and taunts and blasphemies, instead of hosannas and hallelujahs. He exchanged heaven's diadem for Judea's thorns, and the robes of light for Pilate's faded and discarded garment; he forsook the palace where he was sovereign, for the judgment-hall where he was bound and buffeted and scourged and condemned. He left his body-guard of holy and mighty angels, to be at the mercy of wicked and puny mortals who hated him. He was the Lord of the universe, but he was born of one of the lowliest inhabitants of earth's obscurest corner. He was Prince of life, but he tasted death for every man. This the Scriptures call his sacrifice for man's salvation. But they make all this the lightest feature of the image of his cross. When they would start our imaginations on the path to his expiatory sufferings, they drop a few phrases, which are not so much intended to instruct, as to impress and overwhelm us with godly fear and sympathy. "My soul is exceeding sorrowful; yea, it is oppressed by a deathlike sorrow." What made him sorrowful — so sorrowful? Nothing in all that was external around him there; nothing that the Evangelists mention. Again; in the garden his bodily frame passes through an unparalleled excitement of agony; but from no apparent adequate cause. To attribute it to his fear of crucifixion, or to sorrow for his cause and friends, betrays the most entire disrespect. Again; his agonizing cry, Why hast thou forsaken me? permits us to conjecture, that there is something in what the Son of God endured in our stead and for our salvation, which we may understand only when our intellectual powers shall be expanded by the light, and our moral powers purified by the love of heaven. And when Jesus said with emphasis, " God so loved the world, as to *give* his onlybegotten Son," we understand that this gift was so costly, and there was in some way such an expenditure and sacrifice, that it not only showed God's love to man more clearly than all else he had ever said or done, but also, that it shows the immensity of that love. And so, when the apostle reasons for the encouragement of faith ; "If God *spared* not his own Son," &c. we understand that this not sparing, and freely giving up, involve something which we are now incapable of comprehending, but by which God designs to affect our hearts and form our characters more powerfully than by all his words or works. If the understanding of any man forbids the flow of emotion, until this veil is removed, then his heart will never feel fully in this life what Paul felt when he said, " The love of Christ constraineth us, because we thus judge that if one died for all, then were all dead." We were all dead, and he died for the dead; and in dying, he showed his conviction of our state of spiritual death.

But we have done with proofs of man's apostate and ruined state. It is to us a fact. The Word of God declares it. But it also declares another fact. And on all this gloomy cloud rests this rainbow-truth — "The Son of Man has come to seek and to save that which was lost." Oh then, ye scoffing economists! let us hear no more your severe reproofs of our poor expenditures of property in the missionary cause. Jesus is the master whom we follow, though at too great a distance; Jesus is the model we imitate, though very imperfectly. Oh then, covetous, selfish professors of Christ's gospel, imbibe his spirit, and live and labor and expend for the recovery of the lost. Brethren, I must rise now from the attitude of defence, and turn and charge on this practical indifference and on this skeptical philosophy, positive guilt. Had the Bible contained its present amount of wisdom, but on some of men's temporal interests, — had it determined the great questions of finance, — how eagerly would they read it, — how cordially believe it! But as a spiritual book, the one class disregard it, and the other look at it as full of exaggerations. But they should remember that this is the only volume in human language which God has condescended to write. And should it not contain deep, high, wondrous things? Is not this one of its very marks and seals? The Bible is full of paradoxes, because it shows us only fragments of truths, the full magnitude and harmony of which we cannot now comprehend. When God teaches man the dignity of his origin, philosophy denies it, and makes him the birth of chance. When the Bible declares the dignity of man's primeval estate, philosophy denies it, and says he is as good and pure and happy as when God made him. When God pronounces his fearful sentence against sin, philosophy laughs at it, and says it is extravagant. When God proclaims the immense price of our redemption, she laughs again, and says, how absurd to make an expiation to himself, and so costly a one for such trivial offences! But God knows two things which we do not know, and therefore does two things which we would not do. He knows the demerit of sin, and therefore threatens it with everlasting punishment. He knows the value of the soul, and therefore gives his Son for its redemption. Ye that despise this rich gift, — ye that despise us for our efforts to proclaim its story to the world, — let me say to you in God's name — Ye have a double guilt, and must need a twofold condemnation. You believe not, and therefore are condemned already. You also rob the world of its hope. Your theories and your practice would leave mankind in a hopeless condition. You dash from the trembling hand of perishing man the lamp of life, — the cup of salvation; you shatter in pieces the only bark to which poor human nature can commit its hopes for eternity! What have you proved, fellow-man? At best, a negative. You have begun and ended with denying. That there is disorder, wickedness, misery, you cannot deny. That the world is full of it, you cannot deny. And yet you would prevent our going to probe this moral wound and administer God's efficacious remedy. If one finds himself the slave of passion, if his conscience condemns him, if he fears that there possibly may be an hour of retribution and an eternity of wretchedness just beyond the confines of life — what can you say to this troubled spirit? You can sneer; but can you console? You can reason; but can you suppress the instinctive solicitude for a sure and solid hope of immortal blessedness? It was an instructive scene, when the dying Hindoo, representing our common humanity, turned to his priest and cried — Where shall I go when I leave the body? And the priest replied, in the spirit of your philosophy and in the pride of ignorance — Into a bird. But when that bird dies — where then? Into a flower. And where then? The priest became weary with answering; but still the soul cried — And where then? That is the question which must be met — fully, definitely and authoritatively answered. To leave it unsolved, is to mock and deceive the wretched heart of the mourner; to leave it unsolved, and yet pretend to offer the cure for human misery, is charlatanry the most detestable. To answer it by conjectures, or to meet it with inferences from God's mercy which every groan and tear falsifies, is fraud of the most injurious kind. To amuse man with theories, but to leave darkness on this chief point of all his solicitude, is the glory of anti-scriptural philosophy. Just where man most wants light, it is darkness. And just there the Bible pours the effulgence of eternal day. And not to hail that light, not to spread it, is treason to God's mercy, treason to our sacred trust, treason to man's highest interests.

But let me turn a moment in closing, to you, my dear brother, on this momentous hour of your life, when you are come to receive from Jesus, by the hands of his unworthy servants, the investment of this highest office confided to man. Let me say to you:

That deep compassion for men should characterize the whole spirit of the missionary and of missionary work.

Go to the benighted, with as glad a heart as animated the angels when they were commissioned to announce the glad tidings of Heaven's great mission of love. When your feet shall touch the shores of that distant land, sing in the fulness of your spirit — Glory to God in the highest, peace on earth, and good will to man. Be touched, like your high priest, with a feeling of their infirmities. Dwell in your thoughts, on their lost estate; see them as the great Shepherd did, wandering from the fold; until your heart bleeds and breaks with pity. This will animate and sustain you amid difficulties. You can bear them for the sake of the miserable, for yours will then be pity tender and sustaining, like that of the patient mother by the couch of her suffering child. This will make you gentle and forbearing and patient, even with a mother's tenderness, and keep you from crushing the bruised reed, or quenching the faintly-kindled wick. This will speak in heavenly eloquence from your very countenance, and melt the gates of brass in the hard heart of man. This will give you errands to the mercy-seat, and arguments before it. This will nerve you to your work, when a relaxing climate would tend to unnerve you. This will be treading in the footsteps of the Great Missionary.

Let me say again — That the example of Christ is the missionary's encouragement. You leave all for those you would save; so did he. You mean to identify yourself with them in every thing but sin, to bear their infirmities and share their sorrows; so did he. You are acting on the great principle, that to save from overflowing evil, the good of the universe must be diffused, not concentrated; so did he. You are going *to* men, and not waiting for them to come to you; so did he. You are going to seek and to save that which is lost, according to the measure imparted to you of the Father; so did he. And you are not only laboring like Christ, but also for him and with him. He is seeking these very souls. He once did it in person. Now he does it by his Spirit and by his people. But his interest is no less now, than when his sacred feet were traversing the land which your feet shall traverse, to save the perishing sheep of Israel's fold. You are going like him to pray in Gethsemane; but he spares your ascent to Golgotha and the tree. Go, dear brother, moisten with your tears for man the soil which he moistened when he thought of the lost. Go, assured not only that you are seeking them for Christ, but that he is seeking them by you and with you. Urge that, much, and with much faith in your prayers; it will prevail for many a blessing.

Let us conclude by saying — That persuasion to believe in

Christ is the missionary's great work. To effect this, he must commend himself to the conscience. Through an awakened conscience, man learns his need of Christ. Go then, dear brother, speak to the sleeping conscience of man. Let not your attention be fixed upon his peculiarities, his specific qualities as an individual man or his more general features of national character, his theories of philosophy and religion; but meet him as a man, as a lost man; nay, as one that knows he is lost. If your attention is drawn only or chiefly to his corporeal miseries, his social degradation, his intellectual privations, you will incur the danger of diverting his and your attention from that which should arouse your profounder sympathies and all his slumbering energies of conscience. You must indeed attempt the amelioration of his intellectual and social state; but guard vigilantly against letting either your or his anxieties and efforts terminate there. When you have to meet him as the philosopher of another school, you may be discouraged at the sincerity and obstinacy, nay perhaps, plausibility with which he can confront you. But when you meet him in the winning strength of a deep sympathy; — you the lost and recovered, he the lost and perishing man; — then you are in your strongest attitude, he is in his most defenceless. The missionary must speak from deep experience to the consciousness of guilt often stifled, never annihilated in the impenitent bosom; to a conscience often stifled, often cheated, never tranquilized by his vain superstitions. Speak, my brother; now in thunder, — now in the still, small voice. So God speaks in nature and in grace. Man will understand you, when you whisper to his conscience. Yet you may awaken resistance. The light is painful to them that love darkness. And false philosophy, and false religion and practical unbelief will all be resorted to, to shield the conscience. And yet your great work is to bring home on the soul of each man the conviction that he is lost. Trouble yourselves little and others still less with theories of human depravity. They may be important. They have their place. But whatever else they do, they do not awaken the conscience. And if I mistake not, more of them have lulled, than have awakened it. The facts of depravity and conscience are two of the ultimate facts, to be taken as theological axioms. God has not proved the existence of either, but simply asserted it. And so may we, both on his testimony and on men's very consciousness,

And yet if your brethren entertain themselves with theory-making, or deem their theories important; do not therefore separate from them; only you yourself be given to the work of saving the lost. Perhaps one of the mightiest elements of ministerial power, is the deep conviction on the soul, of the lost condition of man. It must give fervor and frequency to prayer, and tend greatly to produce a conviction in others. Your hearer may be proud and powerful in his philosophy, he may be self-complacent in his creed and ceremonies. But whisper to his soul of seasons of shame and self-reproach and fear which forebodes impending doom, and he cannot deny, he cannot argue; for he feels that he is dealing with Truth and with God. In your public addresses, deal with the conscience and you will imitate the greatest preachers. Study the sermons of Elijah to Ahab, of Nathan to David, of Peter to the thousands at Jerusalem, of Paul to Felix. There you find no flattery of human nature, no general descriptions of virtue, but guilt and condemnation described as pertaining to them all. Feel that man is lost; that guilt and condemnation and spiritual poverty belong to every child of Adam. Proclaim that, on the house-top and in the closet. Man may not have thought of it, but when you suggest it, he sees that it is truth. Give him exalted views of human dignity and worth, not as it is, but as it was and may be. Solve the strange perplexity of every man's experience; tell him what you know of former conflicts and present conquests; of noble aspirations after heaven and sordid attachments to earth; of desires to please God and determinations to please self. Speak to his love of happiness; he will understand you. And as you solve the mystery to his astonished soul, as you describe the symptoms of his spiritual malady, as you point him to the balm of Gilead, and the great Physician, — a new life of hope may begin to infuse itself into his soul. — Again I say, your great employment is to bring the individual souls of men to Christ. Be not diverted from this; be not satisfied short of success in this. If you must do other things, consider them collateral and subordinate to this. Your glorious commission is, to seek and save the lost. Be filled, be fired with the spirit of that commission. May you, and may the church, and all of us who announce the gospel, be more and more filled with that glorious object — the recovering to immortal spirits the lost image of God, and guiding the perishing to an almighty Saviour. May the Spirit be poured from on high, until the whole church sees and feels that these facts are now of chief importance — man is lost, and the Son of God is seeking him; man is lost, and the Son of God is come to save him; man is lost, and the church is commissioned to go forth in the might of faith and prayer to his salvation. *To save the lost!* To-night we talk of it, as children talk of the affairs of empires; we see through a glass darkly; our conceptions are low and limited. *To save the lost!* Tell us, ye damned spirits, what it means. Tell us, Son of God, what it means; what stirred thy soul in godlike compassion to seek the lost? Tell us, ye ransomed and ye faithful spirits who never sinned — tell us, eternity — what is this mighty work of gospel missions? Tell us, O Father, tell thy churches; tell thy ministers; until every slumberer awake, every energy be aroused, and the way of life be pointed out to a perishing race!

CHRIST, A HOME MISSIONARY.

BY

REV. WILLIAM R. WILLIAMS, D. D.

And he said unto them, let us go into the next towns, that I may preach there also: for therefore came I forth. — MARK 1 : 38.

It is ever delightful to the Christian, that he can trace in the way, along which he journeys, the footsteps of his Saviour preceding him. The labors, the sorrows and the joys of his course all become hallowed, when it is seen that the Master has first partaken of them. The cup of affliction is less distasteful to the believer, because our Lord has himself drunk of its bitterness, and left on the brim a lingering fragrance. In prayer, he approaches to God with greater confidence, because he names as his intercessor, one who himself prayed while upon earth, with strong crying and tears, watched all night in supplication on the lone mountain side, and bowed to pray, beneath the olives of Gethsemane, with the bloody dews of anguish on his brow. And the preaching of the word derives its highest glory from the fact, that He who descended into the world to become its ransom, was himself a minister of that Gospel he commissioned others to preach. In the words before us we have Christ's own testimony, that the very purpose of his coming was to preach from town to town of his native land. Jesus Christ was, therefore, a Home Missionary. To this end, blessed Saviour, "camest thou forth." To thy servants, who have at this time for the like purpose gathered themselves together, wilt thou not then give thy presence and favor, Head of thy Church as thou art, Master of all her assemblies, and the only effectual teacher of all her pastors and evangelists?

Aid me, my brethren, with your prayers, while from these words I would commend to your notice THE RESEMBLANCE BETWEEN YOUR OWN LABORS, AND THE PERSONAL MINISTRY OF YOUR LORD AND SAVIOUR AS PERFORMED IN THE FIELD OF HOME MISSIONS; and while I urge THE CONSEQUENT DUTY OF THE CHURCH TO CONTINUE AND ABOUND IN THE LIKE GOOD WORK.

I. The title of Missionary denotes, as you know, one *sent forth*, and especially belongs to one whose errand it is to propagate religion. You need not to be reminded how often Christ announced to his hostile countrymen the fact, that he was *sent* from God, to declare the Father, from whose bosom he *came forth*, whom no man had seen or could see. The title of apostles, by which he saw it meet to designate his twelve chosen disciples, is, as you are aware, but the rendering into Greek of the same idea, which, borrowing the word from the language of the Romans, we express by the term missionary; and the Saviour himself is by Paul described as the great Apostle of our profession, or in other words, the chiefest Missionary of the Church. Now the field of his labor and his missionary character may assume different aspects, according to the point of view from which our observations are made. If we look to the original Godhead of the messenger, and to the glory which he had with the Father before the foundation of the world, his mission was a distant one. To bring the glad message to our earth from the far Heavens, he emptied himself of glory, became a voluntary exile from the society of the pure and the blessed, and taking on him the nature of sinful man, became the sharer of his miseries, and the perpetual witness of his iniquities. In this sense it was to a foreign shore that he came, and to an alien race that he ministered; and thus considered, his labors more nearly resembled those of the foreign missionary. But if we confine our regard to the mere humanity of our Lord, his missionary toils assume another aspect. His personal ministry was far more limited and national in its character, than was his message. Although in his relation to our race of every kindred and of all lands, he is the second Adam, and the nature which he took upon him was that common to our whole kind, he was yet born in the land of promise, under the law given to Moses, and within the range of the covenant made with Abraham. By these bounds his personal ministry was for the most part limited.

It might have been otherwise. The same indwelling Deity, that enabled him at an early age to confound the doctors of his nation, beneath the shadow of their own proud temple, might have been displayed, had he chosen it, at a still earlier year of his life; and the holy child might have preached the gospel to that heathenish Egypt, in which his infancy sought refuge. The Being, before whose eye, in the wilderness of temptation, were brought all the kingdoms of this world, with all the glory of them, might, had he so willed it, have traversed all those kingdoms in his own personal ministry. Clothing himself, had he chosen it, with those same miraculous gifts which he reserved for his kingly ascension, then to be showered down on his Pentecostal Church, he might have visited land after land, declaring to every tribe of mankind, in their own dialect, the truths he came to reveal. He might have been the first to carry the gospel to imperial Rome, and hunting the hoary profligate and dissembler Tiberius to his guilty retreat at Capreæ, he might have reasoned before the crowned ruler of the world, of righteousness, temperance, and judgment to come, until he too, like an inferior ruler in after times, had trembled on his throne. He might have anticipated the labors of his servant Paul, by bearing the news of the unknown God, and the resurrection, to the philosophers of Athens. To the Roman people he might have declared himself as that great Deliverer, of whom their Virgil had already sung; and the sages of Greece might have been compelled to own in him that Heavenly Teacher for whom their Socrates had longed. And the nations of the East now intently looking for the advent of a king, whose dominion should be an universal one, might have learned from our Lord's own lips, the spiritual and eternal nature of that kingdom they justly but blindly expected. And thus having filled the whole world with the echo of his fame, as a preacher of repentance and of faith, he might have returned to Jerusalem, out of which her prophets might not perish, there to consummate the atoning sacrifice of which he had testified.

We say, Jesus Christ might thus have carried abroad the word of salvation to many nations. Instead, however, of doing this, he confined himself in his personal instructions to the bounds of Palestine, one visit to the coast of Tyre and Sidon excepted, and even of this it is most probable, that he taught in that region only the Jews there scattered. In his occasional retirement from the violence of his enemies, he neither wandered to Arabia and its roving hordes of the race of Ishmael, on the south; nor did he travel into the country of that powerful people, whose territories skirted Judea on the east, the Edomites, who were the kindred of Israel, as being the posterity of Esau. When the appeals of distress were made to him by those of another race, he himself drew attention to this restriction as being laid upon his own ministry, declaring that he was not sent, but to the lost sheep of the house of Israel, — was not *sent*, or in other language, his commission as a *missionary* preacher, went no further. To their relief he confined well nigh all his miracles. With the devotedness of a true patriot, he labored for the good of his own, although his own received him not. And to the end he persevered in this course. In the last week of his mortal career, when to his divine prescience the awful scenes of the betrayal, the mockery, the scourging, and the crucifixion were already present, as a vivid reality, when, seated with his disciples on the sides of Olivet, he looked with them, upon the city with its battlements and turrets, its long drawn terraces, and its gorgeous temple, spread out on the opposite heights, but saw what their eyes could not see, and heard what their ears could not hear, — when, in the garden that lay at his feet, his prophetic eye already discerned the bloody agony soon to bedew it, and viewed in the palaces of Herod and Pilate rising before him, all the scenes of ignominy and torture he was soon there to encounter, — when along the streets, now sending up but the hum of cheerful industry, his prophetic ear even now heard resounding the yells of the multitude, as they rushed from the place of judgment to the hill of Golgotha, — even with these sights and sounds around him, from the thought of his own overwhelming baptism of anguish, he could turn aside to weep over favored but guilty Jerusalem, with as ardent an affection as had ever filled the heart of a Hebrew, when his eye caught the first glance of its turrets on his yearly pilgrimage, and he hailed it in inspired song, as the city of the great King, seated on the sides of the north, beautiful for situation, and the joy of the whole earth. And after he had wrought out the great work of redemption, and gave his apostles, before his ascension, charge to bear his gospel among all nations, however remote, and however barbarous, he yet added the restriction, that their labors should begin at Jerusalem.

We are ready to admit that all this was needed for the accomplishment of the prophecies that went before concerning him. But Christ had, it should be remembered, the ordering of those very prophecies, for his was the Spirit that prompted them. To refer this restriction of the field of Christ's labors to prophecy, is then only to make his plan of Home Missions a few centuries the older, and leave it still the work of his mind. Into the purposes which may have guided the Saviour in thus acting, we would not here enter. Whatever his intent, in thus narrowing the field of his toils as a preacher, the fact is evident that to the land of Canaan, or the bounds of his native country, his ministerial labors were confined, and Jesus Christ, while upon earth, was a Home Missionary. Now a work which occupied the greatest of preachers, can never be unimportant, and a plan of benevolent effort, which marked the first ages of the Church, and was commended by the example of its great Head, can never become obsolete.

Nor is this, beloved brethren, the only point of contact between the ministerial labors of Christ, and the work in which you are engaged. We have seen how far resemblance to him may be claimed by your society in the *scene* of your labors. Bear with me, while I proceed to consider the *commission* under which he acted, the *message* he bore, the *manner in which he published* it, and the *mode in which his labors were sustained.*

2. Of the commission under which he labored, it may indeed be said, that it was peculiar to himself, and may be claimed by none others, that he spoke by his own authority. It was the natural result of his Deity as the equal Son of the Eternal Father. The scribe and the pharisee quailed before the self-sustained dignity of his teachings. Thus your Missionaries may not teach. They may promulgate only the things His word contains, and in no other name than his are they to speak, or is the Church to receive their testimony. But in this respect they may claim to act under the same commission with Christ, that they are embraced within its ample provision of gifts and blessings to the Church. As the Father hath sent me, said he to his disciples, so send I you. To them thus sent he promised his own perpetual presence and aid. Lo I am with you always, even unto the end of the world. Again in the mission of the Saviour he inherited as a qualification for its varied tasks, the Spirit with-

out measure, and with him is its inexhaustible residue. Now of this Spirit, in its due and needed measure, he has vouchsafed to communicate to the Church and its teachers. To communicate it to his apostles, he employed forms on which the Church dared never venture, and which well betokened his own self-derived and incommunicable right as God, to dispense it. The apostles were wont, by the imposition of hands, an act ever accompanied with prayer, to confer the gifts of the Spirit, acknowledging thus that to God they looked up for the blessing. He, on the contrary, breathed on the twelve, as if to show its native and perpetual in-dwelling within him, and in a brief sentence, which, were he not God, would be condensed and inspissated blasphemy, said: 'Receive ye the Holy Ghost.' Although not thus given, you believe that the same Spirit yet remains to teach and bless the Church. Did not that Spirit, as you trust, first endow them, your Missionaries would not have been accepted. Did he not attend them, and work with them, they could not be prospered. May it not then without irreverence be claimed, that the men sustained by your alms in the mission field, go forth under the same commission with Christ; since he himself construed that commission as including the subordinate laborers of all times, whom he should raise up, — since he has himself promised his personal aid and presence with these to the end of time — since the Spirit that first endowed, and that yet prospers them, is all his own, — and is one with that Spirit by which he himself was anointed for his great work, under the commission by him received of the Father.

3. As to the *message* which he bore, its great burden was repentance and faith, as ushering into the kingdom of God. He taught this truth by his herald and fore-runner John, and continually reiterated it in his own ministry. He veiled it in his parables — he mingled it with his miracles of mercy — he spoke it in the ears of his favored apostles — he published it on the house-top to the indiscriminate multitude. On the mountain side, or sitting in the ship, in the way as he walked, or leaning in weariness on the brink of the well, in the home of his poorer disciples, or the banqueting chambers of some richer host, still this was his theme. And what other dare your missionaries substitute? Varied as may be the garb into which it is thrown, man's corruption and condemnation, the need of repentance and faith, that faith in Christ as a King, and a Redeemer as well, — are not these the topics

still applicable and never trite, of which the Church shall not have exhausted the glories, or fathomed the mysteries, ages after the world shall have been consumed, and all its tribes shall have been adjudged to heaven or to hell for ever? Your laborers then in the far West are yet carrying abroad the same gospel which Christ bore in weariness to the city of Samaria, and scattered along the shores of the lake Gennesareth, and published, as he walked the streets of Jerusalem, or stood and cried in the thronged courts of the temple.

4. But in the *manner*, too, *in which he published his message*, it was said that our Lord had shown himself the great exemplar of the Home Missionary. In this single feature, had he manifested no other claim to a divine mission, our Lord proved himself endowed with superhuman wisdom. We refer to the means he selected for propagating his religion amongst mankind. There had lived in the Gentile world men of high intellectual endowments, who had discerned the ignorance and corruption of their age, and aspired to become its reformers. But although some were deified for their fancied success, futile had been their endeavors; and most cumbrous yet most imbecile the instrumentalities, upon which they had chosen to rely. Some had been legislators, bequeathing to their fellow citizens new forms of government; others, warriors appealing to brute force, and imposing by the strong hand of power their improvements upon the feebler race whom they had subdued; others resorted to what they deemed allowable and pious frauds, forging prophecies, inventing mysteries, and bribing oracles; others philosophized, and yet others, employed the elegant arts to soften and to better the human character. But none of them knew aright the might of the Leviathan they affected to curb and tame. Man, though disguised by civilization, and adorned by science and art, was still the same selfish and godless savage at heart, that he had ever been. Mutually wronged and wronging, the race were yet, as Paul too truly described them, hateful and hating one another. Of the depth of corruption into which alike the Jew who boasted of a law he would not keep, and the Gentile, whom he scorned, were sunk at the time of Christ's coming, Paul has told us in language of fearful significancy. How dreadfully the history of the world filled up the gloomy outlines that master-hand had drawn in the opening of his epistle to the Romans, I need not say to you. And yet all this went on, in spite of efforts the most earnest, the

most varied, and the most costly, to check, or at least to conceal the evil. But it was only to varnish putridity, and to gild over decay, that these earthly reformers came. Of ever profiting the vast mass of the people, the most intelligent of these sages despaired. They had no hope except for the wise and the lettered portion of society. To these they spoke in veiled and guarded language. For these, their select hearers able to bear it, they had an internal or esoteric doctrine. To the multitude they held out doctrines often utterly the opposite of these their private teachings; and the poor and the ignorant they looked upon as an inferior kind, like the 'brute beasts made to be taken and destroyed;' to be entrapped by error, and given over to unpitied ruin. As the larger portion of mankind will ever be found in the classes of neglected and restricted education, to despair of the poor and of the many, was virtually to despair of the well being of the race.*

Another obstacle, which these reformers felt themselves incompetent to assail, was found in the false but received religions. To change the religion of a whole nation, when once established, was deemed an impossibility. Plato, among the wisest of Grecian schemers, makes it an axiom in his celebrated treatise of a republic, " that nothing ought to be changed by the legislator in the religion which he finds already established; and *that a man must have lost his understanding to think of such a project*."† Yet not to change the religion of one nation only, but of all nations, is Jesus Christ come. Look at the varied forms of error that met him, all obstinate by the force of ancient and inherited prejudices, and by the violence of the passions they indulged and sanctified, and made venerable in the eyes of the people by the

---

* A similar feeling with regard to the multitude, the reader may remember, has marked many of the reformers of modern times, who have claimed to release the world from the dominion of Christianity. The private correspondence of the patriarch of French infidelity,—whom his disciples were accustomed to hail, in language borrowed from that Bible at which they scoffed, as their " Father of the Faithful,"—contains the following passage. It is in a letter to his fellow-laborer D'Alembert, and when congratulating his friend on the progress of their principles : " Let us bless this happy revolution, that has within the last fifteen or twenty years taken place in the minds of all respectable people (*tous les honnêtes gens*.) It has outrun my hopes. *As to the rabble, I meddle not with them ; the rabble they will always remain. I am at pains to cultivate my garden, but yet it will have its toads ; they should not however prevent my nightingales from singing*." — Lettres de M. de Voltaire et de M. D'Alembert, 211.

† Warburton's Divine Legation, Book iii. § 6.

lapse of time. In his own nation he encountered truth tenaciously held, but held perversely and partially, and in all unrighteousness. In the lettered classes of the Roman empire, he saw a band of learned and acute triflers, addicted to a heartless and endless scepticism, or of debauched errorists, in whose minds atheism and profligacy, in drunken alliance, leaned each upon the other. The mass of the nation were the corrupt votaries of paganism, in its most corrupt forms; sensual and sanguinary, they had become enervated by luxury, and yet were ravening for blood. Equally fierce and cruel, if not alike sensual, were the superstitions of the savage hordes whom they held in check, or retained in their pay on the borders of the empire. In the East were the worshippers of fire. Arabia, and Persia, and India, and Scythia, and Egypt, all had their national idols. The inquiry had been made by Jeremiah six centuries before, " Pass over the isles of Chittim and see; and send unto Kedar and consider diligently and see if there be such a thing. Hath a nation changed their gods, which yet are no gods?" And the inquiry, made as if to challenge an instance of its occurrence, had remained unanswered. Yet the reputed son of a carpenter, a man of Nazareth, the most despised city of the Jews, the most despised of nations, rises up to make the attempt. And what are his resources? Is he patronized by kings? Is he levying armies, and equipping fleets, or is he compiling new codes of law, or despatching ambassadors and forming treaties? None of all these things. But perhaps he has won to his party the sophists of Greece, and the scholars of Athens, the learned, and acute and eloquent disciples of Epicurus, and Zeno, and Plato, are retained in his interests, and are disseminating his peculiar sentiments? — Not so. The wisdom of this world he has counted foolishness, and his doctrine teaches that the most labored result of human intelligence has been confirmed ignorance, as to the first and most obvious of all truths, — that the wise have failed to spell out the handwriting and superscription of a Creator, though found upon all his works, — and the world by wisdom knew not God. But he has converted, perhaps, the Sanhedrim, and the Rabbies of Israel; the lights of the law and the oracles of the people are with him? No, he has denounced them with fearless severity, and they are plotting his death. But Herod is in his favor, and Pilate is his friend? — No, Herod is seeking to see him, in vain, dreading in him the resurrection of the Baptist he had slain; and Pilate is neither concerned nor able to give him protection from the fury of his own nation. But the Reformer moves on, nothing daunted. Unlike all others who despised the people, or despaired of them, he addresses himself to the poor and the ignorant. It is the mass of the nation he hopes first to reach. But what are his arts of persuasion with the people? Does he hold out the lure of wealth, or earthly honors, or pleasure? Is he slipping the leash of law and order from the passions of the multitude, and cheering them on to the prey that is before them in the possessions of the wealthy? He honestly assures his auditory that they must expect to lose all in following him, that his poorest followers must become yet poorer, and that his disciples are doomed men, bearing their own crosses on their way to death. He writes no books. He forms no plots. He meddles not with political strife; nor interferes with religious sects, but to denounce them all, and to turn their combined enmity on his single and unsheltered head. And the weapon by which he is to foil all his enemies, and to subdue the world to the obedience of the faith, is — hear it, O heavens, and be astonished, O earth!—the foolishness of preaching,—the plain tale of man to his fellow men concerning God and his Christ. By the preaching of the word, and especially to the poor, Christ is come to change the face of society. Jesus Christ was, indeed, the discoverer of these two great truths, that all reformations must begin with the lower classes, and that preaching is the grand instrument of changing the opinions of a nation. The latter had indeed been used in the older dispensation, but its applicability to such a scheme as that of the world's conversion, had never been suspected. Yet how well established are both now become. The man, who in endeavoring to heat a mass of water, should build his fire above the fluid, would in physics be but as absurdly employed, as the man who in morals looks to the highest points of a corrupt society as the first to be reformed. As in the heated liquid, the lower stratum when warmed passes upward, and gives place to another still cold, which is in its turn penetrated with heat, and then displaced by the descending of yet another; so in the moral world, the only efficient reforms are the reforms that begin at the lower portion of society, and work upward. It was so in the first preaching of the gospel. It was so in the English Reformation. It was so in the religious influence that followed the labors of Wesley and Whitefield. And Jesus Christ first discovered and first applied this great but simple principle, that to the poor the gospel should be preached. Again let us consider the character of the instrumentality he selected. It was the cheapest of all implements. And where the many were to be reached by many laborers, and the poor by the poor, its cheapness was a matter of no little moment. A book would be worn out, ere it had taught a thousand readers, or travelled a hundred miles. The living teacher might go on from land to land, and instruct myriads after myriads. If the book were unskilfully composed, its errors must remain unchanged. If addressed to one class originally, one class only it continued to the end to interest. The living evangelist varied his message and form of address, as varying circumstances required, and appealed in different modes to the differing habits of the regions and classes through which he passed. The book might meet many who knew not how to read, but all might hear the living voice. The book could not solicit the careless to hear, or pursue the wanderer who fled from reproof. The living teacher sought his auditory in the retreats whither they betook themselves. The book was a cold and unimpassioned abstraction. The preacher was a living, breathing thing, appealing to all the sympathies of man's nature. His countenance, his gestures, his tones, all sought and won him the attention of men. And it was left for Jesus Christ to discover that this was the great instrumentality for correcting the popular faith of a nation, as being the cheapest, and as having the widest range of influence, the utmost variety in its applicability, and the greatest power and life in its appeals. We speak considerately when we say, that the institution of preaching as the great means of national illumination and conversion, is not one of the least among the evidences of the Saviour's superhuman wisdom, and consequently another argument for his divine mission.

Now while the stationary pastor, in the more abundantly supplied districts of a Christian land, may claim to labor in this our Lord's appointed mode, the preaching of the word, may you not assume, that to the Home Missionary belongs eminently the honor of preaching *to the poor*, and of caring for the neglected and destitute, the class to whom Christ himself chiefly addressed his gospel, and in its being addressed to whom, he bade the anxious Baptist and his disciples recognize one of the many proofs of his Messiahship? The laborer in the field of Home Missions is applying therefore the favorite instrumentality of his Lord in his Lord's favorite mode. And upon this instrumentality, it is your instruction to them that they chiefly rely. And while they may scatter the tract, and gather the Sabbath-school, and use every other means that may aid man in the knowledge of his God, their main business, and your great charge to them given, is that "as ye go, preach."

5. We have seen that in the manner of publishing his message, our Lord was not unlike the laborers whom you employ. Let us lastly observe the comparison you may institute with the ministry of our Lord, in the similar *means adopted for the support of the laborer.* Christ did not, then, like the established priesthood of Israel, find himself sustained by the tithes of the land. No State furnished from her revenues the endowments of his mission, or taxed her subjects to secure through his means their spiritual good. The free contributions of those whom he instructed, enlightened and saved, were the only revenues to which he looked. And these, you will observe, were given not to sustain him in his labors for the donors, so much as to aid him in journeying onward to benefit others. The frugal meal and the sheltering roof were the reward that poverty gave for words such as never man spake. Salvation came to the house he visited, and when he parted, his blessing was left with its inmates. But in addition, he seems to have received from time to time, of the free-will offerings, which, from their abundance or their penury, his disciples contributed, to meet the wants of the morrow, when he should have reached a distant hamlet, and be discoursing to a new auditory. These contributions one of the apostles bore, and dispensed to meet the necessities of that wayfaring company. Pious women followed him, ministering of their substance.

Now it is to such resources that your enterprise looks. You have not been subsidized from the national treasury. Nor have your missionaries been empowered or been willing, to sit them down at the receipt of custom, collecting from the traffic of the land a stinted tithe, in acknowledgment of the temporal blessings with which the gospel has enriched every walk of society. To the free gratuities of Christians, themselves benefitted by the gospel, and anxious to spread before others the word that God has made the power of salvation to their own souls, — to their spontaneous alms, gathered unequally and rather according to the willingness of the heart, than the fulness of the hands, you have been compelled to look as your only treasures. And though the store has often seemed well nigh spent, ever wasting, it has been ever renewing itself, like the widow's cruse, still as it was emptied, still by the goodness of Providence mysteriously replenished. And the relief thus given has resembled that which sustained our Lord's own personal ministry, in the fact, that it was not the giver's own benefit that was immediately sought. The Christian supports at home his pastor to preach to himself and to his children, but he supports the Home Missionary to preach to his destitute neighbors. It was in this way that the disciples of our Saviour sustained their master, not expecting it as the condition of their gratuities, that he should continue day after day to bless with his lengthened stay their own hamlets and households, but that he might journey onward from village to village, and city to city of their native land.

The Redeemer, then, in his own personal efforts as an evangelist, gave himself to the very work in which your Society is toiling, the supply of the religious destitutions of your own land. And ere we pass, let it be remembered, that upon principles unlike the timorous and stealthy policy, which his church in the days of persecution adopted, of choosing rather as the scene of her labors, the retired valley, and the remote and safe wilderness, Christ, as we see in the words of our text,* and in the whole record of the gospels, sought to plant his word, though in the face of fiercer opposition and surer and greater risk, in the towns and cities of the land. He bade his disciples, in times of persecution in one city, to flee indeed, but it was only to another city; and their ministry he at the same time describes, as a going over the cities of Israel. He chose these as the scenes of labor, for his work was with men, and men were there to be found in the greatest number. He did so, because his hours were few, and there the greatest effects might be wrought in the shortest time. He did so, because his gospel was the remedy of human depravity and misery, and in the crowded dwellings of man, his depravity assumes its most aggravated forms, and his suffer-

---

* See also Luke 4: 43. How rigidly the early preachers adhered to our Lord's plan in the dissemination of the gospel, appears from the fact, that the inhabitants of the *cities* in the Roman empire had become nominally Christian, while the rural population remained yet plunged in idolatry, and the word Pagan, or *villager* (paganus) became synonymous with heathen.

ings are most intense and distressing. He did so, because these are the points of radiation, around which the character of the whole nation crystalizes and becomes fixed, and in ancient as in modern times, the impress of the metropolis is to some extent seen upon the most distant and rude of the rural population. Ever then may it be the prayer and the policy of this Society, acting upon the like principles, to plant its missionaries in the towns and cities of our land, till they be fully supplied with the preaching of the gospel.

Yet let it not be supposed, that we would exalt the importance of Home Missions at the expense of the foreign field. We believe the latter, if a division and a choice were admissible, (which they are not,) we should believe the latter, the more needful work of the church. It was indeed one of the characteristics of the superiority of the new, over the older dispensations, that it looked beyond all the former boundaries of national prejudice and selfishness, and taught men that the field of benevolence is the world. Our Saviour himself, during his own more restricted ministry, alluded to these designs of mercy for the Gentile. In his discourses at Nazareth he called his hearers to observe, that the *Gentile* widow of Zarephath had been honored by entertaining a prophet of God, when the many widows of Israel were passed by, and that the leprous nobleman of heathenish *Syria* had been miraculously healed, while the many lepers of Israel were left unrelieved. This was a theme the Jews could least of all things endure. They thrust the Saviour from their city, and would have killed him, just as in succeeding years, their countrymen at Jerusalem heard Paul patiently, until he mentioned a divine mission to the *Gentiles*, when they exclaimed, away with him, he is not fit to live. Christ from the beginning contemplated foreign missions as the field of his church; but his own was a Home Mission. And while the church, from his teachings, and the example of his apostles, learns to regard Foreign Missions as her chief care, she cannot sever it from the work of Home Missions. They are indissolubly united, and each needs the other,—the farther and the nearer sides of the same great net; the fishers of men are needed alike, to bear the one into the bosom of the deep, and to guard the other along the edge of the shore. The true interests of each are necessarily advanced by the growth of the other.

II. We have seen our Lord himself devoting the years of his personal ministry to the preaching of the gospel throughout his own country. With such a sanction of your endeavors, what motives are needed to impel you? His example to guide, His presence to uphold, and His Spirit to prosper you,—if the Lord be thus for you in the splendor of his example, for you in his promises, and for you in his wonder-working Spirit, who can be against you? Whether we look to the advantages which our nation presents for such labor, or to its peculiar necessities, to our duty as Christians, or our interests as men loving their country, to the general obligations of the church, or our own personal and special privileges and responsibilities,—on every hand are teeming incitements to energy and liberality, to perseverance and courageous devotedness.

1. Do we speak of the *advantages*, which our wide-spread land presents for labor of this kind? We cannot forget, that here are none of the impediments of an adverse government, and an alien nation suspicious of your missionaries as foreign emissaries,—impediments with which the laborer abroad must ever contend. From the St. Lawrence to the Gulf of Mexico, and from the Atlantic to the Rocky Mountains, and yet onward to the coasts of the Pacific, a broad and goodly land is open or opening before you,—not the land of strangers, but your own native soil, blest with free institutions, and a government springing from and accountable to the people. Its free institutions invite the free and glad labors of the Missionary. The national appetite for knowledge, and the many endowments and appliances for the diffusion of knowledge, promise you aid, in bringing before the national intellect the only knowledge that is of unmingled truth, and immutable value. The land is inhabited by a people, not divided and isolated, as are the possessors of equal spaces of territory in the old world, by the varieties of dialect and languages, which make man seem as a barbarian to his neighbor, separated from him but by a river, or a range of mountains. The language of your forefathers, the language in which your household bibles are written, is that which its cities, and its hamlet, and its farmhouses alike acknowledge — which its colonists are carrying into the depths of the forest, and the seeds of which its adventurous mariners are scattering along every shore smitten by their keels. To make yet more plain your duties, and to render the wise and beneficent purposes of his Providence yet more easy of translation to the reason and the conscience of this people, God has made their country the point of attraction to the oppressed or the needy of other lands, and

the eyes of many and distant nations are fixed upon you. Our Heavenly Father has made us a national epistle to other lands. See that you read a full and impressive comment to all lands, of the power of Christian principle, and of the expansive and self sustaining energies of the gospel, when left unfettered by national endowments, and secular alliances. The evangelical character of our land is to tell upon the plans and destinies of other nations. See to it, that the men, who quote your democracy, and your enterprise, your energy and your increase, be compelled by glaring evidence, which they may not dispute, and cannot conceal, to add, that for your freedom and all its better fruits, you are indebted to the religion of the Saviour borne throughout the length and breadth of your land. And last among the advantages with which God has endowed you, and bound you, as it were, to this work, let me name the amount of uneducated or perverted mind, which He is daily quarrying from the mines of European superstition, and from the place where Satan's seat is, and casting down upon our shores to be inserted into the rising walls of your republic. At home it was comparatively beyond your reach. The jealousy of priestly and of kingly rule guarded it from your approach. God has brought it disencumbered to your shores. Will you meet it with the gospel — will you follow it to its western homes with the Missionary? Your prayers have ascended to God in behalf of those perishing in the darkness of false religion in other lands. Your prayers have been answered, as God is wont to answer even his own people, in the mode and the hour they were perhaps least prepared to expect the boon; and while your souls thought only of the subjects of your petitions, as dwellers on a foreign shore, He has in his wondrous working made them already the denizens of your own land, and the crowds, to whom you had hoped to send the Foreign Missionary, have already besieged your doors to ask the easier, and the cheaper, care of your Home Missions. Their souls are evidently as valuable here, as they would have been if sought out by your messengers on their native soil, and there won to the faith of Christ. You know not, but that, although transplanted to this soil, they may still retain a hold so strong on the affections, and an influence so controlling on the character and destinies of the kindred and countrymen they have left behind, that converted here by the labors of your Home Missions, they may become the allies, or the channels, or themselves the chosen instruments of your Foreign Missions to the lands whence they came. It was thus in the declining ages of the Roman empire, that the hordes of Paganism, disgorged from their own native seats upon the imperial territories, became themselves christianized by the nation they had invaded, and evangelized the paternal tribes they had quitted. Let us, then, regard the emigrants around us, not as invaders, but as the exiles of a country, of which they or their children may yet become the evangelists. Let us count wisely and gratefully the number of the deathless spirits, who have thus been ushered, under the most favorable circumstances, into our borders. Many of them have been the nurslings of a corrupt or careless hierarchy; and torn from the breasts of European error, they are now committed by the hand of Providence to the fostering care of your Sabbath Schools, and Bible classes, and the pioneer churches planted and watered by the care of your Missionaries.

2. As to the advantages, so to the *necessities* of our case we need ever to look. We may not forget, or hold negligently the civil privileges, the envied but the fragile inheritance which our fathers have bequeathed us. The strangers day by day wafted to your shores become your fellow sovereigns. They choose with you the law-makers. They interpret and modify, sustain or subvert your Constitution. If not converted, under God, by you to the faith, they will with the characteristic energy of evil, sacrifice your dearest earthly interests to their passions, their superstitions and their crimes. Your written constitutions, your declarations of right and of national independence, your books of statute law and of precedent, contain in themselves no inherent principle of vitality. They operate and have life, but in proportion as that life is infused into them by the feelings and conscience of the nation. The reign of violence has passed; men talk now of the reign of written constitutions. But parchment and paper cannot give freedom, or uphold it when given. Ours is a government of public opinion, and each day the channels, by which that public opinion may act upon the laws, tribunals and treaties of the nation, seem shortening and widening, turning each day a fuller and more direct and more rapid stream upon the ostensible rulers, and the written laws of the nation. In the formation of this sovereign principle of opinion, your new-found fellow citizens wish to share, and cannot but share, even did they not wish it. If not educated and sanctified,

they will only lower and dilute the tone of public morals, already alas, too evidently declining; and a vitiated public opinion will send its reeking corruption into your senate-chambers, your halls of justice, your schools, your warehouses, and your homes, until licentiousness, and profaneness, and violence, like the curse of Egypt, be found a croaking and slimy plague infesting the whole land. Nor may we hide from ourselves the fact, that unfriendly influences of the most seductive character are busy—that the work of natural corruption is not left to its own natural course, but superstitions, which have in other lands and ages held the widest sway, are assiduously engaged in the work of education and proselytism amongst us;

> And bold with joy,
> Forth from his dark and lonely hiding-place,
> (Portentous sight,) the owlet Atheism,
> Sailing on obscene wings athwart the noon,
> Drops his blue-fringed lids, and holds them close,
> And hooting at the glorious sun in heaven,
> Cries out, "Where is it?"*

And yet amid these dangers, that self-gratulation "which goeth before a fall" as surely in a nation as in the individual, is so evident, as to be imputed to us as a national foible. Privileges, singular and great, we indeed have; but the only light in which it is safe to view them, is that of the corresponding obligations they impose. Signal mercies, if misused, must provoke judgments as signal; and American Christians, if unfaithful to their high trust, will be made examples of God's sore indignation. And among the difficulties of our situation, felt not indeed except by the church, let us remember the demands of the Foreign Mission field, each day increasing. To meet these, the Home Mission enterprise must be sustained by the churches at home, until made by its influence united, intelligent and devoted, they become the camp and armory, from which shall be sent forth yet other and more numerous levies of conscripts for the foreign service of the Church of Christ.

3. The *motives* which urge you to the work, in view of these considerations, will naturally suggest themselves to all, and are alike varied and powerful. Self-interest and the love of kindred furnish them. The more aged amongst us

---

* Coleridge.

cannot but desire to transmit to the coming generations, unimpaired, the immunities and blessings they received themselves from those who went before. To the young men of our churches, we might speak of the peculiar interest which, as the future inheritors of the land, they have, to escape the evils of ignorance and irreligion, and to avert, if it may be, the storm that will descend on the quiet graves of their fathers, but which they still surviving must buffet for themselves, or be swept before its violence. We might appeal to your love of man as such, or to your love of country, and ask on these grounds your alms and your prayers in this good work. But if the Roman patriot could say of the paramount force and engrossing character of that high motive,— love to our country :— " Dear are the charities of home ; dear are parents, and dear are our children ; but our one country, yet dearer, combines all the charities of us all ; " — I would speak to you, brethren, of a higher love, blending with and absorbing as well this as all minor charities. As lovers of your country I might urge, and as lovers of your kind I might require you ; but by a love which sanctifies, and itself surpasses all others, I beseech you ; as the lovers of Christ, or rather let me say as the beloved of Christ, whom he has loved to the death, has ransomed and is sanctifying ; give to this work your prompt aid, your prayers and your efforts. And while some give of their substance, and some add their counsel, and all their prayers, are there not yet others here, who are girding themselves to a costlier offering, and who are prepared to become themselves a whole burnt offering upon the altars of the church, and as a living sacrifice to spend and be spent, in the personal labor of bearing the gospel to the destitute?

In the consuming flames of divine charity, our Lord became himself a willing victim, and the zeal of his Father's house devoured him. To reach and rescue you, he shrunk from no sacrifice. Requite him by love intense and absorbing, like that love which it reflects. And to those here, who are themselves honored by their personal engagements as the missionary preachers of the church, let me say: Brethren, remember in your most painful sacrifices, in the most distressing repulses that your efforts may encounter, you can never know the peculiar agony of soul which our Lord Jesus Christ, as a Home Missionary, endured. Among the most affecting pages in the history of David Brainerd, is the journal of that

Sabbath which he spent amid the idolatrous revellings of the heathen, who had refused to listen to his teachings. Destitute of all Christian society, he had retired to the forest, and there in desolate loneliness sat him down with his Bible in his hand, while at a little distance, they yelled and danced in honor of their demons. Even that devoted man sunk in the trial, and describes the absence of all sympathy and Christian society as making this the most burdensome Sabbath he had ever known. Now this loneliness, which for the time crushed even the spirit of a Brainerd, was felt by our Lord, as none else could feel it. There was no heart even among his disciples, with whom he could have true and entire communion. Omniscient, he read perpetually the evil in the breasts of all that surrounded him. All was naked and opened to him. The ambition, the jealousy, the distrust, and the avarice of his own apostles, the malignant hatred to God and all goodness that filled the souls of the impenitent around him, were necessarily and ever present to his view. And he himself was all purity, entirely and intensely abhorring evil in its slightest stains. This healthful and sensitive purity was condemned to be continually jostled by our depravity, and how harshly, in the rude collision, must it have been rasped by the hard, dry, scurf of our moral leprosy. His was indeed a peculiar solitariness, as he moved a sinless one among sinners. The anguish of this loneliness, this daily death, endured by our Master, we may never know. But of these the sacrifices of *his* love we do well often to think, that our own may be rekindled.

There are those here, who giving of their substance and their cares to the good work, withhold their own hearts. The yoke of Christ, which is easy, their necks do not yet wear; and his burden, which is light, they refuse to assume. Dwelling in cities each one of whose moving multitudes lives, moves, and has his being in God,—or the tillers of fields which He only has blessed with fruitful seasons, filling your hearts with food and gladness,—in the enjoyment of a plenty, a freedom and a peace which Christ's providence gave,—in the daily hearing of his commands, and with his sacrifice for sin hourly before your view, you yield him no love, and act as if you owed him no allegiance. The Giver is shut out from the heart by barriers which his own gifts have been employed to form. O, remember that a land which sends forth the gospel to other lands, a community that sustain the missionary to labor amid their own and foreign destitution, as they are the most favored, so they may be also the most guilty of all lands and of all communities. Remember the curse of Jerusalem, and the plagues of the nation whose hills had been traversed by a Saviour's feet, and the field of whose home missions a Saviour's own tears and blood had watered. Christ's word and Spirit have come nigh you — your own kindred and friends are found in his church. And God grant that the Redeemer who has thus taught in your streets, and wrought wonders even in your own homes and households, stand not up in the last day, an incensed and inflexible Judge, to condemn you for that gospel which you have sent to others but rejected for yourselves.

EFFICIENCY OF PRIMITIVE MISSIONS.

BY

REV. BARON STOW.

The word of God grew and multiplied.—ACTS 12 : 24.

THE success of the first Christians in their missionary enterprises, has long been regarded as one of the most remarkable facts in history. Their beginning was small, and peculiarly unpromising; but in less time than has elapsed since William Carey commenced in Bengal, they had preached the gospel and organized churches throughout all Palestine, and almost all Asia Minor, through Macedonia, Greece, the islands of the Ægean sea, and along the sea-coast of Africa, and passed on to Rome, the mistress of the world. In a few years more, they were found doing their Master's work, and rejoicing in their Master's blessing, in every known nation, from Cape Comorin to Britain, from Scythia to the Pillars of Hercules. A historian of the second century says that in his time, Asia, Africa and Europe "abounded with Christians."

Yet such were the circumstances under which Christianity was then propagated, that upon the ordinary principles of human calculation, any man, not a lunatic, would have pronounced the enterprise impracticable. A candid consideration of these circumstances has wrought conviction in favor of the divinity of our religion in many a mind that was utterly impervious to every other species of evidence.

Who were the first preachers and advocates of the Christian religion? What was their number? What their origin, their standing, their education, their personal influence? Were they the agents that human sagacity would have selected for such an undertaking?

What was the character of the religion which they would propagate? Was it such as the world, Jewish and Pagan, would be likely to welcome with grateful enthusiasm? What were its doctrines? What its precepts? What did it prohibit? What require?

What was the state of the world, the whole world, to which they were commanded to preach the gospel, and for whose subjugation to Christ they were pledged to labor even unto the death? Had Judaism become superannuated and decrepit, so that its hold of the children of Abraham could easily be relaxed, and Christianity, with little difficulty, be substituted in its place? Was paganism in its dotage, and "ready to vanish away?" Did the systems of philosophy, then popular, pre-dispose the mind of the age to a prompt reception of such a system as that of Jesus of Nazareth?

What were the malignant and persevering efforts, not only to obstruct the progress of the new religion, but to suppress and exterminate it from the earth? So far did one emperor, Diocletian, proudly imagine that he had succeeded, that he caused a medal to be struck with the inscription, *Nomine Christianorum deleto*,—the Christian name obliterated.

Yet the disciples of Christ, nothing daunted, went forward as bidden by their Lord, and, transcending all barriers, and pressing their way through all difficulties, conveyed the life-giving doctrine to millions of the perishing, and caused earth and heaven to exult together over its wide-spread and salutary triumphs. This we have called a remarkable fact. The unbelieving Gibbon so considered it, and, without venturing to question its reality, exhausted his rare ingenuity in the attempt to account for it upon principles that should exclude all recognition of the divine original of the system.

There is another remarkable fact, that we are sure will be so regarded by future generations, and that will be no less perplexing to the philosophic historian;—and that is, *The slow progress of the gospel in the nineteenth century.* The Karen inquirer says to our missionary, "If so long time has elapsed since the crucifixion of Christ, why has not this good news reached us before? Why have so many generations of our fathers gone down to hell for want of it?" But these are not the questions which we would now propose. We ask not, How is it that, after eighteen hundred years, so much of the world is covered with pagan darkness? We ask not, How has it happened that for more than a thousand years so large a proportion of the pagan world has been suffered to remain unvisited by Christian heralds? We leave it for our fathers, now in eternity, to answer for themselves to their holy Judge. We simply inquire, How is it that now, as the church professes to understand her obligation, she does not feel its pressure and act in accordance with its dictates? How is it, that with her present knowledge of the heathen world, her aggregate of numbers, her intellectual and physical resources, her triumphs are so comparatively limited?

Just in proportion as our missionary endeavors, in character, motive, spirit, resemble those of the primitive church, they are unquestionably as effective. But let us compare our circumstances with theirs, and who will account for the mighty difference between the results of their missions and ours?

They had no better truth, nor more of it than we have. The gospel which we preach to a sinful world is precisely the same as they preached. It has lost none of its adaptedness to man's condition,—none of its power to regenerate and save.

They had no better hearts to deal with than we have. It does not appear that man has deteriorated, either in intellect or morals, so as to render our task more difficult than theirs. He was then totally depraved; he is only that now. They did not find the heathen more accessible or more susceptible of impression than we find them. The minds which they addressed, like those which we address, were pre-occupied by opinions, and moulded into habits, all directly and sternly repugnant to the spirit of Christianity. Every thing that most powerfully influences and tyrannizes over the human soul,—as superstition, custom, policy, interest, pride, passion, law, philosophy, religion,—was decidedly hostile to the genius and claims of the gospel.

The divine influence that accompanied their labors, and without which even *they* would have been unsuccessful, was not different in any respect, except perhaps in amount, from that with which we are favored. They lived under the dispensation of the Spirit. We live under the same dispensation. If the Holy Spirit rendered them peculiarly successful, it was not an act of arbitrary sovereignty, but an equitable adjustment, proportioning the blessing to their measure of fidelity and devotedness. Such were the character and extent of their labors, that he could consistently show them special favor. In blessing them, therefore, he offered no premium to indolence, gave no countenance to antinomian presumption.

When we shall live and labor as they did, we shall find, either that there is no truth in the promise, or that our exertions are rendered equally effectual by the Spirit's energy.

In what respect did the ability of the primitive church surpass ours? Had she greater wealth or intelligence, or more of anything which we reckon under the denomination of resources? Was her ministry distinguished by extraordinary talent, or superior intellectual training? A few, we admit, and only a few, were divinely inspired,—and they especially for the purpose of filling up the canon of Scripture; but who can show that their inspiration gave them power over a single heart, or added a single convert to the church of Christ?

All the external advantages are decidedly in our favor. We have knowledge of the state of the world which they had not. We have greater facilities of intercourse both by land and water. We have the printing-press, a potent instrument, whose powers, not yet half developed, shall astonish and bless the nations. We have equally with them the force of the argument from miracles and prophecy, and we have the additional argument derived from the propagation of Christianity, its indestructibleness either by internal corruption or external oppression, the perpetuity of its institutions, the preservation of the Scriptures, the continued fulfilment of prophecy, and the benign influence of the gospel upon individual, domestic, and national welfare. Nor should we forget the fact, that the missionary enterprise has in our day secured to itself no small portion of secular respectability. Multitudes, who have no sympathy with its nobler aims, are disposed to regard it with favor, and to aid it forward, merely on account of its indirect results. If in our main object, the salvation of souls from sin and death, they see no point of attraction, yet in the subserviency of missions to literature, science, commerce, civilization, they find something that is congenial to their taste, something which as scholars, philanthropists, merchants, they can admire, something to prompt them to be liberal to a degree that ought to shame the Christian for his parsimony. Foreign missions have acquired a character and a position in the public mind, to which in the days of the apostles they were strangers.

Yet notwithstanding circumstances are so much in our favor, they made advances in the production of effect, such as we have never witnessed. Without the world's favorite instrumentality, learning, eloquence, wealth, arms,—nay, with all these leagued against them, and in the face of them all, the primitive church expanded, and achieved triumph after triumph, — all the triumphs of truth and holiness. All the apparatus of torture and death was brought out and arrayed in her path to arrest her progress, but heedless of its terrors, she moved forward to the execution of her lofty purpose. Some of her most malignant foes became her devoted champions, and even martyrs, and every day new territories were added to her growing empire. Persecution often kindled her fires, and with her blood she as often extinguished them. Her progress from place to place was marked by the dethronement of idol deities, and the fall of idol temples; on the high places of idolatry she planted her banners; and in all lands, known to the merchant, the traveller, the warrior, the trophies of her power were multiplied. "So mightily grew the word of God and prevailed."

The question recurs: — How shall we account for this difference in efficiency, between their missions and ours? The suggestion of a few considerations by way of reply may not be unsuitable.

I. THE TYPE OF THEIR PIETY.

The piety of not only the ministry, but of the church in general, was missionary piety. Just suppose that the great majority of Christians were as spiritual, as dead to the world, as active for God, as we require our missionaries to be, and as some of them actually are, and you have an approximation to the true idea of the religious character of the early church. When believers then gave themselves to Christ, it was a *bona fide* transaction. They did not enter his service as an experiment, or on probation, but unconditionally, unreservedly, and for eternity. They gave up all for him, — they consecrated all to him. In "simplicity and godly sincerity," with a lively sense of his worthiness, and of the legitimacy of his claims, they surrendered themselves, body and soul, to him as their proprietor and ruler, as well as Saviour and friend. Willing to be his, desirous to be his, they became his by voluntary covenant, — "his own," in every possible sense, nominally, really, and for ever.

The distinguishing traits of their piety were strongly developed, and obvious to all.

1. *Great love.* On no part of the Christian character does the New Testament so frequently and strenuously insist, as on this — on none does it pass so many and deserved enco-

miums. Whatever else a man might have, if deficient in love he was regarded as defective in the primary and essential element of evangelical godliness. They understood that "love is the fulfilling of the law."

The early Christians had great love to *the Saviour*. They remembered the thrice-repeated and searching interrogation, proposed under the most impressive circumstances on the shore of Tiberias, "Simon, son of Jonas, *lovest thou me?*" It burned deep into their souls the conviction that love to him must be the fundamental element of their character, the main-spring of all their action. Hence we find them uniformly and studiously cultivating this affection, that so they may never be lacking in the impulsive power appropriate to their calling, — that so they may ever with sincerity appeal to the Searcher of hearts, "Lord, thou knowest all things, thou knowest that we love thee." When Dr. Doddridge entered the dungeon of a prisoner, with a reprieve which he had obtained for him, the poor man fell down at his feet and exclaimed, "I will be yours! Wherever you go, I am yours! Sir, every drop of my blood thanks you, for you have had mercy upon every drop of it!" Similar were the feelings of the first Christians towards their redeeming Lord, — similar their protestations of gratitude, attachment, and allegiance. "My beloved is mine, and I am his." The love of Christ, — both his love to them, and their love to him, — the latter being only a reduplication of the former, — constrained them to live, not unto themselves, but unto him who died for them and rose again. To please him was their primary object. To please him they cultivated personal holiness. To please him they labored for the conversion of souls. To please him they urged their missionary inroads into remote regions, encountered the most appalling dangers, endured the severest hardships, and faced death in its fiercest forms.

This love unquestionably exists in modern Christians in a degree, but alas! in a too diminished degree. It is not in us, as it was in them, a burning passion, a fire giving impulse to the whole machinery of our being. If it were, it would impel us onward to similar sacrifices, labors, conflicts, victories.

They had great love to *one another*. Brotherly love is seldom seen in our day just as it existed among the early Christians. With them it was a test of discipleship, an elementary principle, devoid of which, a man could not obtain, from saint or sinner, from angel or devil, even the name of

Christian. Without this they did not pretend to consider themselves as the children of God. "We know," said they, "that we have passed from death unto life, because we love the brethren." The absence of brotherly love was one of the criterions by which antichrist was to be known. Its presence was to furnish indisputable proof both of the divine mission of their Master and of their attachment to his cause. Jesus prayed that his disciples might *all* be one, to the end that the world might believe that the Father had sent him. And to them he declared, "By this shall all men know that ye are my disciples, if ye have love one to another." And the world, as they beheld the chain of fraternal affection running through all hearts, uniting them firmly to each other, and connecting the whole inseparably with the throne of love, felt and confessed the force of the demonstration. Their brotherly love, — which was really a divine instinct, an essential property of their new nature, and therefore spontaneous and unmodified by external circumstances, — stood forth in strong contrast with the selfishness of the world around them, like the verdure of paradise set in the desert, and drew forth from their bitterest enemies involuntary expressions of wonder. The unbelieving historian before cited, in his attempt to account for their astonishing success in propagating their religion, alleges as one of the most powerful causes, their affectionate union. Then there was but one denomination of Christians.* "One Lord, one faith, one baptism." Consequently there were no clashing creeds, no sectarian bickerings, no rival interests, no party plottings and counter-plottings, no wasteful expenditure of time, and feeling, and moral energy, in attempts to maintain and fortify party positions. "By one Spirit" they were "all baptized into *one* body," and they regarded themselves, and were regarded by all around them, as members of *one* harmonious and devoted brotherhood. Christ was the centre of attraction, around which they rallied and united, and, like the radii of a circle, the nearer they drew to the centre, the nearer they were to each other. Assimilated by the grace of

---

* It can hardly be necessary to qualify this general statement, by the admission that even before the apostles were all dead, the church was vexed with false teachers and consequent heresies. These were very limited in their extent, and never affected the great body of believers. On some points of unrevealed doctrine there were diversities of opinion; but, in the language of Waddington, "their variations were without schism, and their differences without acrimony."

God, and fused and welded by the fires of persecution, their affinity and cohesion rendered them the admiration of the world that hated them, and gave them a moral power which the modern church does not possess, and never will possess, until brotherly love shall resume its ancient influence, and become, as it then was, a "bond of perfectness,"—until "the multitude of them that believe" shall be "of one heart and one way," keeping "the unity of the Spirit in the bond of peace." O when will the "whole family" of Christ become one, and with "hearts knit together in love," discontinue their petty controversies among themselves, and, following their one Leader, converge and direct their whole energies towards the one point, the salvation of the human soul? We may speculate as we please about the incidental advantages of our division into sects or denominations, comparing them poetically to the prismatic hues of the rainbow, and from the pulpit and the platform shouting in ecstasy, "*E pluribus unum!*" But the practical man will tell us that if we would dissolve the intractable substances of earth, we must have the colorless ray of virgin light.

The religion of the first Christians was essentially *philanthropic*. They had great love to man. As the creature of God, as a fellow-being, as a sinner lost and helpless, as the one for whom their Master died, as bound with them to a common destiny, they loved him and sought his good. O how different was their philanthropy from that of the atheistic philosophers, with which, at the close of the last century, a portion of the eastern hemisphere was deeply cursed. They talked of love, universal, disinterested love. But O, such love! Who ever beheld its parallel? Love to man, but not to men; love to everybody in general, but to nobody in particular; love to the mass, while they soaked the earth around the guillotine with the blood of individuals! The love of the early Christians comprehended mankind not only as a whole, but in detail; and in order to do good to the whole, they sought the improvement of the individuals. If fanaticism be, as defined by an able writer, "Enthusiasm inflamed by hatred," they, admitting them to be enthusiasts, were certainly not fanatics. Militant and aggressive as were their movements, not an enemy, however embittered and prejudiced, could charge them with malignant motives. Their enthusiasm was inflamed by *love*, and "Love worketh no ill to his neighbor." Tender and affectionate, as if they had just come from leaning on the bosom of incarnate compassion, their words melted like honey on the hearts of the people, and by an invisible, irresistible influence, won them over from hostility to friendship. O! yes, brethren, love, love, was one of the secrets of their power. Love of souls was with them both a principle and a passion, and, under its exhaustless impulse, what did they not endure, sacrifice, accomplish!

2. *Vigorous faith.* Nothing so debilitates a moral being, as unbelief. Nothing so girds him with strength, and renders him energetic and efficient, as intelligent confidence.

The primitive Christians had strong faith in the inspired account of man's condition and destiny. Confiding in revealed truth, they looked on him as deeply depraved, guilty, condemned, and, unless saved by the gospel, sure to perish for ever. This they believed in respect to the heathen as well as the Jews. Do we believe it as they did? "If one died for all,"—thus they reasoned,—"then were all dead." How appalling the truth,—"all dead!"—all exposed to hell! They believed it,—they acted as if they believed it. They went forth and labored "unto the end," under the full persuasion that every unbeliever would be damned. With such faith, how could they be inactive? And is not our comparative inertness attributable to our unbelief? "Lord, increase our faith!"

They had faith in the adaptedness of the gospel to the necessities of a depraved and perishing world. They believed what they said, that the gospel is "the power of God unto salvation, to every one that believeth,"—that it could remove from the penitent sinner, not only the external condemnation, but the inward defilement,—not only deliver him from the curse of the violated law, but bleach his polluted nature as white as heaven. They had faith in their own message, and none who heard them and saw the correspondence of their lives with the testimony of their lips, could gainsay their not immodest declaration, "We believe, and therefore speak." Can we, with no misgiving of conscience, with no fear of contradiction, adopt their language? Have we a confidence like theirs in the suitableness and efficacy of the gospel? Do we believe that it is the thing, and the only thing that can save the heathen from eternal hell?

They had faith in the rectitude and utility of their enterprise. They did not consider their time, strength, suffering, blood, as expended in a crusade uncalled for, undignified, misdirected. No, no. They had heard from the lips of their Master, the remarkable words, "As the Father hath sent me, even so send I you," and they had thence learned that their mission was identical with his, a continuation of the one grand design, — the salvation of "a multitude which no man could number." They regarded the cause as his, devised by his love, sustained by his power, and sure to prevail. Hence, in the depths of their dungeons, with the chains of a despot about them, they could exultingly say, "The word of God is not bound," and could even rejoice in the things which happened unto them, because they contributed to "the furtherance of the gospel." If they were mortal, their enterprise was not. They might be "like the foam of the billows which the tempests easily scatter;" but their cause, "resembling the eternal flow of ocean, should roll its fulness upon the most distant shores."

They believed that the work assigned them, — the preaching of the gospel to every creature, — could be done. Consequently they were the people to do it. A doubt as to its practicability would have unfitted them for the service. Brethren, do modern Christians, — do we believe, that the heathen world can be converted to God? Do we believe that with proper effort the earth can be "filled with the knowledge of the Lord," and the kingdom of Christ be made to outstretch its borders, until it shall encompass "all nations?" "If thou canst believe, all things are possible to him that believeth."

They had the Saviour's promise to be with them and defend them, and give them success. His own words, "All power is given unto me in heaven and in earth," were engraven in the metal of their souls, and they felt that he was able, with "all power," to make his promise good. How could they hesitate or falter? "Lo, I am with you," was enough to brace up their courage, and retain it firmly at the desirable point. Hence timidity was not even an accident of their character.

Such, and more than such was their faith, and under its invigorating and impulsive influence they went forward, and quit themselves like men, Christian men. Brethren, is there a large amount of this faith in the existing church? Should the Son of Man come, how much of it would he find on the earth?

3. *Rigid self-denial.* When they gave themselves to

Christ, they counted all things loss for him and his salvation; and the surrender was an honest, whole-hearted transaction, never to be reconsidered, never to be regretted.

Hence, from the hour of their conversion, they made little account of *property*. If it was confiscated by government, or destroyed by the mob, they "took joyfully the spoiling of their goods," assured that in heaven they had a better, an incorruptible inheritance. When the cause required, how ready were they to lay all at the feet of the Missionaries! Generally they were poor. A rich Christian! why, such a thing was hardly known. However it may be now, it was *then*, "easier for a camel to go through a needle's eye, than for a rich man to enter into the kingdom of God." And if, as an act of special sovereignty, a man of wealth was converted, he seldom retained his riches for a long period; for such was his sympathy for the despoiled and suffering brotherhood, and such his solicitude for the conversion of the perishing, that his funds were poured forth as water. Yet poor as were the first Christians, they were liberal to a degree seldom surpassed. We from our much give little. They from their little gave much. Their "deep poverty abounded unto the riches of their liberality." Baptized covetousness was the product of a later age.

Reputation was with them a matter of trivial consequence. We have often so much character to obtain, or to preserve, that we can spare neither time nor resources for the great work of promoting Christ's glory. But the early Christians, bishops and all, while they were careful to maintain consciences void of offence towards God and man, were not very sensitively concerned whether they stood high or low in the world's estimation. It therefore cost them very little to keep up a good reputation. That they left where they left their life, "hid with Christ in God."

They consulted not with flesh and blood, but sacrificed *personal ease*, and submitted to hardships and trials of which we know comparatively, most of us, absolutely nothing. They were "men that hazarded their lives for the name of the Lord Jesus." Yes, for their religion they were ready to die, and for it they did die by hecatombs, and by dying for it they often accomplished more than by living and laboring for it. Hence the triumphant remark of Tertullian had quite as much truth as poetry: — "The more you mow us down, the thicker we rise; the Christian blood you spill is like the seed you sow; it springs from the earth and fructifies the more."

4. *Simple obedience.* They understood Christ to be in earnest, when, standing but one step from the throne of the universe, he said, " Go ye into all the world, and preach the gospel to every creature." It was not therefore with them a matter to be considered whether they should go or not go. The command was positive and peremptory, and how could they escape from the obligation? With us, to stay is the rule, to go is the exception. With them, to go is the rule, to stay is the exception.* Wonder not that they accomplished so much. Wonder not that we accomplish so little. They did not wait indolently for openings, but went forth, either to find them or to make them. If defeated at one point, instead of returning to Jerusalem in despondency, and writing a book on the impracticability of Christian missions, they proceeded to another and perhaps more distant field, and then to another, and still another, until they had gone over the appointed territory. Their piety was ENTERPRISING; the spirit of obedience made it such.

Have we this spirit of obedience to the last command of the Lord Jesus? Let us not evade the question, but answer it. Why then is it necessary for so much to be said and done, by the pulpit and the press, by corresponding secretaries and travelling agents, to obtain our scanty supply of missionaries, and gather from a half million of Baptists, at the rate of a dime each, enough to send these few missionaries to six hundred millions of perishing heathen? O Jesus! is this thy church? Are these the people whom thou didst redeem by thy blood, and who with the first throbbings of the new heart have severally inquired, "Lord, what wilt thou have me to do?" When Ko Chet-thing, the Karen convert, was in this country, he was urged on a certain occasion to address a congregation in respect to their duty to send out and support more missionaries. After a moment of downcast thoughtfulness, he asked with evident emotion, "Has not Jesus Christ told them to do it?" "O yes," was the reply, "but we wish

---

* "It is not, as is commonly done, to be taken for granted, by those who come into the ministry, that they are to remain in their own Christian land, unless a case of duty can be made out for them to go to some unevangelized people: but it is to be taken for granted, that they are to be employed in conveying the gospel to some destitute people, unless a case of duty can be made out for them to remain in their own already Christian country."— *Dr. Wisner.*

you to remind them of their duty." "Oh no!" said the Karen, " if they will not obey Jesus Christ, they will not obey me." He in his simplicity considered the command of the Master as paramount and all-sufficient.

It has been often said that in the hearts of our brethren there are fountains of benevolence. Ice-bound, it is acknowledged they may be, and pent in the rocks of ignorance and prejudice; yet if but a Moses go to them, and smite those rocks, the streams of charity, it is said, will flow forth to gladden all the desert. Indeed! And had the primitive Christians such Horeb hearts, yielding nothing to the cause of God, nothing to the claims of a suffering, dying world, until smitten by foreign force? Was the missionary enterprise in their day, a crouching mendicant, wandering among the churches, soliciting with a pauper's importunity the shreds and parings of liberal incomes, and then proclaiming at every corner the name and residence of every donor of a half shekel, lest, forsooth, unless his reluctantly bestowed contribution should be loudly trumpeted, he might cease to care for the will of the Lord Jesus, and lose his interest in the salvation of a world, and the missionary treasury feel no more of the overflowings of his benevolence? Tell me, men, brethren and fathers, were such the Christians of the age of Barnabas, and Philemon, and Polycarp?

5. *Fervent prayer.* It has been remarked respecting a modern preacher, whose labors while living were eminently blessed in the conversion of his hearers, and who, " being dead, yet speaketh," that the secret of his success lay in his devotional habits. He dwelt on the border of eternity, and carried with him into his pulpit, and into all his intercourse with his people, the very atmosphere that circulates around the throne. Hence a member of his congregation once declared, — " When our pastor prays, it is right into the heart of God. When he preaches, it is right into the heart of the sinner." This description, true perhaps of a few moderns, is truer still of the great body of the ancient preachers. They had peculiar access to the hearts of men, because they had peculiar access to the ear and heart of God. With him and the glories around him they were familiar, and ever as they came forth from his presence, they brought to the people, fresh from the tree of life, the leaves that are for the healing of the nations, — sparkling from the river of life, the waters " clear as crystal," that purify the unholy, and refresh the way-worn and weary.

Another pastor, whose success was proverbially great, when asked how it happened that under his ministry "the word of God" so "grew and multiplied," returned the significant answer, "I have a praying church." The early church was eminently a praying church. The sin of indevotion could not be laid to her charge. The oft-repeated and unanimous request of the apostles, "Pray for us," "Pray for us that the word of the Lord may have free course and be glorified," was never made in vain. Indeed, the request scarcely needed to be made. The Christians of those days waited not for a specified season, but at all times and every where they remembered before God the cause of missions, and the self-denying missionary laborers. In the closet, in the family, in the church, the burden of their prayer was, "Thy kingdom come." Every prayer-meeting was a concert of prayer for the universal spread of the gospel of Christ. And theirs were the effectual, fervent prayers that avail much. They knew how to touch that delicate chain which Jesus had passed over the throne, and by which the faintest spark of holy desire may be easily transmitted; and through it they sent a continual stream of invisible but powerful influence away into the deepest recesses of heathenism.

Such, in five of its aspects, was the type of their piety. Perceive we not good reasons why they were so amazingly successful in propagating the gospel of Christ? And see we not, by comparison, satisfactory reasons why the gospel in our hands is so limited in its efficiency?

Another fact which gave a peculiarity to the missions of the primitive church, and doubtless conduced in a large measure to their success, deserves to be considered.

II. THEIR PLAN OF ACTION.

If indeed that can be called *plan* which indicates no forecast, includes nothing of method, proceeds from no concert, and betrays the entire absence of all worldly wisdom. Yet in all their operations there were certain elements that exhibit, if not human sagacity, the supervision of a master mind that understands human nature, and knows how to adapt the means to the end.

1. *Unity of object.* They considered that it was their calling, their very business as Christians, to propagate the religion that they loved. Hence, every one felt it incumbent on him, whether others joined him or not, to do whatever he could for the object. "I cannot *speak* for Christ," said a

martyr on his way to the flames, "but I can *die* for him." That was the pervading spirit. " If I cannot do every thing, I can do something. 'This one thing I do;' I labor, 'according to the ability that God giveth,' for the conversion of the world." This was the end they contemplated with unwavering eye; this the point toward which they pressed with unfaltering movement. To this end they devoted their thinking, feeling, acting, praying. For this they earned, for this they gave their money, and ever found it, as you may find it to-night, "more blessed to give than to receive." For this they toiled, and suffered, and counted not their lives dear unto themselves. O, they were Christians worthy of the name! Like their Master, they had one thing to do, and how were they straitened until it was accomplished!

What was the master passion of the primitive church? What but a burning desire for the salvation of the guilty and the perishing of their race? Hence, having one object, their feeling and action were intense, and they moved onward with a momentum which the nature of mind forbade to be more, which the principles that actuated them forbade to be less. We occasionally see an individual of our own circle, cherishing the same high purpose, living as if he had one, only one object,—the glory of God in the salvation of souls. But the instances are rare,—rare as light-houses on the North-West Coast. Our sympathies and energies are distributed among a variety of objects. Our eye is not single,—our heart is divided. Undertaking too many things, our resources are dissipated, and we do nothing effectively. Our life is but a span, and our ability is finite; let us endeavor to do one thing, and do it well.

2. *Simplicity of means.* It is an assumption of modern wisdom, that the gospel cannot be made effectual among the heathen, unless civilization precede and prepare the way. "Send first the schoolmaster and the mechanic, and the agriculturist; afterwards the missionary." This counsel we hear not only from the world, but we regret to say from too many of the church. But besides betraying a secret infidelity respecting the real efficacy of the gospel, it is a virtual impeachment of the wisdom of the Lord Jesus Christ, who has arranged an order of things entirely the reverse.

Thus we have been confidently assured, as if it were a settled axiom, that the gospel cannot advance at home, and that we must expect no more revivals of religion in the south or the north, in the west or the east, until certain evils are removed, certain dominant vices suppressed. Moral reform, it is said, must precede the triumphs of the cross. And by these specious theories, have thousands of the people of God been unhappily deluded, and, leaving their appropriate work of preaching the gospel and distributing the Bible, they have seized the pickaxe and gone to beating down the obstacles which they have learned to think the Christian religion can neither remove nor transcend. Sadly for themselves and for the world, do they forget that "the weapons of our warfare are not carnal, but mighty through God to the pulling down of strong holds; casting down imaginations and every high thing that exalteth itself against the knowledge of God, and bringing into captivity every thought to the obedience of Christ."

The primitive Christians acted on the principle that the gospel is the grand pioneer, fitted above all else to make crooked things straight, and rough places plain. If fatigue duty was to be performed, in order to open a way for the easy progress of the King of Zion, they desired no better instruments than the truths of his own glorious gospel. They understood that moral reform proceeds best in the *train* of Christ and his cross, and hence, for the regeneration of a degraded and miserable world, they used no other instrumentality. They, in their simplicity, regarded the gospel as the divinely appointed catholicon,—the one efficacious remedy of all moral evils. They supposed that if individuals or communities could be brought completely under its influence, they would renounce all sin, and cultivate all righteousness. Brethren, if the gospel does not rectify what is wrong in man, can you inform us of any system of truth or of agencies that will do it? You cannot predispose men's hearts to welcome the truth of God by any external means whatever,—not even by the potent influence of grammars and lexicons, globes and orreries, spelling-books and newspapers, spinning jennies and steam engines. But the simple story of the cross does execution in all places,—in the German university and the Northumberland colliery, in the Louisiana cotton-field and the Lowell factory, in the Putawatomy wigwam and the Karen jungle. And when sinners are once converted by the grace of God, then they begin to estimate rightly the importance of their being; then they recognize their relations to Jehovah and to one another, and the work of improvement may proceed successfully, for it has a basis and an object. "Seek first the kingdom of God," and all these minor results shall be superadded.

3. *Judicious application of their means.* You may cool water downward, but you must heat it upward. So with society; it deteriorates downward and improves upward. If the upper classes become vicious, they descend; if the lower become virtuous, they rise. This fact was manifestly recognized by Christ and his apostles, for they directed their attention chiefly to the lower strata of the social mass. Had they commenced with the upper, they would doubtless have succeeded with a single stratum, but all beneath would have remained untouched by gracious influences. But by beginning with the lower, they acted wisely, as he acts wisely who kindles the fire beneath a fluid instead of above it. They wrought upward, and the results amazed even themselves. We reverse the order, and work downward, and then wonder that the effects are so limited. Let us conform to the simple order of nature, as well as to primitive example, and both at home and abroad, PREACH THE GOSPEL TO THE POOR, and we shall soon rejoice in enlarged success.

They did not, like us, expend a large proportion of their resources upon mere machinery. They used but little of it, and the plan they adopted required but little. In rearing the temple of the Lord, we expend largely upon the scaffolding, what they devoted to the edifice. We pay great attention to *modes* of usefulness; they, willing to do good in the way prescribed by their Master, were intent solely upon the *usefulness.* We engage freely in matters remotely connected with our great, our appointed business; they "let the dead bury their dead," and went every where preaching that men should repent and turn to God. We devote weeks and months to the glorious privilege of "free discussion;" they allowed the potsherds to strive, and improved their time in preaching the gospel to the destitute. How long is it since an ecclesiastical body in a single session, squandered seventeen years of ministerial time in the discussion of points very slightly associated with the work assigned them by the Head of the church? As the result of the whole, has there been, or is there likely to be a single soul converted? Alas! results of a very different character may be apprehended, results over which demons will exult, and seraphim weep.

During the next three weeks this great city will be thronged with the servants of Christ, come up from the face of the whole land, like the heads of the tribes to Zion. Are they coming here to preach the "everlasting gospel?" To do good to souls? Will they burn with irrepressible desire for the conversion of the guilty thousands and hundreds of thousands who crowd the broad way to hell? We come here to consult about sending the gospel to the distant heathen, while around us, within a circle of two miles radius, are a quarter of a million human beings as much without hope as any pagans on earth, and for whom it shall be less tolerable in the judgment than for Sodom and Gomorrah! How long ought we to sit here debating a point of order, discussing an amendment to a resolution, adjusting the phraseology of a report, and passing votes of thanks to each other for services which Christ views as culpably imperfect? Oh brethren! if Paul and James were here, what would they do?

4. *Personal effort.* The primitive Christian regarded himself as a centre from which the voice of truth was to go forth over the whole circle of his influence. Every individual added to the church considered himself as an agent for propagating the news of salvation to his neighbors, who were in turn to communicate it to others, and they to others beyond them, and thus onward, till a chain of living voices should have been carried around the globe, and earth from the equator to the poles made vocal with the cry of those whose feet are beautiful upon the mountains, who bring glad tidings, and publish peace. Cherishing a conviction of individual responsibility, they were not content to do good merely by proxy. Their piety, in all its aspects, was essentially missionary, and each member felt himself to be consecrated, by his very profession, to the great work of evangelizing the world. When, therefore, a man was converted, he was immediately found moving among the impenitent, persuading them to flee from the wrath to come. And this he did, not more from a desire for the salvation of souls, than from love to the Saviour, and a conviction that it was his appropriate business, — an essential part of his "high calling." In the aggressive movements of the "sacramental host," he considered himself as drawn to serve, and he neither sought nor desired exemption. In the great cause at issue between God and man, he felt that he was subpœnaed as a witness for his Sovereign, and when his testimony was wanted, he was never among the missing.

The churches were then so many missionary societies. Each congregation of Christians, duly organized according to the laws of Christ, became first a focus into which the sanctified excellence of earth might be collected, and then a centre from which the light of truth and holiness might radiate in all directions. Hence the seven churches of Asia were represented as "seven golden candlesticks." Every church, "holding forth the word of life," was the pharos of a benighted world, flinging a hallowed radiance far over the stormy sea of human existence.

Missionary was than the highest style of ministerial character. The principal men, the most capable and influential, — the "sons of consolation," and the "sons of thunder," — not satisfied with remaining at home, and sending men of inferior powers and endowments, went themselves to the work, and with their own lips related the story of Calvary, and bared their own heads to the tempests of persecution.

It may well be questioned whether the committee of the English Baptist Mission did not perpetrate a grievous mistake when they refused to send to India that eminent man of God, the seraphic Pearce; and whether the London Society did not err exceedingly when they declined the offer of Dr. Reed to proceed to China, and occupy the breach where a giant had fallen. Both societies have unhappily confirmed the popular impression, that men of ordinary ability will do for missionaries, — that ministers who are capable of great usefulness at home, cannot be spared for the heathen.

Let us not wonder that modern missions, when compared with the ancient, are so limited in their efficiency. We probably expend more money in the enterprise than they did; but our piety is not like theirs, missionary piety; our zeal is not like theirs, missionary zeal; our activity is not like theirs, missionary activity. We probably talk and write as much about converting the world as they did; but we act less, we give less of personal labor. To the many designations given to the present age, we may properly add "the age of resolutions." Under the head of "Resolved," we all announce what we believe and what we deny, what we desire and what we deprecate, what we have done and what we intend to do. But the most of these resolutions, contemplating action, are never executed, simply because no one of the conclave that passed them feels personally responsible for their execution. Individuality is merged in the mass, and obligation that presses upon the whole, is unfelt by the separate confederates. I and We, are different words, and it is too often forgotten that the former is included in the latter. If some brother, three years ago had said, "I resolve, by the blessing of God, this year to raise one hundred thousand dollars for foreign missions," very likely it would have been accomplished. A hundred or more of us said unanimously, "WE will do it," and not an additional thousand did the resolution bring into your treasury.

Not thus did the primitive Christians manage their matters. If anything was to be done, instead of calling meetings, making speeches, passing resolutions, and then leaving the work undone, they went directly themselves and did it. How rightly is one book of the New Testament named, not the Resolutions, but the Acts of the Apostles. *Non dicta, sed acta Apostolorum.*

Oh how changed would be the aspect of the church, if her ministers and members would come up to the same standard of feeling, and principle, and action, recognizing in equal degree the claims of a world lying in wickedness, and their obligations to the world's Redeemer! Just suppose that the Church of England should lay aside her secular character, and become strictly a religious body, a missionary church, spiritual, self-denying, enterprising, — how luminous would be her glory, now so tarnished, — how mighty through God her moral power, now so paralyzed! Consecrating all her wealth, talent and intelligence to the cause of Christ, what triumphs might she not achieve? Let her archbishop and all her titled prelates, laying aside the paraphernalia of outward distinction, — the pitiful remnants of Romish folly, — and vacating their seats in the halls of legislation, become missionaries of the cross, such as Paul and Peter, Apollos and Timothy, going forth in the spirit of apostles, not to advance a sect, or to distribute the prayer-book, but to convert the pagan world to Christ Jesus, then would she become what she is not now, and what nothing but humiliation and sacrifice will make her, — "the perfection of beauty, the joy of the whole earth."

What but their Christian simplicity and missionary zeal, have made our Moravian brethren the agents of so much good, — the theme of such universal commendation? They commenced the work of missions to the heathen when their whole number did not exceed six hundred. They now reckon but a few thousands, with a very limited amount of wealth. But they are pre-eminently a missionary church, and are at this time supporting more stations, and more laborers among the unevangelized in both hemispheres, than the whole Baptist denomination in the United States, though we exceed them more than two hundred fold in numerical strength, and more than a thousand fold in pecuniary ability.

Brethren, we are culpably deficient in duty. We are not doing good, either at home or abroad, in proportion to our resources. We act not in accordance with our knowledge of the wants of an apostate world, and the will of our sovereign Lord. However it may be in other departments of moral action, it is certain that here, where the most fervid enthusiasm is but cool sobriety, and where it is hardly possible to be extravagant; here, in the holy cause of missions to the heathen; here, if nowhere else, we actually sacrifice zeal to prudence, or to something which we denominate prudence, but which the apostles would have called timidity, or unbelief, or perhaps covetousness. Anxious, on the one hand, to avoid a blind, headlong impetuosity, we have, on the other, diverged too far into a cold, calculating policy. Acting with cautious reference to the state of the treasury, we lose sight of the promises that encourage adventure, and choose rather to walk by sight than by faith. Reluctant to trust the great Promiser for a long time, or to a large amount, we treat him too much in a commercial spirit, and under the pretext of doing a safe business, we do comparatively nothing. When he sent forth his first missionaries, did he charge them to wait till funds were accumulated? Did he not rather bid them go at once, and assure them of his own gracious presence until the end of their course? Did they ever deal with him as if they suspected either his ability or his faithfulness?

Brethren in Christ, we have scarcely begun to feel, as all the churches must feel, before the world will believe us in earnest, and before we can rationally pray for the divine blessing upon our endeavors. We need more of the spirit of evangelical enterprise; the quenchless spirit of love that glowed in the bosoms of Paul and the primitive disciples; of Luther and his associate reformers; of Brainerd, and Schwartz, and Carey; and more than all, in the bosom of Him who " came not to be ministered unto, but to minister, and to give his life a ransom for many." The energy we want is that which springs from sympathy with the grandeur of our object, and an assured confidence that we have the coöperation of the mightiest agencies in the universe. We need a zeal that shall be kindled by an unclouded view of the condition and prospects of a guilty world; a zeal that shall burn as if fed by visions of the cross — of Heaven — of Hell; a zeal sustained by so much principle as that it can afford to be reproached as extravagant, and to wait until we are laid in the grave to be appreciated; a zeal that no discouragement can repress, no opposition smother; a zeal like that of the incarnate Son of God, which urged him on to his baptism in suffering; a zeal that shall admit of no repose, and intermit no exertion, until the gospel shall have been fully preached to the last of the species, and the Redeemer, surrendering his mediatorial commission, shall proclaim to the universe that he is SATISFIED.

RESOURCES OF THE ADVERSARY AND MEANS OF THEIR DESTRUCTION.

BY

REV. LYMAN BEECHER, D. D.

Thus saith the Lord, Even the captives of the mighty shall be taken away, and the prey of the terrible shall be delivered. — ISAIAH 49 : 25.

Therefore will I divide him a portion with the great, and he shall divide the spoil with the strong; because he hath poured out his soul unto death. — ISAIAH 53 : 12.

When a strong man armed keepeth his palace, his goods are in peace : but when a stronger than he shall come upon him, and overcome him, he taketh from him all his armor wherein he trusted, and divideth his spoils. — LUKE 11 : 21, 22.

And the seventh angel sounded ; and there were great voices in heaven, saying, The kingdoms of this world are become the kingdoms of our Lord, and of his Christ ; and he shall reign for ever and ever. — REV. 11 : 15.

And a voice came out of the throne, saying, Praise our God, all ye his servants, and ye that fear him, both small and great. And I heard as it were the voice of a great multitude, and as the voice of many waters, and as the voice of mighty thunderings, saying, Alleluia : for the Lord God omnipotent reigneth. — REV. 19 : 5, 6.

THE Scriptures teach, that sin commenced its reign on earth under the auspices of a mighty fallen spirit; and that he, having seduced mankind from their allegiance to God, has been constantly employed to maintain his bad eminence over them. They also teach, that the Son of God has interposed to destroy the works of this spirit; and that he will accomplish the object; that the power of Satan shall be broken; and the whole world be restored to loyalty and the favor of Heaven.

The passages which have just been recited, allude to the success with which the enemy of God has fortified his cause — to its final overthrow — and to the exultation and joy with which the event will fill earth and heaven.

I am aware, that with some, the doctrine of fallen angels is but an eastern allegory; and the idea of a conflict, between the creature and Creator, ridiculous and unworthy of the Divine Supremacy. I can only say, that if there be not an order of sinful intelligences above men, the Bible is one of the most deceptive books ever written. The entire history of the world shows, that human depravity, though operating in accordance with the laws of mind, is yet methodized and wielded with a comprehension of plan, wholly inexplicable upon the principle of accidental coincidence among men. That there should have been a system of well-constructed opposition to the Gospel, varying with circumstances, and comprehending the great amount of bad moral influence which has existed, without some presiding intellect, is as improbable, as that all the particles of matter which compose the universe, should have fallen into their existing method and order by mere accident, and without the presiding intellect of the Deity. And as to moral competition between the creature and the Creator, it exists, even if there be no fallen angels. It is a matter of fact before our eyes — a matter of experience too — that the carnal mind is enmity against God; and that God, in Christ, is reconciling the world to himself.

It should be remembered also, that when God has formed moral beings, even He can govern them, as such, only by moral influence, and in accordance with the laws of mind: mere omnipotence being as irrelevant to the government of mind, as moral influence would be to the government of the material universe. Nor must it be forgotten, that an alienated world requires more moral power for its restoration than that of simple law, which proved insufficient to maintain its allegiance. It requires a new moral influence so introduced and applied, as to corroborate law, and strengthen the loyalty of all the good, while rebels are reconciled and pardoned.

The reconciliation, through Christ, of such a world as this, in opposition to the rooted aversion of every heart, the concentrated power of social wickedness, and the ceaseless counteraction of mighty intelligences, principalities, and powers, does not seem to us an achievement unworthy of that Being who numbers the hairs of our head. By prophets and apostles, it is represented as exhibiting the height and depth and length and breadth, of the wisdom, and goodness, and power of God.

In this discourse, it is proposed to consider,

THE DEFENCES AND RESOURCES OF THE ENEMY, AND THE MEANS OF THEIR OVERTHROW.

We shall suppose, as the language of the text does, that

the Christianity, which is to prevail on earth, is the Christianity of the heart, rising to high eminence, and extending its blessed influence through all the relations of society, until the kingdoms of this world shall become associations of holiness — the Gospel become the predominant spring of action, and its morality the governing rule of all mankind. The array of opposition to such a glorious change on earth, now demands our attention.

1. At the head of opposition to the Gospel, in numerical power, must be placed *Idolatry*. To banish from the earth all knowledge of God and his government, and substitute a worship composed of lust and blood, seems most desirable to the great adversary, where circumstances allow it to be done: and this he has achieved in respect to about six hundred millions of the human family. In all that world of mind, knowledge is in deep eclipse, intellect slumbers, conscience is paralyzed, and all holy intercourse between earth and heaven is cut off; while passion and appetite, inflamed by sin, are suffered to prey uncontrolled.

2. The next form of opposition to the march of holiness, is that of *Imposture*. This was introduced by Mohammed. It was a system accommodated to the condition of a mingled population, composed of Pagans, Jews, and nominal Christians, all in a state of great ignorance and deep moral debasement. By complimenting Abraham and Moses, he beguiled the Jew; by conceding to the Saviour the rank of a prophet, he seduced the degenerate Christian; and by giving ample license to sensuality, in time and eternity, he secured the pagan: and what persuasion failed to accomplish, was finished by the sword. Thus one hundred and forty millions have been grouped together under the most ferocious and horrid despotism that ever warred against heaven, or tormented man. Over all these the smoke from the bottomless pit has ascended, intercepting the light of heaven, and dooming them for centuries to " darkness visible."

3. Cotemporaneously with this system of imposture, and like it a subject of prophecy, arose the *Papal superstition*, in the form of a corrupted Christianity, and adapted to a state of intellectual improvement where the grossness of Mohammedan imposture might not be likely to prevail. This has been, and is still, the master-piece of that wisdom which is from beneath; concentrating the bad influence of all past systems; satisfactory to the pagan, and not alarming to the degenerate

Christian; dazzling through the medium of sense; and giving such a license to sin, or such a cheap escape from its penalties, as allayed all fear, and stimulated to boundless indulgence.

Until this horrid system arose, the resistance made to the church of God had been planted without her walls. Now the sacred citadel is assailed and entered. Her friends are driven out, subjected to obloquy and death. The perverted authority of Heaven, and the sacred name of Christianity herself, and all the glorious and fearful sanctions of eternity are arrayed against the pure Gospel. Instead of the fold of Christ, the church became a ferocious beast, not sparing the flock: instead of a pure virgin,—the mother of harlots, corrupting the nations. Instead of reflecting the light of the Sun of righteousness, every orb was eclipsed; every candlestick removed out of its place; while the night of ages settled down upon the earth. In this tremendous period, knowledge and virtue expired, and corruption and violence, as before the flood, filled the earth. The great merchandise was in the souls of men; the chief staples, indulgences to sin; and nothing but holiness of heart and life was absolutely unpardonable.

Here, around the standard of Christ, the kings of the earth took counsel against the Lord and his anointed, to break his bands and cast away his cords. And here the atheist and the Jew, the infidel and the libertine, could wear the sacred vestments, and make war upon the Saviour and his friends.

Popery is a system, where science and ignorance, refinement and barbarism, wisdom and stupidity, taste and animalism, mistaken zeal and malignant enmity, may sanctimoniously pour out their virulence against the Gospel, and cry, Hosanna, while they go forth to shed the blood, and to wear out the patience of the saints. And though by revolutions it has been shaken, and compelled by motives of policy to cease a little from blood, not a principle of this system has been abandoned. All the wiles of ages past are put in requisition now, to heal the fatal wounds which the beast has received, and to render the system still more powerful and terrific. The leaven is in secret and in open operation in this country; and the quick action of the beast to the touch of the spear in Palestine, shows that he is neither dead nor asleep. And considering the civilization, and wealth, and science, which the system comprehends, it is from popery, no doubt, that the Gospel is destined to experience the last and most determined resistance.

4. Another form of resistance to the Gospel is to be anticipated from the *despotic governments of the earth* — so inconsistent in their influence with that illumination of mind and melioration of heart, which, it is predicted, shall prevail, and which the blessed Gospel never fails to produce. Hence it may be expected, that despots will take counsel against the Lord, as the march of intellect, and piety, and civil liberty, shall minister alarm.

To what extent forcible resistance will be made to the Gospel, it is not our object now to inquire; or whether republican forms of government will supplant the ancient dynasties. It is enough to know, that all the governments who yield to the intimations of that providence which sends out religion and civil liberty upon the earth, will be safe and happy; and that all who make resistance will be agitated by revolutions, and destroyed by heavy judgments. "Be wise now, therefore, O ye kings; be instructed, ye judges of the earth: serve the Lord with fear, and rejoice with trembling; kiss the Son, lest he be angry, and ye perish from the way, when his wrath is kindled but a little."

5. Another source of resistance to Christianity is that of *crime in its varied forms.* A vast amount of capital is embarked in enterprises which directly or indirectly war against morality. All this, when the spirit of Christianity shall prevail, will be contraband, and withdrawn. The power of steam shall not needlessly violate holy time, nor the sail, without cause, whiten in the Sabbath sun, and spread itself to pervert the breath of heaven. Theatres, those "schools of morality," falsely so called, shall cease to beguile unstable souls, whose feet go down to death, whose steps take hold on hell. Christianity, as she prevails, will form a public sentiment that will make virtue blush at the thought of meeting within the same walls, and breathing the same polluted air, and applauding the same exhibitions, with the most debased and wretched portion of the community. All who thrive and grow rich amid the desolations of inebriation, and all who desire to do wickedly without loss of character, or annoyance of conscience, will feel instinctively the approach of religion: and as their craft shall be in danger, will raise a loud and bitter cry — " Great is Diana. Great is Diana."

Nor are the maxims of more reputable trade in such nice

accordance with the "golden rule," as to need no revision, or to present no resistance to the Gospel, as she moves on to make it the universal actual law of commercial intercourse; while the entire world of honor must be expected to stand against that Gospel, which forbids murder, and inculcates forgiveness, and arrays public sentiment against the guilty.

If the Gospel would prohibit only acknowledged immoralities, and wink at human weaknesses, the whole pleasure-loving world would consent to an armistice, and permit her to move on without much complaint. But the inexorable requisitions of purity of heart and self-denial cannot fail to bring out against her a multitudinous and determined resistance. The haters of her uncharitableness, and the lovers of a more liberal way, and all classes of the openly wicked, will, it may be expected, as the light increases and enmity rises, be condensed into a firmer and firmer phalanx of opposition. And now will the alarm be sounded about popery and priest-craft, by just that class of men, who, in papal countries, love darkness, and most cheerfully purchase indulgences to sin; and who, in this country, should the darkness of popery be permitted to come upon us, would be the first to hail it as a covert for their crimes and a quietus for their consciences. And yet panic-struck will many become about liberty of conscience, who long since have ceased to have any conscience; and suddenly will many fall in love with civil liberty, who, all their days, and with all their might, have, by their pernicious influence, been employed in attempts to undermine her deep foundations.

6. To cover the nakedness of this forlorn hope of opposition to the Gospel, *a more liberal sort of religion* must be introduced, which shall keep men in countenance, and enable them to wield the name and institutions of Christianity against Christianity — including so much truth as may serve to beguile, but so little as cannot avail to save — sustained by such as live in pleasure, and will not bow the knee to Christ. The time will have come, when the light of science and of Christianity will have rendered obsolete the grossness of idolatry, the imposture of Mohammed, the superstitions of popery, and the impurity of infidelity. A religion must rise, therefore, under the last touchings and finishings of art, where infidels may be received without conversion; and where they may be converted with scarce a perceptible change in doctrine, heart, or life; and where, as in papal countries, the thoughtless,

and the gay, and the beautiful, and the dissipated, may float together down the stream, to the sounds of music, and drink the Lethean cup, and wake not till their redemption has ceased for ever. All this abomination of desolation is predicted, as attending the last triumphs of pure Christianity. " And he said, Go thy way, Daniel: for the words are closed up and sealed till the time of the end. Many shall be purified, and made white, and tried; but the wicked shall do wickedly: and none of the wicked shall understand; but the wise shall understand."

7. One other source of opposition to the progress of vital Christianity remains to be mentioned. There may be an attempt to wield the church against herself, by *corrupting the purity of revivals of religion.* Terrible, by the power of revivals, as an army with banners, her victory is secure, unless fanaticism can be substituted for pure religion, and her compact masses be broken and scattered by the commotion of unhallowed passions within. In this manner was the glory of the Reformation eclipsed, and vital religion, in the time of Cromwell, made a scoff and a by-word. The same attempt was made in New England early in the days of our fathers. It was repeated in the time of Whitefield and the immortal Edwards, with lamentable, though with but partial success. As revivals shall become more extensive, and the Spirit of God shall awaken larger portions of the community at once, opportunity will be afforded to the enemy — and, apprised of his devices, we ought not to think that the opportunity will be neglected — of mingling false fire with holy zeal, for the purpose of throwing discredit upon a work which threatens a speedy overthrow of his empire.

All these great divisions of systematic opposition to the Gospel have, where circumstances allowed, been defended by the sword. Christianity, in her first attempts to disenthral the world, met the storms of ten persecutions, protracted through a period of three hundred years.

The false prophet established, and still maintains, his empire by force. It is death to turn from Mohammed to Jesus Christ. And as to Popery, in her dominions, all the wiles and corruptions of idolatry and imposture have been condensed and wielded with infernal wisdom and malignity against the Gospel, ever since the apocalyptic kings gave their power to the beast. And when atheism, for a little moment, abolished popery, its terrific power was, at the same moment, directed with indiscriminate fury against Christianity. The Bible was burnt; the Sabbath blotted out; the existence of God denied; and death proclaimed an eternal sleep.

The Arian heresy, protected by the sword, wielded against the truth a furious persecution. In Holland, Arminius attempted to enlist both literature and the civil arm for the propagation of his sentiments, and, to some extent, succeeded. At Geneva, the enemies of evangelical sentiment, as appears from recent events, do not rely on charity, and enlightened reason, and liberty of conscience, but upon the civil power, to protect them in their usurpations, and to keep back the truth.

And now, can such varied and mighty resistance be overcome? Can the earth be enlightened? Can the nations be disenthralled? Can the whole creation, which has groaned and travailed together in pain until now, be brought out of bondage into glorious liberty? Yes, all this can be done, and *will* be done. Our next inquiry then is,

BY WHAT MEANS SHALL EVENTS SO DESIRABLE BE ACCOMPLISHED?

First — By the judgments of heaven, in which the Son of Man will come upon the strong man armed, and take away his armor.

Secondly — By the universal propagation of the Gospel; before the light of which, idolatry, imposture, and superstition, will retreat abashed.

Thirdly — By frequent, and, at last, general revivals of religion; giving resistless power to the Gospel, as it is preached to every creature.

Then will come to pass that which is written. Great voices will be heard in heaven, saying, *The kingdoms of this world are become the kingdoms of our Lord and of his Christ:* as the voice of many waters, and of mighty thunderings, saying, *Alleluia! for the Lord God omnipotent reigneth.*

It is manifest from prophecy, and clearly to be anticipated from the existing state of the world, that *great commotions and distress of nations* will exist, antecedent to the spiritual, universal reign of Christ on the earth. Some have supposed that these calamities will fall alike upon the church and the world; that as yet the witnesses are to be slain; and that, for three years at least, Christianity will seem to be blotted from the earth. Whereas, manifestly, the judgments which are to precede the glory of the latter day, are to fall almost exclusively upon antichristian nations. And if the witnesses are yet to be slain, they are to be slain in the street of that great city, which, spiritually, is called "Sodom and Egypt"— prophetic symbols, which have been understood to designate countries subject to the dominion of antichrist. The very struggle to suppress vital Christianity in papal countries, called the slaying of the witnesses, may be, and probably will be, the result of moral causes now in powerful operation. Science, and commerce, and the progress of evangelical religion, are fast apprising mankind of their rights, and awakening the desire of civil and religious liberty. And this slaying of the witnesses may be the last struggle of those despotisms, to arrest the march of truth and freedom. It may be the collision between light and darkness — between despotism and liberty — which shall call out the kings of the earth to the battle of the great day of God Almighty; when he, whose eyes are as a flame of fire, on whose head are many crowns, and whose vesture is dipped in blood, shall smite the nations with the sword that goeth out of his mouth, and rule them with a rod of iron, and tread the wine-press of the fierceness and wrath of Almighty God; when the angel standing in the sun, shall summon the fowls of the heavens to the supper of the great God — to eat the flesh of kings, and of captains, and of mighty men.

But without attempting a minute exposition of prophecy, nothing is more plainly revealed, than the visitation of the earth with unparalleled judgments and revolutions, preparatory to that state of light and peace which is to bless the world. So long as Satan can wield the power of despotic governments against the truth, he can hold his goods in peace. But these defences a stronger than he will take away, when, in awful judgments, He will come upon him. "He shall overturn, and overturn, until He, whose right it is, shall reign. The day of vengeance is in his heart, because the year of his redeemed is come. The foundations of the earth do shake; the earth is utterly broken down; the earth is clean dissolved; the earth is moved exceedingly; the earth shall reel to and fro; and the Lord shall punish the host of the high ones that are on high, and the kings of the earth upon the earth; and they shall be gathered together as prisoners are gathered in the pit; and shall be shut up in the prison. Then the moon shall be confounded, and the sun shall be ashamed, when the Lord of hosts shall reign in Mount Zion, and in Jerusalem, and before his ancients gloriously. And the seventh angel poured out his vial into the air; and there were voices, and thunderings, and lightnings, and there was a great earthquake, such as was not since men were upon the earth, so mighty an earthquake and so great."

One of these moral earthquakes has already shaken Europe to its centre; and the thunderings and heavings of the unquiet earth proclaim, that one wo is past, and behold, another wo cometh quickly.

When these systems of physical resistance are destroyed, then will the time have come to extend the institutions of the Gospel throughout the world. Benevolence, like the air, will move to fill up the vacuum. Like the light from its great fountain, it will fly to cheer the nations who sit in darkness. And having no resistance to encounter, but the simple power of error, the conflict will be but momentary, and the victory complete. This also is in accordance with prophecy: for immediately after the downfall of Babylon is announced, all heaven breaks forth in ecstasy, saying, *Let us rejoice and give honor to him, for the marriage of the Lamb is come, and his wife hath made herself ready.* The church of Christ is called his bride; and the conversion of the nations to Christianity and to God, the day of her espousals.

That this glorious victory is to be consummated by the *special influence of the Holy Spirit,* is equally manifest. The simple presence of Christianity would no more convert the heathen, than it converts those where it already exists. Were every family on earth now blessed with a Bible and a pastor, these, without the effusions of the Spirit, would not maintain upon the earth an uncorrupt nominal Christianity, for one hundred years. Revivals of religion are alone adequate to the moral reformation of the world. All other means — science, legislation, philosophy, eloquence, and argument — have been relied on in vain. The disease is of the heart, and they reach it not. But revivals touch the deep springs of human action, and give tone and energy to the moral government of God. They multiply families that call upon the name of the Lord, and train up children in his fear, and churches, constrained by the love of Christ to propagate the Gospel. They elevate the standard of liberality, and augment the capital which is consecrated to the renovation of the world, and the importunity of prayer which secures its application and efficacy. They multiply the host of evangelical ministers and missionaries. They repress crime, and purify the public morality, and breathe into legislation and the intercourse of nations that spirit of the Gospel, which shall banish wars, and introduce peace upon earth and good-will towards men. They pour day-light upon darkness, and destroy, with a touch, the power of sophistry. Hence nothing is so terrible to the enemies of evangelical truth as revivals of religion, because nothing is so irresistible. If they oppose them by violence, they move on. If they misrepresent them, they move on. If they ridicule them, they move on. If they imitate them, the imitation fails, and they move on. While, often, the chosen vessels of opposition fall under their power — sending panic and rage through the ranks of the enemy. It is owing to this power of revivals, that they are every where, by the wicked, so much spoken against; and all the infirmities of humanity, which attend them, gathered up with such exultation, and urged as confirmation strong, that they are the work of man, and not the work of God. It is reserved, therefore, for revivals of religion to follow in the train of the means of grace with increasing frequency and power, until a nation shall be born in a day. This also is predicted. — " Who art thou, O mountain, before Zerubbabel? Thou shalt become a plain. Not by might, nor by power, but by my Spirit saith the Lord. Drop down, ye heavens, from above, and let the skies pour down righteousness. I will pour water upon him that is thirsty, and floods upon the dry ground. It shall come to pass in the last days, saith God, that I will pour out my Spirit upon all flesh. And then shall that wicked be revealed, whom the Lord shall consume with the spirit of his mouth and shall destroy with the brightness of his coming."

The judgments which are to shake down antichristian empires, and cast down high imaginations, and lay open the world to the entrance of truth and the power of the Spirit, are to be closely associated with a new and unparalleled *vigor of Christian enterprise*. Until now, the church will have been the assailed party, and stood upon the defensive : but henceforth the word of command will not be, *Stand*, but MARCH. The gates of the holy city will be thrown open ; the tide of war will be rolled upon the enemy ; and one shall chase a thousand, and two put ten thousand to flight.

The means and efforts for evangelizing the world must correspond, however, with the magnitude of the result. The idea that God will convert the heathen in his own good time, and that Christians have nothing to do but to pray and devoutly wait, is found in no canonical book. It is the maxim of covetousness, and sloth, and uncaring infidelity. We have no authority for saying, what some, without due consideration, have said, that God, if he pleased, could doubtless in a moment convert the whole heathen world without the Gospel. It might as well be said, that he can, if he please, burn without fire, or drown without water, or give breath without atmosphere, as that he can instruct intellectual beings without the means of knowledge, and influence moral beings without law and motive, and thus reclaim an alienated world without the knowledge and moral power of the Gospel. It is no derogation from the power of God, that, to produce results, it must be exerted by means adapted to the constitution of things which himself has established. God has no set time to favor the husbandman, but when he is diligent in business; and no set time to favor Zion, but when her servants favor her stones and take pleasure in the dust thereof. From the beginning, the cause of God on earth has been maintained and carried forward only by the most heroic exertion. Christianity, even in the age of miracles, was not propagated but by stupendous efforts. And it is only by a revival of primitive zeal and enterprise, that the glorious things spoken of the city of our God can be accomplished.

Nor need we be disheartened. We possess a thousand fold the advantage of apostles and primitive Christians for the spread of the Gospel. And shall the whole church on earth — shall the thousand thousands who now profess the pure religion, be dismayed and paralyzed at an enterprise, which had once been well nigh accomplished by the energies of twelve men?

But what can be done? It would require ten discourses to answer this question in detail. We can only sketch the outlines of that moral array, by which Jesus Christ is preparing to come upon the strong man, and overcome him, and take from him all his armor.

1. There must be *more faith* in the church of God.

All the uncertainties and waverings of unbelief must be swept away by the power of that faith, which is the substance of things hoped for and the evidence of things not seen.

Those "scenes surpassing fable," when Satan shall be bound, and an emancipated world shall sing hosanna to the Son of David, must rise up before us in all the freshness and inspiration of a glorious reality. Such faith, and only such, will achieve again the wonders it wrought in other days. It has lost none of its power. Again, it will subdue kingdoms, work righteousness, obtain promises, stop the mouths of lions, quench the violence of fire, escape the edge of the sword, out of weakness become strong, wax valiant in fight, and put to flight the armies of the aliens. For this is the victory over the world, even your *faith*.

2. There must be *a more intense love for Christ* in his church.

Such love as now burns dimly in the hearts of Christians; a low, and languid, and wavering affection; halting between the opposing attractions of earth and Heaven; may answer for standing upon the *defensive*, but never for making that *vigorous onset* which shall subdue the world to Christ. Effort will never surpass desire. And as yet our hearts are not equal to those efforts needed for the achievement of victory. They linger and look back upon the world. They hesitate, and slowly, and with a sigh, part with substance in penurious measure. Weight hangs as yet on the wheels of the Victor's chariot: and never, on earth, as in heaven, will it move,

> "Instinct with spirit,
> Flashing thick flames, ... unless
> Attended by ten thousand thousand saints."

3. There must come an era of *more decided action*, before the earth can be subdued to Christ.

Compared with the exigency, we have not, as yet, the semblance of an army in the field; and our munitions are yet to be collected. Two hundred souls constitute the entire force, which twelve millions of freemen, cheered and blessed with the light of the Gospel, have sent forth to bring the world out of bondage. And yet one half the nation is panic-struck at the drafts thus made upon her resources! What has been done, however, is but mere skirmishing before the shock of battle. Half the subjects of Satan's dark empire on earth have not heard, as yet, that we have a being. And were none but such feeble efforts to be put forth, he, instead of coming down in great wrath, would keep his temper, and leave the war to his subalterns.

Nothing great on earth, good or bad, was ever accomplished without decisive action. The cause, in the moral world, as really as in the natural, must ever be proportioned to the effect to be produced. And what have we done, as yet, to justify the expectation, that God, by such means, is about to *make all things new?* Could our independence have been achieved by such indecisive actions as we put forth for the emancipation of the world? Dear brethren, we must fix our eye earnestly on a world lying in wickedness: our hearts must be fully set upon its deliverance: our hands must be opened wide for its relief. Not only the ministers of religion must give themselves wholly to this work; but all who prize civil and religious freedom — all who exult in these blessings must come forth to the help of the Lord against the mighty. And when, to all who are now cheered by the light of revelation, the deliverance of a world in bondage shall become the all-absorbing object, and the concentrating point of holy enterprise; then speedily will the angel descend from heaven, with a great chain, to bind and cast into the bottomless pit him who through so many ages has deceived the nations. But,

4. For this glorious achievement, there is demanded *more courage* than has, in modern days, been manifested by the church of God.

Wherever circumstances have precluded the application of force for the defence of his cause, there the god of this world has attempted to fortify it by a *perverted public sentiment.* This, while it predominates, is as terrific as the inquisition; and if not as bloody, it is unquestionably as virulent, overbearing, and severe. Multitudes shrink before it, who would not hesitate to storm the deadly breach; and one half the power of the Christian church is doubtless this very moment paralyzed by it, if not even arrayed by its influence against the cause of Christ. Fashion is the Juggernaut of Christian lands; around whose car pilgrims of all conditions gather, and do homage.

Here, then, in communities civilized and nominally Christian, is to be fought one of the keenest battles; for after every strong hold is demolished, if Satan can but frame the laws of honor and of fashion, he will not fail to govern by maxims which will shut out the Gospel, and perpetuate the dominion of sin. And Christians are the first to be emancipated. While they are in captivity, the world will be in chains. Jesus Christ must have entire possession of his own soldiers, before the armies of the living God can put to flight the armies of the aliens.

This conflict for dominion over public sentiment is coming on, and by this generation, in city and in country, it is to be decided, whether an evangelical or a worldly influence shall prevail — whether the landmarks of Christian morality shall stand against the inundations of vice, or, with every thing that is pure, and lovely, and of good report, be swept away. Emboldened by the pusillanimity of the friends of virtue, the enemy have become audacious, and scarcely covet the veil of darkness, but seem even to glory in their shame. And if no stand is made, we are undone. The church in this land will go into captivity, and the nation is undone. Our prosperity and voluptuousness will be our ruin; and short and rapid will be our journey from the cradle to the grave. But if resistance is made, then will the waves rise, and foam, and roar, and dash furiously upon those who shall dare to make a stand; and birds of ill-omen will flap their sooty wings, and croak, and scream, to intimidate and dishearten the fearful, and the unbelieving; and all the engines of bad influence will be applied to prevent that coalition of patriotism and of virtue, which would set bounds to the encroachments of evil, and shed day-light upon the works of darkness, and stamp with indelible and intolerable infamy, wickedness in high places and in low places.

And now, *custom*, with silver tongue, will plead *prescription* — "It always has been so, and always will be, and why should we attempt innovation?" And *interest*, too, will plead *necessity* — 'How can I withdraw my capital, or alter my course? To refuse to do wrong a little, would be to take away my children's bread." And now, *difficulty*, with good wishes and sorrowing face, will plead, "Spare thy servant in this thing — is it not a little one?" While *fear* will see the giants, the sons of Anak, and call out for care, and prudence, lest we should act prematurely, or be righteous overmuch. *Petulance*, too, will lift up her voice, with vexation at our presumptuous meddling, wondering that we cannot mind our own affairs, and let other people alone. And even *charity*, so called, will draw aside her veil, for the archers with poisoned arrows to hit us. While *liberality*, provoked beyond endurance, will hail upon our heads the hard names of "bigot, enthusiast, fanatic, hypocrite."

All this, however, we could easily sustain, were there no treachery within. But our hearts are yet in too close consultation with flesh and blood. "What will the world think? What will the world say? How will it affect my reputation — my interest — my ambition — or even my usefulness? — Suppose I step in as a kind of candid mediator between the world and my too zealous brethren, taking the prudent course, and not carrying matters too far?" O that prudent course — that middle ground — so crowded, when the lines are drawing between Christ and the world! Satan desires no better troops than neutral Christians. And the Lord Jesus Christ abhors none more. He prefers infidelity to lukewarm Christianity. "I would that thou wert either cold or hot; so then because thou art neither, I will spew thee out of my mouth."

As to cheating Satan out of his empire over men, by a reversed course of warfare, he has no objection that Christians should dream about it, and try it. But we mistake, if we suppose our wisdom a match for his wiles; or that we can so prudently drive him out of this world, as that he will find no pretext for controversy. Whenever we do enough to give to religion a solemn reality upon the minds of men, and draw the cords of evangelical morality with such power, as shall compel reformation, or inflict disgrace; we must calculate to meet his resistance who reigns in the hearts of the children of disobedience. And the time will come, when men must take sides. For as the conflict between virtue and vice waxes warm, neither side will tolerate neutrality; and he who plants his foot upon neutral ground, will select just the hottest place in the battle, and receive the fire from both sides.

Two things are required of all who would be found on the side of liberty and evangelical morality. One is, that we will not do wrong in obedience to custom: the other is, that we will not be accessary to the wrong done by others — that we will give to the cause of virtue the testimony of correct opinions, the power of a correct example, and the influence of our inflexible patronage. There are piety and principle enough in the community to put down the usurpations of irreligion and crime, if the sound part of the community will only awake, and array itself on the side of purity and order. But we must come out and be separate, and touch not the unclean thing. The entire capital in the hands of honest and moral men, which is employed in establishments that corrupt society, must be withdrawn; and that patronage which has swelled the revenue of establishments that lend their aid to the cause of licentiousness, must be turned over to the side of purity and order. Until this is done, we shall not cease to be partakers in other men's sins. The press, that mighty engine of good or evil in a free country, must be enlisted decisively on the side of virtue; and its perverted influence, if it continue, must be sustained only by those whose guilty cause it espouses. We cannot, as Christians — we cannot, as patriots — give our patronage to that press which will not plead the cause of virtue, and which will prostitute its fearful energies to the cause of sin.

5. There must be new and more vigorous efforts to increase the number and power of evangelical churches in our land.

In all countries the tone of piety and evangelical morality corresponds exactly with the number, and purity, and energy of the churches of our Lord Jesus Christ. The want of this organized moral power in many parts of our land is appalling. Our population multiplies, and the ratio of good moral influence declines, and ignorance and crime are coming in like a flood. All that has been done by Tract Societies, by Sabbath Schools, by Education Societies, and by the National Society for Domestic Missions, is as the drop of the bucket to the ocean. A new and mighty effort is demanded to send light through the territories of darkness — to repress crime, and perpetuate our civil and religious institutions. In our large cities, especially, is the increase of ignorance and licentiousness lamentable and ominous. Here wealth and temptation concentrate their power upon masses of mind, whose influence cannot fail to affect deeply the destiny of the nation. If they send out a vigorous current of healthful life-blood, the whole nation will feel the renovating influence: but if, with every pulsation, they send out iniquity and death, no power on earth can avert our doom.

A *moral* power is the only influence that can save our cities. Mere coercion in a land of freemen, will not avail. Nor will a lax nominal Christianity suffice, where offenders may find access to the table of Christ, and protection by the horns of the altar. The new churches, to succeed, should be composed of persons of real piety, of kindred sentiment, and of decided character; and, from the beginning, consist of so many members, and be blessed with such talent and devoted piety in the ministry, and be so countenanced and sustained by other churches, as that their attraction shall not fail to bring under the sacred influence of the Gospel the surrounding community. Until our cities shall thus be made to feel, in every part, the purifying power of the Gospel, the whole land will continue to send to them, as it has done, hecatombs of youthful victims, to be repaid by disappointed hopes and moral contamination.

6. Special effort is required, to secure to the rising generation an education free from the influence of bad example, and more decidedly evangelical.

The atmosphere which our children breathe, from the cradle upward, should be pure. Instead of this, it would not be difficult to find common schools, in which ignorance and irreligion predominate. Even where the intellect is cultivated, the heart not unfrequently is corrupted, and the child made wise only to do evil. In a great proportion of the higher schools, to which Christians send their children, little exists of a decidedly religious tendency; while in some, a powerful influence is exerted against evangelical sentiments and piety.

And though in many of our colleges there is a salutary religious influence, and repeated revivals of religion are enjoyed, in none is the influence of religion so decisive as it might be; while in some, to which pious parents send their children, the influence is directly and powerfully hostile to religion.

I am aware, that not a few regard religious influence in our colleges as already too great, and that an effort is making to separate religion from science, during the progress of a collegiate education. And those who choose to rear colleges, and send their offspring where the power of the Gospel shall be excluded, have, doubtless, a right to do so — answerable for their conduct only to God. But no Christian can do this without violating the vows of God which are upon him, to train up his child in the nurture and admonition of the Lord. And, instead of a compromise in the evangelical colleges of our land, there should be, as easily there may be, a more decided tone of religious influence. Our colleges should every one of them be blessed, not only with preaching, but with kind, discreet, and assiduous pastoral instruction and care.

Why should these precious communities of inexperienced youth, separated from parental inspection, and exposed to peculiar temptation, be deprived of the watchful eye and parental voice of pastoral exhortation and advice? What parent would not pray with more faith, and sleep more quietly, if he knew that some one, acquainted with the youthful heart, and appointed to watch over his child, had gained his confidence and affection, and was praying and laboring for his salvation?

There is no period in life when the heart may be more successfully assailed, than that which is passed in a college. And there is no class of human beings, among whom revivals may be promoted, by proper pastoral attention, with greater certainty, or with greater power and glory. Nor can it be expected, that the church will ever look forth fair as the morning, until effectual care is taken, that in her higher schools and colleges, her children shall be induced to consecrate to God the dew of their youth.

7. The vigor of *charitable effort* must be greatly increased.

As long as rich men shall trust more in uncertain riches than in the living God, and the covetous shall dare to heap up treasures to themselves, consecrating to God scarcely the crumbs that fall from their table, and the ambitious shall insist that they will roll in splendor, and give only the pittance which can be spared from the expense of a wanton ostentation — as long as professors shall consume, in extra gratifications of sense, to the injury of health, sums that, if consecrated to Christ, might suffice to extend the word of life and the institutions of the Gospel all over the world — as long as avaricious Christians shall so extend their plans of business, with the increase of their capital, as always to be straitened in the midst of their gains — and as long as parents shall labor to amass wealth for their offspring, only to paralyze their enterprise, and corrupt their morals, and ensure their ruin, — so long the cause of God on earth must move slowly. But the blame must rest on us. There is at this moment, in the hands of Christians, capital enough to evangelize the world in a short period of time, and without the retrenchment of a single comfort, and only by the consecration to Christ of substance, the possession of which would be useless, and often injurious. It is not required of Christian nations to sustain the entire work of preaching the Gospel to all the unevangelized population of the earth. Nothing is needed but to erect the standard in pagan lands — to plant the seed — to deposit the leaven, in schools and in churches, until each nation shall support Gospel institutions. This is the work to which God in his providence is calling the churches. Now, and for fifty years to come, the substance and enterprise of good men are imperiously demanded. Within that period, it is not improbable, that every nation may be so far evangelized, as that the work may move onward to its consummation, without extraneous aid.

8. The jealousies of Christians, who are united substantially in their views of evangelical doctrine and religion, and who are divided only by localities, and rites, and forms, must yield, and give place to the glorious exigencies of the present day. The amalgamation of denominations is not required. The division of labor may greatly augment the amount; and the provocation to love and good works may be real and salutary, and still be conducted without invidious collision. Like the tribes of Israel, we may all encamp about the tabernacle of God — each under his own standard — and when the ark advances, may all move onward, terrible only to the powers of darkness. And if the enemies of righteousness are not sufficient to rebuke our selfishness, and force us into a coalition of love and good works; then verily it may be expected — and even be hoped — that God, by the fire of persecution, will purge away our dross, and take away our tin, until we shall love him, and his cause, and one another, with a pure heart, fervently.

9. Let me add, that we must guard against the dangers peculiar to a state of religious prosperity.

There is no condition in which an individual, or the church at large, can be exempted from temptations. And especially as the church shall become formidable, and bring upon the great enemy of God the pressure of a desperate extremity, we are to expect, that his rage will increase, and his wiles be multiplied. For he will leave the world only when forced; and will fight upon the retreat — giving many a desperate battle, when it shall seem as if the necessity was past of watching against his devices. Never, therefore, has the necessity of vigilance and prayer been more imperious than now. Let all the churches, then, with their pastors, feel deeply their dependence on God; and when their alms come up before him, and his Spirit shall descend in new and glorious showers, let them watch and pray that they enter not into temptation, and experience an overthrow in the moment of victory.

To fear revivals, because attended by some indications of human imperfection, would be weak and wicked: and far from the church of God be the presumptuous confidence, that nothing deeply injurious to the general interests of religion can be blended with a real work of the Spirit. But though I am not without solicitude on this head, I do trust and expect, that God will preserve his churches, and cause pure religion and undefiled to prosper, and not permit the adversary to turn our glory into shame. O, could he do it, how would his minions scream out their joy! and how would Zion be confounded, and in this day of rejoicing, be compelled to hang her harp upon the willows, and sit down to weep in sackcloth and ashes! To conclude,

Will any of you, my hearers, in this glorious day, take side against the cause of Christ! It will be a fearful experiment. What the mind and counsel of God have purposed to do for the melioration of man is now hastening to its consummation, with the intenseness of infinite benevolence, under the guidance of unerring wisdom, and by the impulse of almighty power. And wo unto him who contendeth with his Maker. The lines are now drawing, and preparation is fast making for the battle of the great day of God Almighty. And who is on the Lord's side? Who! Will any of you, in this sublimely interesting moment, stand on neutral ground! Remember, that neutrality is treason: and if persisted in, is as fatal as the unpardonable sin. Jesus Christ will have the decided services of his people. Already has he denounced as enemies, all who will not labor and suffer for him. *He that is not for me, is against me: and whosoever shall deny me before men, him will I also deny before my Father which is in heaven. Think not that I came to send peace on earth;* (that is, that the progress of truth will be without resistance and persecution;) *I came not to send peace, but a sword. For I am come,* (that is, the effect of my coming will be, as the Gospel prevails,) *to set a man at variance against his father, and the daughter against her mother; and a man's foes shall be they of his own household. He that loveth father or mother more than me, is not worthy of me: and he that taketh not his cross, and followeth after me, is not worthy of me. He that findeth his life, shall lose it; and he that loseth his life for my sake, shall find it.* These statutes are not repealed. And if the laws of Christian discipleship could bind men to give up every relative, and even life itself, for Christ and his Gospel, no excuse, surely, will screen from condemnation those who flinch and temporize, where the sacrifices required are comparatively trivial. If such as would not lay down their life for Christ, cannot be accepted — what will become of those, in Christian lands, who will not lay down their substance, nor risk their reputation, nor lift a finger, to advance his cause?

Is there a Christian here, who cannot, for the year to come, double the amount of his charities? Is there one who will not now purpose in his heart to do it? Brethren, the time is short in which we here have opportunity to express our boundless obligations to the Saviour. The fashion of the world passeth away. Next year, our tongue may be employed in celestial praises, and our substance be in other hands. What remains, then, but that this day we dedicate ourselves, and our all, anew, to Him, who washed us in his blood? The tone of feeling which we cherish to-day, may, by a holy sympathy, and by the power of the Holy Ghost, be propagated through this great city — through this powerful nation — and through the world. The augmented religious enterprise, to which we pledge ourselves this day, may tell quickly in the very heart of Satan's empire, and cause light to spring up in retreats of deepest darkness.

If any man, however, is smitten with fear, let him retreat. If any man is faint-hearted, let him draw back. If any man tremble at his proportion of the charges for evangelizing the whole world, let him depart. If any man is alarmed at the noise which precedes the last conflict, let him hide himself, with his talent, in the earth! But let all who love our Lord Jesus Christ in sincerity, and wait for his appearing and glory — give themselves anew to his service; and break the earthen vessel; and lift up their light; and shout, *The sword of the Lord and of Gideon:* and the victory, and more than the victory, shall be given to the people of the saints of the Most High God. And a great voice out of heaven shall be heard, saying, *Behold, the tabernacle of God is with men, and he will dwell with them, and they shall be his people, and God himself shall be with them, and be their God.*

THE EARTH FILLED WITH THE GLORY OF THE LORD.

BY

REV. SAMUEL MILLER, D. D.

And the Lord said, I have pardoned according to thy word: but as truly as I live, all the earth shall be filled with the glory of the Lord.—NUMBERS 14: 20, 21.

THESE words were spoken on a very distressing, and, to the eye of man, a very discouraging occasion. When the twelve men who had been sent from the wilderness of Paran to spy out the land of promise, brought back their report, the mass of the people were almost overwhelmed with alarm and discouragement. Nay, overcome by apprehension, and infatuated by a spirit of unbelief and rebellion, they proposed to make choice of another leader, and return back to Egypt. With this ungrateful and daring revolt the Lord was greatly displeased, and threatened to give them up to his destroying judgments, and to disinherit them forever. Moses, however, interceded for the people in a most touching strain of importunate prayer: and he prevailed. The Lord said, "I have pardoned them according to thy word. But as truly as I live, the earth shall be filled with the glory of the Lord." As if he had said—" Unbelieving and rebellious as this people now appear, and utterly desperate as their prospects may seem;—neither my plans nor my promises, in regard to them or the world, shall be frustrated. My cause shall finally triumph over all the infatuation and rebellion of man. *The whole earth shall*, in due time, *be filled with my glory.*"

There are *three* things in the passage before us which demand our notice — *the import of the promise which it contains;—the reasons which we have for believing that this promise will, in due time, be realized; and the duty devolving on us in relation to the promise.*

I. Let us attend to THE IMPORT OF THE PROMISE BEFORE US. This import, expressed with so much solemnity of asseveration, is large and precious. "As I live," saith the Lord, "all the earth shall be filled with the glory of the Lord."

Glory is the manifestation of excellence. The glory of God is that display of his most blessed character and will, which opens the way for his intelligent creatures to know, to love, and to obey him. This glory is exhibited in various ways. It shines in all the works of creation. All the works of God, we are told, praise him. "The heavens declare his glory, and the firmament showeth his handy work. Day unto day uttereth speech, and night unto night showeth knowledge. There is no speech nor language where their voice is not heard. Their line is gone out through all the earth, and their words to the end of the world." Again, the glory of God is manifested by the works of his providence. Here his wisdom, his power, and his benevolence, gloriously shine. *The Lord, we are told, is known* — that is, is made known — *by the judgments which he executeth.* But above all, is the glory of God displayed in the work of Redemption; in that great plan of love and mercy by a Redeemer, which was first revealed, to the parents of our race immediately after the fall; which was more and more unfolded in the ceremonial economy; and which reached its meridian brightness, when the Saviour, the blessed "Sun of Righteousness," rose upon a dark world. In this wonderful plan of salvation, the glory of God shines with its brightest lustre. Here all his perfections unite and harmonize, and shine with transcendent glory. Now, when the gospel, which proclaims this plan of mercy, shall be preached and received throughout the world; when every kindred, and people, and nation, and tongue, shall not only be instructed in its sublime doctrines, but also brought under its benign and sanctifying power; then, with emphatic propriety, may it be said that "the earth is filled with the glory of the Lord." As the highest glory of which an individual creature is capable, is to bear the image of his Maker; so the highest glory of which our world at large is capable, is to be filled with the holy and benevolent spirit of Him "who is the brightness of the Father's glory, and the express image of his person;" is to have the knowledge and love of the Saviour reigning over all the population of our globe, "from the rising of the sun even unto the going down of the same."

It is this universal prevalence of the true religion; that religion which alone can enlighten, sanctify, and save; that religion which imparts the highest physical and moral glory, wherever it reigns, and in proportion as it reigns;—it is the universal prevalence of this glory which is promised in our text. When this holy and benevolent religion shall fill the world, then shall be brought to pass the promise which is here recorded. Yes, when the benign power of the Gospel, and all the graces and virtues which it inspires, shall reign over all the family of man; when the highest intellectual and moral culture shall be everywhere enjoyed; when the voice of prayer and praise shall be heard in every tabernacle; when the Sabbath shall be universally kept holy to God; when the Christian law of marriage, that noblest and most precious bond of social purity and happiness, shall be universally and sacredly obeyed; when the temperance reformation, without any unscriptural extremes, or fanatical perversions, shall pervade the world; when "wars shall cease to the ends of the earth;" when fraud and violence shall be banished from the abodes of men; when the voice of profaneness shall no more pollute the lips or the ears of creatures claiming to be rational; when tyranny and oppression, in every form, shall come to an end; when sectarian feuds and jealousies shall be unknown, save only in the pages of history; when all heresy and error shall give place to the power of truth, and all vice and profligacy to the reign of Christian purity; when the Mosque and the Pagoda shall be transformed into temples of the Christian's God; when the habitations of savage cruelty shall become the abodes of holiness and peace; when the activity of a greatly extended commerce shall be directed chiefly to the intellectual and moral culture of society; when justice, order, industry, brotherly kindness, and charity shall universally reign; — in a word, when the church of God, with all its choicest influences, shall fill the earth; — then shall the promise before us be gloriously realized. This will be emphatically "the glory of the Lord;"— the glory of his power; the glory of his holiness; the glory of his love. It will be, in its measure, the same glory which forms the blessedness of the heavenly world; the same glory in which those "whose robes have been washed in the blood of the Lamb, walk in white raiment before the throne of God." O, how glorious shall this fallen world be, when all the nations which compose it shall be "just, fearing God;" when those who are nominally "the people of God, shall be righteous;" when every family shall be the abode of purity, order, and love; when every individual shall be a "temple of the Holy Ghost;" and when, from pole to pole, the song of jubilee shall be heard — " Blessing, and honor, and glory, and power be unto Him who sitteth on the throne, and to the Lamb, for ever and ever! Alleluia! for the Lord God Omnipotent reigneth!"

Such appears to be the import of the promise before us. Let us next inquire,

II. WHAT REASON HAVE WE FOR BELIEVING THAT THESE SCENES OF GLORY WILL ONE DAY BE REALIZED?

This is to the Christian's heart a most interesting inquiry. Let us ponder it with a seriousness corresponding to its unspeakable importance.

And here it is obvious to remark, that there will be no need of *miracles* (in the ordinary sense of that word) to bring about the accomplishment of the promise before us. Only suppose the genuine power of the gospel, which we see to reign in thousands of individuals and families now—actually to reign in all hearts, and to pervade the world,—and the work is done. But how can we hope for this? I answer—

1. First of all, and above all, our hope is founded on *Jehovah's faithful and unerring promise.* This is, undoubtedly, the chief ground of confidence. For that a religion which has been preached for eighteen centuries, and which has been as yet received, even nominally, by less than a fourth part of mankind, will one day, and, at most, in a century or two from this hour, pervade and govern the world, we can expect with confidence only on the promise of Him who is Almighty, and who cannot lie. But this promise is, surely, enough for the most unwavering confidence. "Hath he said, and shall he not do it? Hath he spoken, and shall he not make it good? Jehovah is not a man that he should lie, nor the son of man that he should repent." Heaven and earth shall pass away, but one jot or tittle of all that has gone out of his mouth shall not pass away, until all be fulfilled.

Let us attend, then, to some of the promises on this subject with which the word of God abounds. Take the following as a small specimen of the "exceeding great and precious" catalogue found in the inspired volume. "The kingdoms of this world shall become the kingdoms of our Lord, and of his Christ," Rev. 11 : 15. "Ask of me, and I will give thee the heathen for thine inheritance, and the uttermost parts of the earth for thy possession," Ps. 2 : 8. "All the ends of the earth shall remember and turn to the Lord; and all the kindreds of the nations shall worship before him," Ps. 22 : 27. "From the rising of the sun, even unto the going down of the same, my name shall be great among the Gentiles; and in every place shall incense be offered unto my name, and a pure offering; for my name shall be great among the heathen, saith the Lord of hosts," Mal. 1 : 11. "And I will gather all nations and tongues, and cause them to come and see my glory," Isa. 66 : 18. "And it shall come to pass in the last days, that the mountain of the Lord's house shall be established in the top of the mountains, and shall be exalted above the hills, and all nations shall flow unto it," Isa. 2 : 2. "His name shall be continued as long as the sun; men shall be blessed in him, and all nations shall call him blessed," Ps. 72 : 17. "The wilderness and the solitary place shall be glad for them, and the desert shall rejoice and blossom as the rose. It shall blossom abundantly, and rejoice even with joy and singing; the glory of Lebanon shall be given unto it, and the excellency of Carmel and Sharon; they shall see the glory of the Lord, and the excellency of our God," Isa. 35 : 1, 2. "And the dominion, and the greatness of the kingdom under the whole heaven, shall be given to the people of the saints of the Most High; and all dominions shall serve and obey him," Dan. 7 : 27. "He shall say to the North, Give up; and to the South, Keep not back: bring my sons from far, and my daughters from the ends of the earth," Isa. 43 : 6. "His way shall be known upon earth, and his saving health among all nations," Ps. 67 : 2. "And the glory of the Lord shall be revealed, and all flesh shall see it together, for the mouth of the Lord hath spoken it," Isa. 40 : 5. "Ethiopia shall stretch forth her hands unto God," Ps. 68 : 31. "The isles shall wait for his law," Isa. 42 : 4. "He shall have dominion from sea to sea, and from the river unto the ends of the earth," Zech. 9 : 10. "All the ends of the earth shall see the salvation of our God," Isa. 52 : 10. "We see not yet all things put under him," Heb. 2 : 8. "But he must reign until all enemies shall be put under his feet," 1 Cor. 15 : 25. "At the name of Jesus every knee shall bow, and every tongue shall confess that he is Christ to the glory of God the Father," Phil. 2 : 10, 11. "For the earth shall be filled with the knowledge of the glory of the Lord, as the waters cover the sea," Hab. 2 : 14.

Such is a specimen of Jehovah's promises respecting the future prevalence and power of the gospel. Read them, Christians, with joy and confidence. Ponder them daily and well in your hearts, as a source of continual encouragement. And remember that they shall all, without failure, be gloriously accomplished. I cannot tell you precisely *when* this happy period shall arrive; but I can tell you, on authority not to be questioned, that, at the appointed time, this earth, so long the abode of sin and sorrow, shall be restored from its desolations, and made to bloom like "the garden of the Lord." I can tell you that her Almighty King will yet, notwithstanding every unfavorable appearance, " make Zion beautiful through his own comeliness put upon her; that he will yet cause her righteousness to go forth as brightness, and her salvation as a lamp that burneth," Isa. 62: 1. These promises may not, indeed, be all fully accomplished, until we, who now listen to their recital, shall be all sleeping in the dust; or, rather, if by the grace of God, we be made meet for it, — rejoicing before the throne, in possession of still brighter glory. But, "though we die, God shall surely visit his people" in mercy. Though neither we, nor even the next generation shall be permitted to witness on earth the complete development of "the latter day glory;" yet let us rejoice in the assurance that it will come in due time, and in all its promised blessedness. "The vision is yet for an appointed time; but in the end it shall speak and not lie; though it tarry, wait for it; because it will surely come, it will not tarry," Hab. 2: 3.

2. But further, our confidence that the religion of Christ will, one day, fill the whole earth with its glory, is confirmed by the consideration, that *this religion is, in its nature, adapted above all others to be a universal religion.*

In all the forms of false religion with which our world is filled, there is something which renders them unfit or impracticable for universal adoption. Some are adapted to particular *climates* only; others to particular states of *society;* a third class to particular *orders* of men; so that, in their very nature, they cannot be universal. Indeed none of the Pagans seem ever to have thought of a universal religion, as either to be expected or desired. Nay, even the true religion, as it appeared in its infant and ceremonial form, under the old economy, was not, in its external method of dispensation, adapted to be universal. For, not to mention many other circumstances, it required all its professors to go up " three times a year" to the same temple to worship. And, accordingly, long before the Messiah came in the flesh, it was made perfectly apparent, from so many of the descendants of Abraham being scattered abroad in different and distant parts of the world, that it was becoming to the Jewish people, as such, an impracticable system. Suppose all the four quarters of our globe to be filled with zealous, devoted Jews. Every one sees that a rigid compliance with their ritual would be physically impossible. And, therefore, when the time for *Shiloh's* appearance drew near, it became, every year, more and more plain, — however slow some of that "peculiar people" were in learning the lesson, — that the ceremonial economy *must* come to an end; — must, of course, yield to a system less restrictive in its character, and more fitted for "every kindred, and people, and nation, and tongue."

Accordingly, when we examine the religion of Jesus Christ, in its New Testament form, we find it divested of every feature and circumstance adapted to confine it to any particular territory or people. Its *doctrines*, its *worship*, and its system of *moral duty*, are all equally adapted to universality. It teaches "that God has made of one blood all nations of men to dwell on the face of the whole earth," Acts 17 : 26. — "That he is no respecter of persons, but that in every nation he that feareth God and worketh righteousness is accepted of him," Acts 10 : 34, 35. That he is alike related to all the children of men, as their Creator, Preserver, and Benefactor; and that the high and the low, the rich and the poor, the monarch and the slave, all stand upon a level in his sight, and have all equal access, if penitent and believing, to the throne of his heavenly grace. It proclaims one method of justification for all classes of men; one kind of preparation for heaven; and that not ceremonial, but moral and spiritual; and one great code of moral duty, equally applicable to the learned and the ignorant, the polished and the rude, the civilized and the savage. And as all the great doctrines and principles of the religion of Christ are equally adapted to the whole human family; so the rational and benevolent laws, the unostentatious rites, the simple worship, and the whole spirit and requirements of this religion, are no less adapted to be universally received as the religion of the whole race of man. It has nothing local; nothing national; nothing exclusive, except its uncompromising holiness; no burdensome ritual; no tedious or expensive pilgrimages; no blazing altars; no bloody sacrifices; no intricate genealogies; no special adaptedness to any particular form of civil government, or occupation in life. In short, every thing in this blessed religion; — the simple costume which it wears; the heavenly spirit which it breathes; its law of marriage; its holy Sabbath; its meekness, forgiveness, humility, and benevolence; applying alike to all classes of men, and to all states of society; — proclaim that it is suited to the condition of man, in all nations and ages; to meet the exigencies of all; to supply their wants; to refine and invigorate their talents; to elevate their character; and to unite all who receive it, into one sanctified and happy brotherhood. Surely this character of our holy religion is adapted to confirm our confidence that it will, one day, as Jehovah has promised, gloriously fill the world; and that, literally, in Christ, "all the families of the earth shall be blessed."

3. I have only to add, under this head, *that the present aspect of the world furnishes much reason to hope that the accomplishment of this promise is drawing nigh.*

It cannot be denied, indeed, that, on the principles of worldly calculation, there is much in the present condition of mankind to distress and dishearten. More than *seven parts out of eight* of the whole population of our globe, are still sunk in deplorable darkness and corruption. Of the eight hundred millions of immortal souls, which the earth is supposed to contain, only about *sixty*, or, at most, *seventy millions* are nominally Protestants. The great mass of the remaining *seven hundred and forty millions,* are either Pagans or Mohammedans, or nearly as destitute as either, of saving, evangelical light. Of these sixty or seventy millions of nominal Protestants, only about a third part, or a little more than twenty millions, can be said to have the real gospel of Christ, in anything like its purity, so much as preached among them. Of those, which, in a large sense of the word, we may call *evangelical* congregations, probably not more than one half, or *twelve millions,* are even professors of religion, in any distinct or intelligent import of the terms. That is, of the *eight hundred millions* of the world's population, but little more than an EIGHTIETH PART are even PROFESSORS OF RELIGION, in any scriptural form, or claim to know anything of its sanctifying power. How many of these professors of religion we may calculate upon as probably real Christians — ah! — that is a question on which the humble, enlightened believer, though he may hesitate and weep, will forbear to attempt an estimate!

Such is, confessedly, at present, the dark and distressing state of the great mass of our world's population. To what a lamentably small extent is that "glory," of which our text speaks, found to reign among our fellow men! What a little remnant, among all the multiplied millions of mankind, have any adequate or saving knowledge of the religion of Christ! O what a moral charnel-house does our world appear! What a valley of "dry bones! — exceeding dry!" "Can these dry bones live?" Yes, they shall live! *The mouth of the Lord hath spoken it.* And even NOW, amidst the darkness and misery which brood over the greater part of the earth, there are appearances, every where, which promise the approach of better days. It is but a short time since a large part of the inhabited globe was absolutely closed against the missionaries of the cross. Ten or fifteen years ago, Egypt, Arabia, Persia, China, the Burman Empire, and a large part of Africa and her islands;—in short, by far the greater portion of the Pagan and Mohammedan world, were rigorously shut against the Gospel. Missionaries could not so much as enter those countries, without incurring either certain death, or the most immediate risk of it. But now it may be said, without exaggeration, that the whole world is opened wide to the bearers of the Gospel message. I know not that there is, at this hour, a single portion of the globe, to which the enlightened and prudent missionary may not obtain some degree of access,— unless it be some portions which bear the Christian name, but are under the spiritual despotism of "the man of sin, the son of perdition, who exalteth himself against all that is called God." He who "sits as Governor among the nations," seems to be spreading a *natural preparation*, if I may so express it, around the world, for the preaching of the Gospel among all nations. He seems to be slowly and silently laying a train for mighty movements in time to come. He seems to be showing us how easy it is for him to incline the hearts even of his enemies—from worldly motives—not merely to *permit* the Gospel to enter their territories, but to *invite* its ministers to come in and proclaim their message. Never before was so large a portion of mankind accessible to the evangelical laborer. Never before was there so much evidence that the most massive fabrics of superstition are crumbling to the dust, and ready to give place to a more pure and rational system. Never before were there so many appearances which promise the fulfilment of that prediction, that "nations shall be born in a day." It is believed by some that there are at this moment, in the city of Calcutta, several thousands of young Hindoos, who are disposed seriously to inquire on the subject of salvation, and by no means indisposed to exchange their miserable superstition for a better form of religion. Only suppose such a body of young men prepared by the grace of God, and going forth in the spirit and power of Christ into every part of Hindoostan, and how might that deplorable moral wilderness be transformed into a fertile and delightful garden of the Lord! How might a thousand Asiatic deserts be made speedily to "rejoice and blossom as the rose!" What say you, my Christian friends, to appearances and opportunities such as these? O ye who profess to know something of the sweetness of redeeming love, and the preciousness of Christian hopes, shall we be blind to these wonderful openings of Providence? Shall we be deaf to these importunate invitations to enlighten and save perishing men?

Contemplate, further, the singular progress of various forms of improvement throughout the civilized world; all of which may be considered as bearing on the great promise contained in our text. Behold the *intercourse* between distant portions of the globe increasing every day with a rapidity, and to an extent, beyond all former precedent! Think of the endless improvements in the means of *conveyance* from one part of the world to another; thereby investing missionary enterprises with facilities for carrying on their operations unknown to our fathers. Consider the wonderful improvements in the art of *printing*, and indeed in all the mechanic arts, rendering the multiplication of bibles, and other pious writings, for the benefit of the world, practicable and easy to an extent formerly thought incredible. Contemplate the extension of *commercial enterprise*, which late years have produced, presenting the means of benefiting mankind to an amount altogether new and extraordinary. Think of the enlargement of our acquaintance with the different *languages* of the globe; it being probable that ten persons, if not twenty, now understand other living languages than their own, where one had this knowledge fifty years ago. Think of the Bible having been translated into more than one hundred and fifty languages at this hour spoken among men; and of the process of preparing the Scriptures for circulation in every part of the globe, still going on with increasing rapidity. And dwell, for a moment, on what is no less remarkable — the *progress of public sentiment* in regard to the conversion of the world to God. What, ten years ago, would have been thought the extravagance of visionary dreaming, in regard to this great enterprise, is now looked at, and talked about, with a grave familiarity and confidence which it is delightful to contemplate. It is less than ten years since a proposal from a warm-hearted Christian in the State of New York, to supply the destitute of one populous *county* with Bibles, was regarded as a bold attempt, and received with thrilling interest. Not many months afterwards, the young men of the college at Princeton, resolved, with a moral daring which was then almost ridiculed as presumptuous, to attempt to supply the destitute of the whole state of New Jersey with Bibles in two years. Yet bold, and almost hopeless as this pledge appeared at the time of its adoption, it was, substantially, and with wonderfully apparent ease, redeemed. Hardly was this accomplished, before a resolution was adopted to attempt the supply of the destitute in the *whole United States* with Bibles within a specified time. For this resolution, when adopted, many even of the warmest friends of the Bible cause were not prepared; but feared it would prove a presumptuous and abortive undertaking. Yet, as far as anything of the kind is practicable in such a country as this, it was faithfully and happily accomplished. But scarcely was this done, when the enlarged spirit of public benevolence — still augmenting in a geometrical ratio, called for a still wider and nobler field of pious effort. To supply *all the accessible portions of the whole* WORLD with the word of life, within a specified time, was the sublime enterprise proposed to the American Bible Society, and to other Bible Societies in our own and foreign lands. A like rapid increase has been observable in the means furnished by public liberality, for carrying on the great enterprises of Christian benevolence which distinguish and adorn our age. They are, in all, from thirty to fifty fold, and in some more than a hundred fold, beyond what they were a quarter of a century ago. Now, in regard to all these, and other striking analogous facts, I ask, my friends, how shall we account for this *astonishing progress of public sentiment* in regard to plans for the conversion of the world to God? Can we possibly consider it as merely accidental, and without meaning? Surely such a conclusion would be as much opposed to reason as to piety. May we not rather consider it as a precious omen, that the great work which it contemplates is happily drawing near, and will, before long, be gloriously realized?

And to me, it appears worthy of special notice, that there are so many indications that the *English language,*—the language of those parts of the world which are most favored with Gospel light, will probably, ere long, become *the prevailing language of the whole world.* The extensive and rapid progress of this language on the American continent; in all the British possessions and dependencies in the Eastern world; in the continent of New Holland; in many of the islands of the sea; and, in short, in every part of the earth where American or British missionaries are permitted to lift up their voice for Christ, is truly one of the most striking and interesting spectacles now passing before the contemplative mind. If the time should ever again recur, when the "whole earth shall be of one language and one speech," the *English,* I am persuaded, is more likely to be that language than any other. And may we not consider its gradual and remarkable extension, as one of the means by which the "earth is to be filled with the glory of the Lord?"

While we contemplate some of those prominent features in the aspect of the present day, which seem to portend an unexampled spread of the Gospel;—we ought not to overlook some shades in the picture which certainly wear a very different appearance. Infidelity and heresy were, probably, never more busy in circulating their virulent poison, than at the present hour. Principles at war with all social stability and order, were, perhaps, never more widely extended in civilized society; and in both the civil and religious community, the ebullitions of morbid excitement have never been more threatening in their appearance. That there is a *great battle* yet to be fought with these opposing powers, no reflecting mind can for a moment doubt. How violent or long-continued the conflict may be, I presume not to calculate. But let no man's heart fail him on account of these approaching struggles. A little before the advent of the Messiah, it was said, "I will shake all nations, and the desire of all nations shall come; and I will fill my house with glory, saith the Lord of hosts." And, in like manner, may we not hope that all the corruption in principle, and all the morbid feverishness in practice, which exhibit so revolting an aspect at the present time, may result, like many a process in the natural world, in which the animal body is renovated and strengthened by the consequences of a subdued fever; and in which the gradual and complete subsidence of feculent matter is hastened even by the violent agitation of an impure fluid? It is no new thing either for infidelity or fanaticism to furnish an antidote to its own poison, by disclosing the malignity of its virus, in the deadliness of its effects; and thus creating an extensive and permanent loathing of those moral potions which allure but to destroy. Many are "running to and fro;" but my hope is, that "knowledge will be thereby increased;" and that the present febrile state of the social body, will soon terminate, under the control of Him who is able to bring good out of evil, — in more firm and established moral health; and in more widely extended, and better directed efforts than ever, for promoting the universal reign of knowledge, religion, and happiness among men. It remains that we

III. Inquire, WHAT IS OUR PRESENT DUTY IN RELATION TO THE PROMISE BEFORE US ? And here,

1. Undoubtedly, our *first* duty is *to believe the promise.* This is the very least that can be demanded. Unbelief "makes God a liar;" poisons the very fountain of Christian confidence; cuts the nerves of all spiritual exertion; and tends to discouragement and despondency. To what purpose has Jehovah promised, if even his own people will not hear and believe? We may say now, I fear, to the great majority of those who bear the Christian name, as the Master himself said to the desponding disciples on their way to Emmaus — "O fools, and slow of heart to believe all that the prophets have spoken!" Ah, my friends, the lack of faith is the great, crying sin, not of an ungodly world only, but eminently of Christians. It is the littleness of our faith which makes us dwarfs in spiritual stature; cowards in conflict and in enterprise; narrow-minded in our views and plans of duty; and niggards in sacrifice and in contribution to the cause of Christ. Yes, it is the sin and the misery even of the sincere disciples of Christ, that the promises of God have so little daily influence on their practical habits. Christians! be afraid of unbelief; be ashamed of unbelief; only believe, and act as if you believed; and you shall see the salvation of God.

2. Another duty incumbent upon us, in relation to this promise, is to *labor and pray without ceasing for its accomplishment*. They are undoubtedly guilty of an unwise and criminal perversion of God's word, who infer, because he has promised a specific and rich blessing, and will certainly bring it to pass, that *therefore* they may repose in a state of entire inaction and unconcern respecting the event. There is no piety, my friends, in that confidence which neglects *prayer*, and which does not add to prayer *diligent effort* to attain that for which it prays. *Show me thy faith by thy works*, is a maxim equally of reason and revelation. God's kingdom is a kingdom of means. He never did, and probably never will, convey the light of the Gospel to any people, by direct miracle; but by the agency of man. He "will be inquired of," he declares, by us — to accomplish even that which he has promised, and which he fully intends to bring about. And although he is able to effect all his purposes of mercy and salvation without the instrumentality of man's labors, yet he condescends in all cases to employ them. And is it not a mercy that he *does* require and employ them? Does not every reflecting man perceive that it is a wise and benign arrangement of Providence which renders constant activity of body and mind indispensable to the highest physical, intellectual, and moral enjoyment? And can any one doubt that it is an equally wise and merciful arrangement which makes it our duty to pray, and exert ourselves without ceasing to promote the reign of salvation throughout the world? Not only is it certain that the great King of Zion has commanded us to send the Gospel to every creature; not only is it manifest that we may properly estimate our Christian character by the degree in which we take an active interest in the conversion of the world; but it is equally plain, that every fervent prayer we offer, and every sincere effort we make for hastening this great consummation, has a tendency to benefit our own souls, as well as the souls of others; to increase our faith; to inflame our love; to enlarge our visions; in a word, to make us more like Christ, and to impart a richer preparation for the holy joys of his presence. In short, we may say of him who is much employed in fervent prayer, and in diligent labor and sacrifice for the conversion of the world to God, — that he is *twice blessed;* blessed as a benefactor of his fellow-men, and as the receiver of a blessing, by the very act of conferring benefits on others.

3. A third duty, in relation to the promise in our text, is, that in laboring for the spread of the gospel, *no adverse occurrence, however painful, ought ever to discourage us, or at all to weaken either our confidence or our efforts.* What could be more discouraging than the state of the visible church when the promise before us was given? Yet the promise itself really prohibited all despondency. If, indeed, we had anything short of Jehovah's promise to rely upon, when difficulties or disappointments arose, we might despond. But *with* that promise, we may meet the most distressing difficulties without fear. What though some of our fondest hopes and plans are frustrated? What though some of those instruments on which the highest confidence was placed, unexpectedly fail? What though the lamented *Evarts*, and *Cornelius*, and *Wisner*, follow each other in quick succession, to their eternal reward, and leave us to mourn over the sore bereavement of the missionary cause? What though one beloved brother and sister after another falls, in the flower of life, and on the fields whitening to the harvest? What though even the hand of savage violence be permitted to cut down young, zealous and promising heralds of salvation, when just about to present the glorious Gospel to their merciless murderers? Our tears may flow over bereavements such as these. They ought to flow. But let no thought of discouragement arise. Frail instruments may die; but the "Captain of Salvation" lives. Is the military commander disheartened, when, in the shock of battle, some of his choicest subalterns fall around him? Not if he has the heart of a soldier. And shall "the good soldier of Jesus Christ" have less courage? In fact, every adverse occurrence ought only to constrain us to turn our confidence from the creature, and to place it more firmly and entirely on the Lord of all creatures. Tell us not, then, of the difficulties which beset our enterprise for the conversion of the world. Tell us not, that, going on as the Christian church has done for eighteen centuries, it will take thousands of ages completely to evangelize all nations; or rather, that, at that rate of progress, there is little hope that the work can ever be accomplished. We know it all. And if our dependence were on the wisdom and power of man, we might abandon all hope. But in the name and strength of Jehovah, our covenant God, who can never fail or grow weary, we may go forward with confidence, in the face of every difficulty; intimidated by no

danger; disheartened by no disappointment or adverse occurrence. Nay, how often has it happened that those events, which we considered as deeply calamitous, and over which we mourned, as greatly hindering the Gospel, — have resulted in its signal and extensive furtherance! When Stephen, the first martyr, was stoned to death by an infuriated mob, to whom he came with a message of love, "devout men," we are told, "carried him to his burial, and made great lamentation over him." But, mark the event! That persecution, though not so intended by the persecutors, became the means of sending many ministers of the Gospel away from Jerusalem, in various directions, and thus of extending and building up the church of God, instead of effecting its destruction, as the malignant adversary had confidently expected.

4. A further duty, in reference to the promise before us, is, that we *pray without ceasing for the power of the Holy Spirit*, to render all the means which are employed for its accomplishment, effectual. When we recollect the extent and difficulty of the work to be done; how many millions are yet in darkness and misery; how hard and full of enmity the human heart; and how obstinately the warnings and entreaties of mercy have been resisted; we may well despair of human wisdom and strength, and look to Almighty power alone for success. " It is not by might or by power, but by my Spirit," saith Jehovah, that means are attended with a saving energy. Had we millions of the most learned, eloquent, and holy preachers in Christendom to send forth, and all the funds that could be asked or desired for this enterprise; — all would be in vain, unless the power of the Almighty Spirit went along with the laborers. While, therefore, we labor with unwearied perseverance for the conversion of the world; while we raise funds with growing liberality; while we select, instruct, and send forth the most able and devoted missionaries that we can find, and while we employ all the means in our power for imparting the Gospel to every creature; let us remember, that all will be unavailing, unless the Holy Spirit accompany and give efficacy to the means employed. Let every thing pertaining to the spread of the Gospel, be done under the deep impression, that, in our own strength we can effect nothing; that as the promise is Jehovah's word, so the accomplishment of it is Jehovah's work; that to *Him*, of course, for bringing to pass what he has promised, every eye and every heart ought to be directed.

And allow me, my beloved friends, to say, we are never likely to be either so happy, or so successful in any enterprise for extending the Redeemer's kingdom, as when we lie in the dust of abasement, sensible of our utter inability to command, by our own power, the least portion of the blessing which we seek; and placing all our dependence for success, at every step, on the Holy Spirit's life-giving energy. And I must also be allowed to say, that in my own view, this doctrine, viz., *that success is all of God*, instead of being a legitimate source of discouragement, is, while it humbles, at the same time, one of the most comforting and animating of all doctrines. For though it be most true, that "he who planteth is nothing, and he who watereth is nothing — but God that giveth the increase;" — it is also equally true, that all hearts are in his hands, and that he is able to turn the most blind and hardened to himself, "as the rivers of waters are turned." O, it is sweet to the believing heart, to lean on God; to plead his promises, and to rejoice in the assurance, that, though man cannot do it, by reason of weakness, He, "with whom all things are possible," and who "cannot lie," hath promised that the whole "earth shall be filled with his glory;" and that He is at once able and faithful to bring it to pass.

5. Finally; if so great a work as evangelizing THE WHOLE WORLD, is promised, and is certainly to be accomplished, *then our plans and efforts for promoting this object ought to bear a corresponding character;* that is, they ought to be *large, liberal,* and *ever expanding.* We ought to consider it as our duty to devote to this object our utmost resources, and to engage the co-operation of all, over whom we can exert an influence.

The promise of God to his people is, "Open thy mouth wide, and I will fill it." It is spoken of in various passages of Scripture, as an excellence in Christian character, that the *heart be enlarged;* — that is, filled with large affections, large desires, large hopes, and large confidence. Never were Scriptures more applicable than these to the case before us. When we direct our attention to the spread of the Gospel, our views, our prayers, our efforts, are all too stinted and narrow. We scarcely ever lift our eyes to the real grandeur and claims of the enterprise in which we profess to be engaged. We are too apt to be satisfied with small and occasional contributions of service to this greatest of all causes, instead of devoting to it hearts truly enlarged; instead of desiring great things; expecting great things; praying for great things; and nurturing in our spirits that holy elevation of sentiment and affection, which embraces in its desires and prayers the entire kingdom of God; and which can be satisfied with nothing short of the "whole earth being filled with the glory of the Lord."

We now and then meet with a professing Christian who really does seem to regard the kingdom of Christ — its enlargement and glory — as the greatest interest in the universe; and who does seem to desire unfeignedly to consecrate all that he has and is to promote its progress. But, Oh, how small is the number of those who manifest this spirit! My dear friends, the number of such must greatly increase, before the church at large can be expected to "rise from the dust, and put on her beautiful garments." The whole style of Christian character — if I may be allowed the expression — must become, generally, more decided; more active; more unreservedly devoted; — more abundant and fervent in prayer; more enlarged and liberal in the system of giving — *far more*, before the spread of the Gospel can correspond with the divine promises; before it is possible that our raised expectations with respect to the conversion of the world can ever be realized. Yes, life and power must be greatly increased *within the church*, before her *power on the world* can be widely extended and triumphantly glorious. Professing Christians must be seen to be really in earnest in their faith and hope, before they can be expected to make a deep impression on the impenitent around them. We often come to you, Christian brethren, soliciting your pecuniary aid, in bearing the Gospel and its heralds to the ends of the earth. And, truly, without this aid, we cannot carry on our benevolent operations for a single day. But, after all, we are much more anxious to see your souls swelling with holy love, and holy zeal, and holy activity; because we know that *this* indicates more deep and enlarged spiritual advancement; and because it is a pledge, not of a mere fitful gush of liberality; but of a perennial stream of Christian *bounty*, flowing from love to the infinitely precious cause.

This character was once much more common, than it is at the present day. How ought we at once to be humbled and animated, when we read the history of the *primitive Christians!* Many of them literally and cheerfully gave up all for Christ. Contemplate, my beloved friends, — contemplate the affecting narrative! Ah! how they labored, and denied themselves, and made sacrifices, and gave their substance — sometimes to the last farthing — for the cause of Christ. See them " counting all things but loss," and even cheerfully going to the stake, when the Saviour's honor required it. Read this narrative, professing Christians, and then say, whether those who feel reluctant to give the price even of a few luxurious dinners for promoting the Redeemer's kingdom, can seriously believe that they are actuated by the same spirit with those devoted disciples?

But how ought we to be still more deeply humbled and animated, when we call to mind what our blessed Saviour has done for us! I have sometimes heard professing Christians talk of doing and giving as much toward the spread of the glorious Gospel, " as they *conveniently* could." Surely this is wonderful language for the professed followers of a crucified Redeemer! Did our blessed Master do no more for us than he " *conveniently could!* " Did He not give *his life* for our redemption? Did He not, in offering up himself a sacrifice, that we might not die, yield himself to sufferings unparalleled and indescribable? Shall not every one, then, who calls himself by the name of Christ, make the language of Paul, in all its force and tenderness his own? — " For the love of Christ constraineth us; because we thus judge, that if one died for all, then were all dead; and that he died for all, that they which live, should not henceforth live unto themselves, but unto him which died for them and rose again."

Lift up your eyes, Christian brethren, on the unnumbered millions of our globe, sunk in ignorance, pollution and misery! Think of their condition — a condition in which *you* must have been at this hour, had it not been for the wonderful grace of God. Contrast with that condition your own mercies and privileges, and then ask, whether you ought not to feel for those who are thus miserable, and try to help them? Christians! can you enjoy your Bibles, your Sabbaths, your sanctuaries, your sacramental tables, and all your precious privileges and hopes *alone?* Can you enjoy these hallowed scenes and heavenly gifts, and know their value, and yet slumber in ignoble indolence over the moral desolations of those who are perishing for lack of them? Can you calmly sit by, and see million after million of treasure cheerfully expended for amusement, luxury and sin, and only a few stinted thousands devoted to the greatest, best work of enlightening and saving the world? O whither has the spirit of the Bible fled? May He who gave the Bible, and the promise before us, restore it in His time!

Let us then, with one accord, rouse ourselves, and endeavor to rouse others to new zeal, and larger enterprise in spreading the knowledge and glory of the Lord. Every heart, every tongue, and every hand that can be stirred up to engage in this great work, from infancy to old age, is needed. And remember that the more thoroughly any of the children of men can be excited and consecrated to this work, the richer the benefit they gain for themselves. Christian brother! Christian sister! whoever you are, in this large assembly!— you have each, respectively, a duty to perform in reference to this mighty work. It is incumbent upon you to do *all in your power* for sending the light of life to the benighted and perishing. Nay, upon every human being, whether in the church or out of it, there lies an obligation to aid, as far as God gives the opportunity, in sending to "every creature" that gospel which is "the power of God unto salvation to every one that believeth." We invite you all, my hearers, not merely to the *duty*, but to the *precious privilege*, of coöperating in this holy and blessed enterprise. And we can venture to assure you, that, if the day should ever come, in which your heart shall be thoroughly imbued with the *spirit of missions*, it will be the happiest period of your lives; as well as the pledge and the dawn of that wide-spread glory, which our text proclaims as certain and approaching. We can point you to no higher honor, no richer pleasure on this side of heaven, than that which is found in enlightened, zealous, active, absorbing zeal for spreading the holy, life-giving religion of Jesus Christ from the rising to the setting sun.

We are now celebrating the *twenty-sixth* anniversary of our Board; and, instead of being weary of our work, we can sincerely declare, that in looking back on our past course, our only regret is, that we have not labored with far more diligence and sanctified ardor in the cause of the world's conversion; that our plans have not been more enlarged; and that we have not prayed more and done more in this greatest of all causes in which Christians can engage. Yes, brethren, beloved of the Lord, we come to mingle our vows with yours, to proclaim with deeper conviction than ever, that we consider the cause of missions as the most precious cause in the world;

and to bind ourselves by new resolutions, that we will, by the help of God, with greater zeal than heretofore, "spend and be spent" in this most blessed service. What more worthy object can we seek, than contributing to fill the earth with the glory of the Lord? Brethren, pray for us, that we may be faithful to our sacred trust. Pray for yourselves, that you may not be found wanting in the payment of that mighty debt you owe to your Divine Master and to a perishing world. And let us all, more and more, aspire to the honor of being "workers together with God" in hastening the triumphs of Immanuel's universal reign. *Come, Lord Jesus, come quickly; and let the whole earth be filled with thy glory!* Amen! and Amen!

INCREASE OF FAITH NECESSARY TO THE SUCCESS OF CHRISTIAN MISSIONS.

BY

REV. WILLIAM R. WILLIAMS, D. D.

—— But having hope, when your faith is increased, that we shall be enlarged by you according to our rule abundantly, to preach the Gospel in the regions beyond you. 2 CORINTHIANS 10: 15, 16.

THE language of the Apostle evidently implies a gentle reprehension of the Corinthian church. The poverty and imbecility of their faith embarrassed him in his ardent aspirations after more extended usefulness. He was anxious to enter upon a new field, and to proclaim the Gospel throughout other and more destitute regions. But he must await in prayerful hope the increase of their faith, and at their hands expect an enlargement. This enlargement, might be, on their part, an advancement and confirmation in Christian doctrine, which should permit him to transfer the charge of these, his children in the faith, into the hands of less skilful pastors; or a rapid growth in Christian holiness, which should justify the Apostle in presenting them as his epistle, to be seen and read of all men, attesting alike the power of the Gospel, and the reality of his mission. Or he might desire the vindication of his own apostolical character, which had been cruelly assailed in their midst, and ask the transmission of his name, with its well-won honors, to the neighboring heathen. Or it had been, perhaps, his hope, from their liberality and wealth, to have received aid in his missionary journeyings; or he had anticipated from their position in a great commercial metropolis, assistance in their sending the Gospel to other havens and cities of the empire. Whether he expected from their increased and matured faith, any one, or the union of all these advantages, and whatever be the decision as to the mode in which enlargement was sought by him, one fact stands forth on the face of these words, manifest and unquestionable. He was now fettered in his plans of benevolence, and it was from the Corinthian disciples that he expected his release. Either from their confirmation in the truths he preached, or in the holiness he enjoined and exemplified; or from their assertion of his just honors as an apostle; from the bestowment of their free alms, or the employment of their mercantile influence, he hoped to obtain the removal of the restraint from himself, and to secure for their pagan neighbors blessings untold and priceless. The fulfilment of his hope depended upon their progress to higher attainments in faith. There is involved, then, in these words of an inspired and most successful missionary, a principle which we would now endeavor to bring before you, that

The missionaries of the church require at her hands, for the extension and success of their efforts, an increase of faith.

Looking to the divisions and scandals he had so sternly rebuked, and to the peculiar temptations of the infant church, which had been gathered amid the luxury, gayety, and profligacy of the licentious Corinth, we might have expected, from one versed as was Paul in the weakness of our nature, and in the wiles of its great adversary, that he would have chosen to specify, instead of the one evil of unbelief, other and numerous impediments to his success. And using the term here employed by him, as we too often do, to describe a knowledge merely speculative and theoretical, we should have supposed that in a community indoctrinated by the personal labors of an apostle, as well as in the churches of our own age and land, the deficiencies of Christians were to be sought, rather in their works of obedience, than in the amount of their faith. Yet such was not the fact then. Such is not the root of the evil now. It is in faith that we are wanting. The elder and parent grace is maimed and infirm, and the whole family and sisterhood of the Christian virtues languish at she decays, and can be reanimated only by her restoration. Having considered, therefore,

I. THE NATURE AND IMPORTANCE OF TRUE FAITH,

II. THE INTIMATE CONNEXION BETWEEN ITS HIGHER DEGREES AND THE MISSIONARY EFFORTS OF THE CHURCH will naturally follow and prepare us to examine,

III. THE DEFECTIVE FAITH OF OUR OWN CHURCHES, AS INTERPOSING A HINDRANCE TO THE TRIUMPHS OF THE GOSPEL OVER HEATHENISM.

And may the Father of lights, by His own Spirit of illumination and power, unfold to the mind, and impress upon the heart, the humbling but the salutary truth contained in these words.

I. The *importance* of faith may be discerned from the dignity and rank assigned it throughout the New Testament. In the commencement and at the close of our Saviour's ministry; in his own private conference with the anxious, but irresolute Nicodemus, and in the public message with which his apostles were charged, as he sent them forth to the evangelization of the world, it is alike represented as the only mode — the one condition of salvation. He that exercises it is not condemned, while he that believeth not shall be damned. To this principle is ascribed our immunity from the terrors of the law, for we are justified by faith. As a shield, it repels the fiery darts of temptation that come from the great adversary of God and man; while within, it purifies the heart, working by love; and, in our contest with the ungodly precepts and example of our fellow-men, "this is the victory that overcometh the world, even our faith." The long and glorious list of its strifes and its trophies, contained in the closing portion of the Epistle to the Hebrews, commences with the announcement that faith is the substance of things hoped for, the evidence of things not seen; and is terminated with the triumphant recapitulation that all these, the worthies of the earlier dispensations, obtained their good report through the same simple, but mighty principle — that of faith.

And although the world are accustomed to dispute the necessity of this principle, when exercised respecting the realities of a world as yet hidden and invisible, they are perpetually employing it with regard to the visible but transient scenery of the present life. Compelled to give their faith to testimony as to those things which might be seen, and often giving it even where they might substitute personal observation for faith in the evidence of others; they refuse to extend it to those objects which, from their very nature, cannot become the subjects of immediate vision and examination. Yielding credence to the testimony of their fellow-mortals, though the witnesses are alike fallible and perfidious, they refuse it to the revelation of their God. Preferring to give it where it is often not required, (did they choose to employ their own natural faculties,) they withhold it where it is inevitably necessary. All the commerce of this world is predicated on the faith which man puts in the skill, integrity, and diligence of his fellow-man; and a writing, of which he never saw the author, shall be to him a sufficient warrant for transmitting, far beyond his own sight and control, his whole property. By the exercise of a just and sober faith in the testimony brought into her halls, the national jurisprudence administers to our citizens the redress of their wrongs, and the punishment of their crimes. The learning dispensed in our colleges is, by the mass of minds, received without personal examination, upon the credit given to the ability and honesty of previous investigators. And all education, whether in the most recondite science, or in the most humble and handicraft art, proceeds upon the faith which the pupil is required to exercise in the superior skill of his instructor, and in the value of the knowledge his teacher is preparing to communicate.

It is only by the confidence they have learned to place in the narratives of the traveller, that the majority of society know the nature and extent of the country, of which they are themselves the inhabitants; or that they can form any idea of the great and magnificent cities, the goodly prospects, and the splendid wonders that adorn some foreign and unseen coast. And with regard to the facts which we have thus gathered, we feel no suspicion, but use them as the current coin of the mind, both in our private meditations and our social intercourse, without fear as to their genuineness and validity. Even the skeptic, loud and boisterous in his rejection of all faith, as being an invasion of the province, and but an usurpation upon the rights of human reason, is most rigid and constant in exacting from his trembling child an obedience to his will, and a subjection to his opinions, which can rest only upon the faith, the tacit but implicit faith, which he requires his family to exercise in his superior wisdom and larger experience.

And if it be objected, that the faith of the gospel differs widely from that which we so readily and commonly render, in that it brings to our minds deep and difficult mysteries, we answer that it would be less evidently the work of God, if it did not come, contradicting the first and rasher conclusions of human ignorance. It would be a departure from the analogy which exists among all the works of our God, did it only reveal what man had previously conjectured, and were Faith employed merely to endorse and register, in silent acquiescence, the rescripts which had been prepared for her by human reason. And even in the sciences of this world, narrow and near as is the field of their labors, there are the same inscrutable yet inevitable difficulties, of which the sceptic complains in religion. We expect it of a cultivated and advanced science, that it should assail and overturn many opinions, which to the first glance of ignorant presumption seem indisputable truths. Contradicting the first and incomplete testimony of our senses and the general impressions of mankind, Geography comes back from her voyages of discovery with the annunciation that the earth is not an extended plain, but one vast sphere. And though the eye sees no motion, and the foot feels no unsteadiness, and no jarring is perceived within or around us, Astronomy comes back to the inquirer with the startling assurance, that, notwithstanding all these seeming evidences to the contrary, the earth on which he reposes is ceaselessly and most rapidly whirling along its trackless path in the heavens; and that, moment by moment, he is borne along through the fields of space with a fearful and inconceivable velocity. And when, from further wanderings, but on better testimony, — when from a higher and stranger world, but with fuller evidence and with more indubitable tokens of her veracity, Faith comes back, bringing assurances that tally not in all things with our preconceived conjectures, shall she be chidden and blasphemed for the difficulties that arise from our own ignorance? Without the mysteries of the Gospel, revelation would be unlike all the other provinces of human knowledge, and the domains of Faith would be dissimilar from all the rest of the handiwork of God.

But although the importance of faith is thus apparent from the rank assigned it in the scriptures, and from its necessity even in the petty concernments of this present life, we shall learn to appreciate true belief yet more highly, when we see mankind, by a heedless but perpetual infatuation, allowing themselves in errors the most absurd and dangerous, with regard to its character and claims. By some it is confounded with a blind and irrational credulity, although evangelical faith is based only on evidence the most satisfactory and sufficient; and although the book of God, when demanding our credence, proffers to the inquirer testimony, not merely abundant, but overwhelming, as to the nature of its authorship. It is as adverse to the character of scriptural faith to believe without a divine warrant, upon authority that is merely traditionary and human, as to refuse the assent of the soul where God has spoken. True Faith is not more allied to superstition than she is to skepticism; and, determined as he is to believe all that God has testified, the Christian, wherever the oracle is silent, suspends his decision, and anxiously excludes from his creed all the inventions of man, whether they come from the school, the synod, or the council.

Others delight to speak of faith in the religion of our Lord, as if it were but an opinion, and the religion it embraces but a hypothesis, of little practical moment or influence; while, on the contrary, the faith of the Gospel is as rigid and experimental in its character as the strictest science of the schools. It makes no arbitrary assumptions, rests on no disputed axioms, but, upon the foundation of facts of the most impressive and varied character, it builds up, patiently and surely, its doctrines and its precepts; invites the most searching scrutiny into the testimonials which it adduces; and having by them established its first principles, gives not only for its fundamental axioms, but for its every inference, and for each subsequent deduction, the word of a God. As well might we call arithmetic or history a mere theory, as to apply that title to the religion which is embraced by our faith. Do the self-satisfied philosophers of this world tell us of the necessity of facts? We answer, the incarnation, the personal character, the crucifixion and resurrection of the Saviour, are facts most fully proved, and standing alone, would be in themselves sufficient to prove the divinity of the revelation that is entwined about them, and of which they constitute the central supports, the chief and favorite theme. And every convert, ransomed by the power of this faith from the tyranny of evil habits, affords in himself a new fact, augmenting the mass of her evidences, and swelling her far-spreading and splendid "cloud of witnesses."

Nor are those men safer or wiser than the undisguised scoffer, who, professing to receive the religion of the Bible, flatter themselves that a mere assent of the understanding to the historical portions of the record, constitutes that faith which shall justify at the bar, and admit them to the heaven of JEHOVAH. The Bible is to be regarded as a whole, and as such is to be received and obeyed. The Gospel is a code of laws, no less than a volume of annals. It has not only narratives, but precepts, and asks the consent of the whole man, and his entire soul, to its undivided and unmutilated contents. And as that man could not maintain his arrogant pretensions, who should claim the honors of devoted patriotism merely because he had studied intently the annals of his country's history, whilst he was trampling upon her laws, and imprinting every leaf of her statute-book with the hoof of swinish indulgence, thus must the man fail of sustaining his claim to the character of Christ's disciple, who, professing to credit and revere his record, treads down into the mire his laws, and has but the faith of historical assent for the narrative, without the faith of love for the precepts, and the faith of affectionate conformity for the character of the Saviour. The Bible contains not only the story of our creation, ruin, and recovery, but it includes as well the indictment of our crimes, and the proclamation of our pardon; and there is no true reception of the history, unless there be also, personally, the humble confession of the imputed guiltiness, and the grateful pleading of the proffered discharge.

Equally erroneous, and chargeable with a kindred folly, is the man, who, passing beyond the vain figment of a faith merely historical, professes to receive the whole system of revelation, in its doctrinal, no less than its narrative portions, and triumphing in the orthodoxy of his tenets, seems anxious to shelter himself from the practical influence of faith, by pleading the freeness of the salvation it brings. The whole necessity of salvation grew out of the practical depravity of man's nature, and the whole errand of the Bible was but the restoration of practical holiness. For this end prophets and apostles wrote; for this it was that a Saviour descended and bled — rose, and reigns, to furnish, to bestow, and to fulfil that Bible. And until this effect be wrought, nothing is gained, and if this be refused, the very object and intention of the religion is rejected. It is surely vain toil to implant in the mind a faith, the vital germ of which is carefully removed, a dead root, which shall never send forth the springing leaf, or bear the ripened fruit.

An error now popular, and not less fatal, is one which the skeptic has borrowed from the armory and champions of the truth. It consists in a perversion of the great scriptural truth, that it is God who worketh in us to will and to do, and that all our thoughts are under his control. Using the theological labors of Edwards for a purpose, which that holy and master mind never intended, the advocates of this dangerous error contend that our belief is beyond our control, that faith is not voluntary, and unbelief is therefore not criminal: forgetting, that, though a gift of God, faith is withal an act or habit of the human mind; that, like every other virtue, it is on the one hand, a boon of heaven, and on the other, the exercise of unfettered human agency — that it is the natural result of evidence duly and impartially considered, and that no man can be guiltless who wilfully turns away from the contemplation of that evidence. The religion of God asks but a verdict according to the weight of proof which she brings. To prevent the admission of that evidence, or wilfully to pronounce a decision against its weighty and sufficient testimony, would not be deemed guiltless in any cause that should be brought before an earthly tribunal; nor shall it be held a venial offence at the bar, and by the laws of an insulted Deity.

From the errors which human perverseness has invented to obscure the character of faith, we turn to review its true *nature* and *office*. It is most simple, as much so as the confidence of a prattling child in his father's kindness and wisdom; yet at the same time as expansive in its views, as the loftiest science that ever tasked the powers of a created intellect. It is but a hearty assent to the whole testimony of God — a submission of the entire soul, not of the intellect only, but also of the affections and the imagination, to the testimony of God; whether that testimony be employed in prescribing a duty, or in establishing a privilege. It is the acknowledgment of human ignorance, united with the profession of confidence in Divine wisdom, and of subjection to Divine authority. Making no reservations, prescribing no terms of limitation, claiming no power of revoking or abridging its grant, it is a surrender of the intelligent spirit to the word of God as its rule and its stay; in conformity to it as the one standard of human conduct, and in dependence upon it as the only fitting nutriment of the spiritual life. It thus restores again the communication which at the fall was severed. In his temptation Satan persuaded our parents to discredit the testimony of God; and the consequent interruption of faith was the hewing away of that channel, through which they had heretofore received from their God knowledge, truth, and love. The human mind became at once an exhausted and rifted reservoir, "a broken cistern," into which no longer welled the outgushing streams from "the Fountain of living waters." By faith the communion is restored, and man is again the dependant and pupil of his God.

It is his natural and rightful state, not for this life only, but forever. The apostle, when enumerating the graces that abide, has spoken of faith as if it too continued. Indeed, the very nature of a created and limited intelligence, involves the necessity of continued faith. Long as we are not omnipresent, and cannot perceive with our own eyes what is every where transacted — long as we are not omniscient, and there are portions of knowledge, which we have not yet acquired — long as man is not invested with the attributes of the Deity, so long must we depend upon His testimony for the truth of that which He has seen and we have not seen; so long must we learn from Him the nature of that which He has known, but which we may know only from his words. The perfection of the heavenly world does not imply illimitable knowledge, either as to the present or the future; and as to all those portions of God's ways, which thus remain concealed from our personal examination, the spirits of just men made perfect, will, with their first-born brethren, the angels that have kept their original estate, remain the pensioners of faith, dependent upon the declarations of God for continual instruction.

And how glorious are the objects which faith brings into the mind of man, even during his sojourn here. He learns from her the secret of his own misery and guiltiness, and its remedy. He is told of a law condemning irrevocably for the first offence, yet now fully satisfied for his hourly infraction of its precepts — a Saviour divine to redeem and human to compassionate — a salvation not of his own procurement — the Spirit of God descended to be his teacher and consoler — troubles sanctified — snares broken — and an eternity of purity and blessedness made his certain inheritance; and are not these truths of surpassing splendor and inestimable worth? They enter into the soul, not so much destroying as be-dwarfing its former ideas, and the original furniture of the mind, which it has obtained from the knowledge and literature of this world. Faith has suddenly widened the mental horizon, letting in the vision of realities before present, but hitherto unseen. Or rather, as has been beautifully said, it is the floating into view of another and a lovelier world, with its glories and its harmony drowning the din and beclouding the splendor of these terrestrial scenes.

The believer judges by a new standard; sees by a new and heaven-descended light; and lo, in the change, "all things have become new." And though the men of this world may question and deride the renovation, because the man's earthly condition, and the powers of his mind remain apparently the same; it is evident to those who will reason, that the man is essentially renewed; for his views, his feelings, his hopes and fears, his prospects and his purposes, his conduct and language, have undergone a marked and strange modification. True it is, the man's garb is still coarse, and his person ungainly, and his mind is not graced with the refinements and adornments of education; but the change is as yet merely initial. Death and the resurrection shall consummate it. And even already the internal process is to his own mind alike evident and delightful; and with tears of gratitude he receives it as the earnest of that thorough renovation, which shall transform him, body, soul, and spirit, into the likeness of his Lord. Thus might we imagine an aged and lonely cottager, musing at nightfall in his desolate home, upon the partner of his bosom, now tenanting the grave, and his children, who have long since wandered from his hearth to a distant land, and are there regardless or ignorant of the sorrows with which his declining years are darkened. And as he cowers over his scanty fire, the unbidden tear will fall, and his heart is full of the bitterness of despair. But enter with the unexpected tidings that his children live; that, prospered and wealthy, they are yet affectionate; that their hearts still yearn towards their early home and the parent who holds it; that they are even now on their way to soothe and gladden his few remaining days: and although you have made no immediate change in the man's lot — although the hovel is yet dark and cold, and the embers emit but the same dull and saddening light; the whole scene is changed to his eyes, and instead of its former desolateness, it has become radiant with the lustre of his new-found happiness. A new element is poured into his mind, and the faith of your message has changed his whole soul. Is there no reality, no enjoyment in this translation from despondency to hope, from comfortless and unpitied helplessness to the glad expectation of attached and watchful children? Yes; let his lot remain long but what it had been, he feels, and you cannot but feel, that the credence given to your tidings has renewed his youth within him, and thrown a new coloring over the whole scene of squalid poverty that surrounds him. And, if you deny not the reality of the happiness because of the absence or present delay of any outward change, should you dispute the reality of the believer's peace, because as yet he is but the expectant heir, and not the joyous possessor, of a heavenly mansion?

Of a principle thus efficient and delightful, what shall secure the preservation and increase? Divine truth is its aliment, and the Holy Spirit its author and upholder. In the language of scripture it will be observed that the term faith, (as in the instance of the exhortation to contend earnestly for it, as it was once delivered to the saints,) is employed not only in the sense above given, but also to describe a system of doctrines; but it is as the *food* of that spiritual principle which we have endeavored to describe. And as the principle of life, and the mode or means by which it is sustained, may be, and, in common speech, often are confounded; so is the same word used in the New Testament to signify both the truth received, and the temper or habit of mind receiving it. But the two dissimilar ideas are not to be blended; nor are we to suppose that the form of sound doctrine will necessarily insure a living faith in the heart. The experiment, often and anxiously repeated, has ever failed. Creeds and confessions have been adjusted and balanced with the utmost nicety of discrimination, and with the greatest precision of language. But in the church at Geneva, planted and watered by the cares of Calvin and Beza, and in the English Presbyterians, the descendants of the holy non-conformists, it has been but too fully proved, that correct symbols of faith may be inherited from a pious ancestry and for a time be retained with great reverence, but without any portion of the indwelling spirit which once framed and pervaded them. Indeed, in the history of Protestant Germany, it has been found that the fallen and corrupted fragments of a traditionary " form of sound words," have been most prolific in the production of heresies, alike strange and revolting. The fat and heavy soil of an inert and " dead orthodoxy," was to that national church the hot-bed of skepticism, nurturing errors of the rankest growth, and the most deadly nature. The stubble, which had well sustained the former and the proper harvest, but served to enrich the field for an after growth of weeds the most noxious and luxuriant. However useful in its place, (and, properly employed, its usefulness is great,) the most correct and scriptural creed is but the outward and inanimate portraiture of an inward and living faith ; and it is as idle to expect that confessions and symbols, alone and unaided, should create faith, as to imagine that a definition of honesty and benevolence, rigid and accurate, should of itself be sufficient to reform the inmates of our prisons.

"Leviathan is not so tamed."

It is not with such weapons that the enemy is to be vanquished, or a living faith perpetuated from age to age. The affections, no less than the intellect, must be reached and won. The continual interposition of the Holy Spirit, the renewed and personal application of truth to the human conscience, are requisite to attain the end. And it is only from a personal faith, in all her members, thus produced — thus fostered — and continually increasing, that the church can expect prosperity. It is thus that she is to be prepared for conflict with her internal foes, and for the subjugation of new territories to the obedience of the cross. From a faith thus established and made general, what may not be hoped — what conquest shall seem too arduous, and what peril too fearful?

We have seen the dignity of faith and its simplicity; the errors which misrepresent and assail it; its nature; the magnificence of its effects; its necessity and eternity; and the mode of its preservation. It remains now to examine,

II. THE INTIMATE CONNEXION EXISTING BETWEEN THIS FAITH AND THE MISSIONARY EFFORTS OF THE CHURCH.

Having observed that this principle is the source of knowledge, and the parent of motives and feelings to the Christian, it is at once evident that the largeness or the narrowness of the knowledge thus gained, the weakness or the strength of the feelings thus excited, and of the motives which are in this mode implanted, will constantly affect the character of all the Christian's doings, but especially those which depend most upon faith for their inception and completion — his doings in behalf of his impenitent fellow-men.

Upon the *enterprises* of the church, it is immediately apparent, whether the faith of the believers who compose that body is in a state of feebleness and declension, or of energy and growth. He who looks much to the parting commandment of his Lord for the universal proclamation of his truth, and much to the repeated assurance of his Lord that his truth shall prove itself mighty, and his word not return void, will be prepared to hope and to attempt much, in obedience to the commandment and in inheritance of the promise. He, on the contrary, who sees eternity but indistinctly, seldom and afar, and whose faith takes but short and occasional flights into the enduring world of realities that surrounds us, will be prone to exhibit in his plans timidity and despondency, in his efforts remissness and apathy. And if we look to the period when the limits of the church were most rapidly and widely extended, it will be found not the era when the worldly power, the learning and the wealth of the church were at their highest elevation, but in the age when, though lacking all these, by the energy of an overmastering faith, she rose superior to every impediment, and destitute of all earthly aid and encouragement, dared to hope in God. Wise in His wisdom, and strong in His might, she devised her plans of conquest upon the broad and magnificent basis of the Saviour's promises, and then, in humility, diligence, and simple devotion, called upon the Saviour's faithfulness to accomplish the plans His own word had warranted, and His own Spirit incited. And in most of the great revivals of faith and godliness in the modern church, it will be discovered that the rising flood of religious feeling has opened anew, or found and followed the already open channel of missionary enterprise. The revival of religion granted to the early labors of the Puritan fathers in New England, saw also the rise of Eliot and the Mayhews, the first evangelists of our Indians. The energetic faith of Wesley sought for its first field a mission to the savages of our southern coast. The era of Edwards, when the faith and love of the church received so wide and mighty an excitement, was also the era of Brainerd, his friend and disciple, a missionary of the rarest endowments. The revival of faith in Protestant Germany under Francke, Spener, and the Pietists, founded the Orphan House at Halle, and saw go forth from its walls Swartz and others, his associates, to labor amid the heathenism of India. The accession of strength to the faith of the Moravian brethren, by the labors of Zinzendorf, soon found an outlet in missionary enterprises of apostolical simplicity and successfulness. The established church of England, in her recent return to the faith of her early founders, has also been aroused to the cause of missions, and already rejoices in the record of her Heber, her Buchanan, and her Martyn. And in our own division of the Christian host, the energetic labors of the elder Hall, Fuller, and the younger Ryland, to restore to the faith of our churches its proper and practical character, were soon followed by the establishment of those missions, which have given, as we trust, an impulse to the energies of the church that shall go on, with greater extension and deepening intensity, until the time of the Messiah's second advent.

The same increased faith which excites the enterprise, serves withal to multiply the *resources* of the church for the successful development and prosecution of the plans she has formed. Consecration to God of our hearts and our substance will produce a liberality which would, to a lukewarm age, seem fanatical and extravagant. Living as in the constant view of the last judgment; estranged from the world, and thus exempted from the various and costly sacrifices it requires to fashion, to pride, and to luxury; the conscientious frugality of the church would enable the poorest and the richest members to unite in habitual contribution. A simple-hearted faith would banish also from the confines of the church that pretended spirituality which anxiously excludes religion from the scenes of business, and shuts her out from all interference with pecuniary matters, under the pretext of guarding her sanctity, but in truth for the protection of a hidden covetousness. In the better and happier era of her history it is found that religion is a familiar and every-day guest, visiting not the chamber of social or secret prayer and the sanctuary only, but passing through all the scenes of human industry, and shedding over every occupation her mild and hallowing influence. Systematic contribution to every form of religious benevolence, will then be regarded as a necessary mark of true piety. But the chief treasures of the church are not her stores of silver and gold, but her living members, with their spiritual endowments of varied character and grades. And how greatly would a revival of primitive faith draw upon these her spiritual resources, for the supply of the perishing heathen. The missionary cause would not be considered as making well nigh its exclusive appeal to ministers of the church; but the merchant, the artisan, and the farmer, each anxious to give himself to the Lord's service, would present not a stinted tithe of his earnings, but himself, his personal labors, and his life, as an offering to the great work of evangelizing the heathen.

How evident and vast the increase of missionary power given to the church, in the influence of a purer and simpler faith upon her *doctrines*. We have viewed incidentally the errors that usurp the name of Christian faith. When these should have been outgrown and superseded by a true and hearty acceptance of God's whole testimony, how immense the amount of moral power thrown into benevolent action. Again, even where true faith exists, it is now embarrassed in its operations by its union with more or less of error. Every admixture of human tradition, and each addition of extraneous and irrelevant authority, has served but to disfigure and weaken the truth it was intended to adorn. When these cumbrous appendages shall be relinquished, and the oracles of truth shall be consulted more habitually in prayer for the teachings of the Spirit, what may not be hoped from the blessing of that God who is jealous for the honor of His own word? What may not be hoped from the temper and edge of the sword of the Spirit, when it shall have been disencumbered of the scabbard, that has so long served only to conceal and corrode its brightness?

The transition is a natural one from the doctrines of the Gospel to the *motives* which they suggest and sustain. And much aid will have been won for urging onward the cause of the Saviour in heathen lands, when a higher standard of faith shall have trained up the church in greater simplicity of purpose, and in pure and single-hearted desire for the glory of God. How much effort is now lost to the world and the church, because polluted by motives which God cannot deign to bless. When this transparency of purpose shall become prevalent, how strong and general the tendency towards a cordial union of all Christians in the common cause. How much of the time and strength of brethren is now wasted upon unbrotherly divisions. Bigotry and partizanship are dividing those who should never have been sundered. And how much useful and needed power is now withholden, because its possessors are at present unwilling to bestow it, accompanied, as it would be, with an exposure of their personal inferiority. The talent being but one, they deem it but Christian modesty to enwrap and inter it. A faith which shall purge the heart of these base and earth-born feelings, and make the motives of action necessarily more powerful, as they were more simple and pure, would evidently strengthen the aggressive energies of the church for her inroads upon the dominions of spiritual darkness.

The *force of pious example* in the Christian church, as

influencing the world, is yet but scantily developed. But when there should prevail a general union amongst the disciples of our Lord, one of the most common topics of reproach, employed by the world, would be taken away. Affecting, also, as an increase of faith would do, the personal character of each member in the various divisions of the Christian church, what would be the influence of the resplendent and consistent holiness thus cherished, upon the families and dependents, the neighbours and friends of Christians! And this influence would be felt, not merely inviting their coöperation in the missionary alms of the church, but attracting and awakening them to inquiry and repentance, and drawing them into the same bonds of tender and heavenly brotherhood. How much of the reasoning and zeal and energy of the church is now wasted, because counteracted by the lukewarm remissness or the undisguised scandals exhibited in multitudes wearing the Christian name. And when a vigorous and wholesome faith should purify our churches; when the unhealthy and diseased portions should be seen sloughing away under the searching influence of Christian discipline, and the faithfulness of an evangelical ministry; and the church should shine forth in the healthful beauty and symmetry of holiness; what would be the boldness of her advocates, the power of her appeals, and the confusion of her enemies! And all these would be felt immediately in the fields of missionary labor; the Christian mariner, the Christian merchant, and the Christian traveller, would strengthen by a holy example, in the sight of the heathen, the hands of the Christian missionary.

But the most important advantage thus gained, for the cause of our Lord in unevangelized lands, would be the enlarged channel for the communication of the *Divine Influences*. Without faith, it is impossible to please God. Great faith delights, as a weak and narrow faith dishonors and grieves Him. And when the thousands of Israel shall go up with the ardent though humble expectation of receiving an answer to their prayers, whilst the supplications of primitive faith should again ascend, who shall say that the wonders of the early church may not return; and men, in the spirit and power of the early believers, rise up to become the heralds of salvation to the most distant and most brutified tribes of mankind? Assuredly those who shall honor Him by a childlike dependence, would be honored of Him. Then, as the early and the latter rain descended, and when the "fountains of the great deep" of moral power now unemployed, should be broken up from beneath in a wrestling church, and "the windows of heaven" be opened from above by a favoring God; how rapidly would the waters of salvation rise and swell and diffuse themselves, till the knowledge of the Lord should cover the earth,

> "And like a sea of glory
> It spread from pole to pole."

III. From this review of the possible and legitimate fruits of Christian faith, let us turn to its actual results in our midst, that we may learn THE DEFICIENCIES IN OUR FAITH WHICH RETARD THE TRIUMPHS OF CHRISTIAN TRUTH OVER ITS ANTAGONIST ERRORS.

We are accustomed to look abroad to the mass of evil with which the Christian missionary must contend in heathen lands, and to suppose that here are the chief obstacles to his success. The language of the text and the previous considerations brought before you, would lead to the conclusion that this is not the truth. Not in the gorgeous temples, and the costly images, and all the imposing pageantry of idolatry, by which he is environed; not in the wiles and violence of an organized and interested priesthood; not in the deep hold which a false religion has taken upon the arts, and customs, and literature, and every institution, political and social, of the nation; not in any of these, nor in all of them united, is the most formidable resistance to his labors to be found. The stress of battle is in a remoter and unobserved portion of the field. His foes and his hindrances are rather to be sought in the land he has left, and in the very bosom of the church which has commissioned and despatched him. It is because their faith is not increased adequately to sustain him, that his heart languishes, and his soul is faint within him; and while he calls upon the obstinate and besotted pagan before him to repent of his unbelief, he sends back over the intervening ocean, to the churches of his native land, an appeal not less earnest and yet more touching, that they too repent of the poverty and pettiness of their faith, and that they enlarge him in his labors according to the apostolic rule, and upon the primitive model.

The existence of such deficiencies in our faith is painfully evident, in the inadequacy of the *views* which that faith ministers, of the *external fruits* which it produces, and of the *internal spirit* which it breathes; or in its influence upon the intellect, the conduct and the affections.

1. The views with which their faith furnishes the majority of those attached to our churches, are then singularly inadequate with regard to the *miseries of the world.* Of the fearful condition of the vast mass of our race, the hundreds of millions ignorant or neglectful of the Gospel, we think little and inquire still less. Of temporal suffering — of the anguish which ignorance, vice, and unrestrained passion are working merely for this life, how immense is the amount; for gross darkness covers the nations, and the dark places of the earth are necessarily and ever full of the habitations of cruelty. How fatal is the influence upon human happiness, even for the few days of our earthly career, of vice, not merely legalized, but sanctified and deified in the national idols, as we find it under every form of paganism. But what is even this, compared to the hopeless and unending woe into which death shall hurl the tribes of heathenism. And yet those, who thus, whilst groaning under present misery, work out fiercer sufferings for eternity, are our brethren, like us fallen and vicious, but like us, immortal and accountable. Of this fearful wretchedness our perception is indistinct and transient. We have no deep and abiding conviction of the evil of sin, and the necessary misery of its captives.

There is equal deficiency in our views of the *promises of Scripture.* How large a portion of prophecy is given to the glories of the Messiah's kingdom! They occupy a prominent room and large space in the brief form of supplication given by our Saviour to his disciples. Redolent as these promises are of the most delightful hopes, how seldom do we remember, and how faintly plead them; though the kingdoms of the world shall become the kingdoms of God's Son, the Gentiles shall be his inheritance, and the uttermost parts of the earth are his assured possession.

> Come then, and, added to thy many crowns,
> Receive yet one, the crown of all the earth,
> Thou who alone art worthy!—
> The very spirit of the world is tired
> Of its own taunting question, asked so long,
> "Where is the promise of your Lord's approach?"
> Come then, and, added to thy many crowns,

> Receive yet one, as radiant as the rest,
> Due to thy last and most effectual work,
> Thy word fulfilled, the conquest of a world.

Nor are our views more just and complete as to *our own obligations* and vows. Although our entrance upon the course of Christian profession was by devoting ourselves to the service of the Lord, and having given ourselves to Him, we gave ourselves into the church by His will; has not the dedication been forgotten, or practically revoked by too many of our number? The lights of the earth, — we are shedding around but a dim, flickering, and uncertain lustre. The salt of the world, — who has perceived in us the savor of Christian vitality?

But especially do our views assume the appearance of meagre insufficiency, in the estimate they afford of the *peculiar opportunities of the age* for Christian usefulness. "Ye hypocrites," exclaimed our Lord, "can ye not discern the signs of the times?" Are the larger number of Christians at all awake to the fact, that the signs of our times call upon the believers of the nineteenth century for unprecedented exertions? The advance of popular freedom and general education, the unrestrained commercial intercourse of nations, the wide-spread peace now enjoyed, the improved speed and lessened expense of travelling, the newly-developed powers of the press, the powers each day more apparent of voluntary associations, the extensive and daily extending use of the language we have inherited from England, and which is now becoming intelligible in the chief maritime ports of the world — all require at the hands of American Christians no ordinary exertions. The daily enlargements of the mission field, and the success of truth's first onset upon the powers of darkness, are summoning us most impressively to action. The institutions of Hindooism, of such vaunted antiquity, and rooted in the veneration of ages, seem already tottering to their overthrow, ere the generation is gone from the earth that first sapped their base. The barrier which long closed the vast empire of China is now found to be but the brittle seal of an imperial edict, unsustained by the national feelings. The word of God, as recently translated and published in languages never before taught the name of JEHOVAH, is calling for the living preacher to scatter and to interpret it. Amid all these omens of good and incentives to diligence, are we found awake to the fact, or conscious of the majesty and splendor of the scenes now opening? On the contrary, is not the church protracting her slumbers, while the whole heaven above her is reddening with the dawn of that day, which shall usher in her restoration and the redemption of all the earth?

But the most afflictive defect in our views, is the slight and irreverent estimate we form of our *Divine Ally*. The King of kings is our intercessor, the Omniscient Spirit is our teacher; and we are invited to counsel with Divine Wisdom, and to stay ourselves on the arm of Creative Power. Yet how do we narrow down the magnificence of the Divine promises, and compress the hopes, large and grand, offered by the gospel, into some petty and pitiful request, that, as we imagine, bespeaks Christian humility, but in truth displays contemptuous unbelief. What! when God is for us, is it not most guilty to hesitate and linger in minor and facile enterprises? What would have been thought of him whose memory we are wont to hail as the Father of his country, if, when joined by the fleets and army of our foreign ally, he had gathered the combined hosts to the siege of some petty barrack, garrisoned by a few disbanded invalids? The greatness of the God we serve, demands on our part a large and manly, a far-sighted and far-reaching faith.

2. The same odious discrepancy between its privileges and doings, its powers and its results, is seen in the *external fruits* of our faith, or its influence upon the conduct. In the prayers of the church, as offered in her solemn assemblies, is there the due and earnest remembrance of the missionary laborer, who has, like Jonathan and his armor-bearer, clambered up into the high places of heathenism, and finds himself alone in the very midst of the enemy? In the Monthly Concert, that touching union which brings the Christians of every hue, and language, and kindred, into one assembly, and blends their hearts in the utterance of one petition, is the meeting maintained with that general and devout attendance demanded by the beauty of its conception and the grandeur of its object? Of the alms of the church — how pitiful the amount compared with the free and glad sacrifices made on the altars of dissipation and intemperance, in games of chance, in fashionable equipages, furniture, and dress, in the support of the theatre, the race-course, and the lottery, in the extravagance of our tables, and the sumptuousness of our homes.

Of that which is given, how much is the niggardly parings of a plentiful income. We have begun by devoting to God the choicest of the herd and the firstlings of the flock; and have finished by laying on His altars but the offals of the victim. In our labors and our sacrifices for the cause of God, how rarely is found the noble disinterestedness, or the humble and retiring generosity that distinguished the faith of the primitive times. But, above all, is there not need of a wide and deep renovation throughout the mass of our churches, ere the standard of personal holiness can be deemed at all comparable with that which sprung from faith, as apostles preached it, and as its first confessors received it?

3. The *internal spirit* which it breathes, was spoken of as betraying a deficiency in the faith of modern believers. If love to man be the second great commandment of the Scriptures, is it sufficiently awakened within us, and in proportion to the dignity which revelation has thus assigned it? But in love to God, in anxiety for continued communion with Him, and deepening conformity to His image, in desire for the honor of His name, are we not verily guilty of a fearful deficiency, and needs not our faith immediate renovation and increase? Have we that intense fear and abhorrence of sin which a lively faith ever displays? The confidence of the faithful anciently inspired them with a holy and dauntless courage, as they faced and rebuked the world. Is ours thus operative? Theirs was a humility, which, springing from conscious weakness, clung the more closely to God, and amid the largest success, resigned to Him the undivided glory; is our faith thus lowly in its spirit and tendency? The voice of inspiration has said, " If any man have not the spirit of Christ, he is none of his." Is the faith, in the possession of which we exult, thus attended and verified? Have we been fashioned into his likeness and imbibed his temper? Is ours the life of cross-bearing and watchfulness and prayerfulness? if not, is it a life of discipleship to Christ — is it the race of faith, swift, direct, and onward? and shall it win at last the crown of the triumphant believer?

Church of the living God, is there not utterly a fault amongst us in this matter? And until our faith increase, can we hope that, according to the rule of Paul's apostolic labors, the destitute Gentiles should be evangelized? Is not an enlargement now demanded and now due in the labors, prayers, and alms that go to sustain the cause of Christian missions? and what but the renovation of faith shall work that enlargement? Let us not contrast our sacrifices and zeal merely with those of the Master whose name we bear, and whom we have avouched as our Great Exemplar: let us but measure our endeavors, in their number, and in the prudence, liberality, and perseverance that mark them, with the efforts and spirit of the men of this world, who are without hope and without God. Yielding up the comforts of home and the society of friends, forswearing ease, periling character, lavishing life, and venturing even upon eternal ruin, as they do, the walks of this world's business and of this world's pleasures are strewed with the voluntary and costly sacrifices of time, property, comfort, life, and salvation. But we, with a soul to save, a heaven to lose or win, a Christ to publish, and a God to serve — how shamefully calm are we found, and timid and half-hearted! And this, while the world is rushing into ruin, and bearing on its swollen and rapid stream our friends, our neighbors, and our children; — while the earth which God has promised to bless, (and that by human instrumentality,) lies as yet, prostrate and groaning, under the curse poured out through all her coasts. The time is coming, and prophecy has foretold it, when in every land there shall be offered to God a pure offering — when, from the closet and the sanctuary, from the hill-top, the field, and the forest-side, where the children of God shall, like Isaac, walk forth at eventide to meditate, the voice of pious supplication shall ascend in one continuous stream; until our globe, as it rolls along its orbit, shall seem but a censer revolving in the hand of the Great High Priest, and pouring out at every aperture a cloud, dense and rich, of incense, fragrant and grateful to God. But, as yet, the ascending cloud is one of far other kind. Its skirts are dark with sullen gloom, and its bosom is charged with indignation and vengeance. Wailing and blasphemy, oppression and outrage, pollution and falsehood, have swollen and blackened it; and with it, a cry goes up, like that from the cities of the plain, piercing the ear of God. Day unto day uttereth speech of human wretchedness, and night unto night sheweth knowledge of human wickedness. What has *our* faith, my brethren, done for its relief? What will be the fruits of our belief in the alms and the prayers now demanded; what its share in the services of this assembly? Shall we not exclaim, reviewing the greatness of the task, on the one hand, and, on the other, the greatness of the guilt which has neglected it, as did the apostles, whilst their Lord was enjoining a duty alike necessary and difficult, "LORD, INCREASE OUR FAITH."

THE CROSS.

BY
REV. RICHARD FULLER, D. D.

And I, if I be lifted up from the earth, will draw all men unto me.—JOHN 12: 32.

THAT is a singular account given by Eusebius of the conversion of Constantine. He was marching, says the historian, at the head of his army from France, to encounter his rival Maxentius in a conflict, upon the issue of which his empire depended. Oppressed with anxiety, he prayed that some God would aid him; when, in the heavens and higher than the sun, a luminous cross appeared, emblazoned with these words: "*By this sign thou shalt conquer.*" He did conquer; and ever after the cross was displayed as the banner of the Cæsars.

The truth of this narrative I, of course, shall not now examine. It is certain, Fathers and Brethren, and all important for us to recollect, that, in the noble enterprise in which we are engaged, there is but one standard which can be upreared successfully — but one banner which, star-like, must flame above our ranks, and lead us on to victory — and that this is the Cross, — the Cross of our Lord Jesus Christ.

How exactly to the subject in hand is the prediction uttered by a prophet, and cited by Paul in the fifteenth chapter of Romans. "In that day there shall be a root of Jesse, which shall stand for an ensign of the people; to it shall the Gentiles seek." And although it is probable that Isaiah himself did not comprehend "what the spirit of Christ which was in him did signify," (for a cross! a gallows! — even upon the vision of that most rapt of all the Seers of Israel, could *this* have streamed as an ensign for man's deliverance — for the gathering and disenthralling of the nations?) yet we, my brethren, understand the prophecy and its fulfilment.

The very act, indeed, of the crucifixion, and the hour, furnished remarkable proof, or rather a significant type and adumbration, of the influence which the cross would exert. On that day and witnessing that spectacle, were present, in truth, the very "all men"— that is, all classes of men — to whom the text refers; and observe the effect on them. In the Roman centurion, behold a representative of the intellectual and skeptical; and what is the effect on him? He is convinced; he "feared greatly, saying truly this was the Son of God." In the multitude, remark the careless and thoughtless; and what are their emotions? Roused and agitated, they leave the spot, " smiting heavily on their breasts." And in that poor thief — in his conscious guilt, his penitence, his imploring cry for help, and the answer which at once dispels his fears, and sheds joy throughout his soul, and opens to him the gates of Paradise — see there the influence of the cross upon a sinner, its power to stir, and then to hush, the guilty clamor within.

Behold the might of the cross, as exhibited in the very act of the crucifixion, and on that memorable day when the Saviour was lifted up. But was this power confined to that time, and to that place? No, my brethren. As Paul said to the Galatians who had heard the Gospel, "Jesus Christ hath been evidently set forth crucified among you," although Galatia was some hundreds of miles distant from Calvary, — so, wherever the gospel is now preached to a people, there the Saviour is set forth lifted up among that people, and there the same influence will be felt, the same potency exerted. Still it is true, (and I here indicate the subject and division of my whole discourse) still it is true, that whatever the intellect of a man, there is an argument in the cross to convince him; whatever the heedlessness of a man, there is an energy in the cross to rouse him; in fine, whatever his guilt, there is in the cross a magnetism to draw, and a magic to change, and a mystery to save him. Let us resume these thoughts. I beg you, my hearers, to honor me with all your attention. And, "O Thou that hearest prayer," vouchsafe me the adorable succors of thy grace, and hasten the time when "unto Thee shall all flesh come!" Amen.

I am going to consider the cross, in the first place, simply as an argument; and recollect, the Saviour himself declares that one object of his mission and death was the assertion and establishment of the truth. It was just before he died upon the cross that he said, "To this end was I born, and for this cause came I into the world, that I should bear witness to the truth." And the apostle represents the "truth in Jesus" as the only truth that can really master the intellect of man, and make him wise unto salvation, because this alone converts speculation into certainty, and substitutes assurance as to eternal things, for those vague and confused and unsettled conjectures which may exist in truth out of Jesus, but are wholly incompetent and ineffectual.

Only "the truth as it is in Jesus" will avail, says the apostle, and with reason. Why, just reflect for a moment — just consider, my brethren, what it is the gospel requires in calling us to be Christians. It is to immolate self — it is to be divorced from the world, to renounce the world, to be crucified to the world.———Renounce the world! be crucified to the world! And of whom is this required? — of angels? — of beings all soul, all spirit? — by no means; — of men — of beings carrying within them a thousand appetites, a thousand passions, a thousand propensities, and around whom are strewed, from their cradles to their graves, objects most seductive, and solicitations most refined and delicate. All these inclinations must be subdued, all these importunities repelled, all these fascinations surmounted. And for what? What does the gospel propose in their place? Things unseen, a world buried in the darkness of futurity; objects which eye hath not seen, nor ear heard, neither hath it entered into the heart of man to conceive.

Now I need not tell you, that against this sweeping demand of the gospel there is not a taste or affection in the natural heart but will rise up in resistance. No language can convey more forcibly the idea of violence, of a painful and protracted struggle, than the very expression "crucified to the world." And nothing is more proper, then, than that the mind insist upon conclusive evidence as to these objects which are to "overcome" and displace the world. From what source, however, can this evidence be derived? From our senses? They give us no sort of information as to such things. From our reason? We feel that this is inadequate. From the books of philosophers? But, besides that their lessons are such subtilties as the multitude could never understand,* the truth is, the philosophers themselves felt but little confidence in their own reasonings. Socrates, when dying, said, "I am going out of the world and you remain in it, but which is better is known only to God. I hope," continued the old man, "I hope there is something reserved for us after death." Cicero confesses himself unable to decide any thing here; and introduces one complaining "that while he was reading the arguments for immortality, he felt convinced, but as soon as he laid aside his books, his belief was gone." And Seneca well remarks, that "the philosophers rather promised, than proved an existence beyond the tomb."

But if the testimony of the senses, and the decisions of reason, and the systems of philosophy, are impotent for the extirpation of our earthly preferences and passions, where can we find that conviction which shall possess the ascendant power? Only in the truth as it is in Jesus. The cross is the only argument; but it is an argument all-sufficient — an argument so conclusive that no power of intellect can refute it, and so simple that there is no ignorance which cannot comprehend it.

Yes, my brethren, Jesus Christ "brings life and immortality to light." He comes, "a witness to the people," "to bear witness to the truth." And he supports his doctrines by his life, and vindicates them by his miracles. Bring forth, he says, your sick, your blind, your lame, and your dead; and at his bidding, the sick are restored to health, the blind receive their sight, the lame walk, and the dead are raised to life. These were sufficient attestations, ample credentials, and ought to have satisfied all. These, however, did not satisfy the Jews. They ask another, and, as they themselves admitted, a conclusive testimony; and he gives even that. He seals his doctrines with his blood. And while evil men and evil angels are exulting in the seeming extinction of the truth, he bursts the bands which held him, and, rising, stamps upon that truth the broad bright signet of Deity confessed;— of a God who could not only bend to his will and at a word the hidden mysteries and ministries of nature, but could invade the pale dominions of Death himself, and grappling

---

* It was expressly taught by the Platonists, that none but the philosopher living in meditation could attain to the spiritual knowledge of religion. To him pertained the ἐπιστήμη; the people must be satisfied with the δόξα, a compound of falsehood and truth. Hence the distinction between the esoteric and exoteric religion.

there, and in his grave-clothes, with the tyrant, could tear the black diadem from his brow, and wrench from him his cruel sceptre, and shiver at a blow his skeleton empire, and plant his bruised heel in disdain upon the prostrate monster who sought to detain him captive.

O yes, dying and standing a mighty conqueror over the tomb, the Redeemer graves as with sunbeams the proof of his doctrines. It is impossible now to doubt. If ever incredulity was personified, and skepticism incarnate, it was in those men who witnessed the Saviour's miracles, and who crucified him; but, by his death and resurrection, Jesus in a most illustrious manner accomplished even the sign, and achieved even the argument which they demanded. Of that death and that resurrection I will not stop here to marshal the array of evidence. They are facts incontestable; and if any man doubt, I cut the matter short with that man — he has never examined the subject. No honest mind can examine and not confess the impregnable stability of the truth. It is of great moment, however, to remark, that these facts being proved, the demonstration they furnish is precisely as conclusive to us, as to those who witnessed them; for we believe, and they could do no more. The demonstration is the same to us, and wherever the Gospel goes. The truths the Saviour preached are equally proved, the doctrines equally established.

But these truths thus certain — these doctrines thus established — what becomes of the world, with all its attractions? How is it dwarfed! How are all sublunary splendors eclipsed, shined into darkness; — and all mortal glories withered, dimmed, shrunk, and spurned into contempt! Ye charms, ye flatteries, ye fascinations of earth, what are ye? Ye pleasures, ye riches, ye grandeurs, to which men crawl and before which they prostrate themselves, what are ye? Come, let me estimate you now, let me see your worth, let me institute a comparison. . . . . . But, my brethren, is this necessary? Ah! do not your hearts already feel the force of the argument? What! will ye compare the deceitful pleasures of sin to the "fullness of joy which is in God's presence?" What! will ye prefer the stinted and polluted drops here to the torrents, the rivers of delight which are "at his right hand?" "What! will ye lie down in hell and become a prey to devils, for the gratification of a vile passion? All pomps and glories of this world, — are they worthy to be compared to "the glory which shall be revealed in us," "the exceeding," "the more exceeding," "the far more exceeding and eternal weight of glory?" To "see God;"—to "be changed into the same image;"—to "go to Mount Zion, to the city of the living God, to the heavenly Jerusalem;"—no more to know sin, and sickness, and pain, and sorrow;—to be forever united to saints, and cherubim, and seraphim, shouting "Alleluia, Salvation, and glory, and honor, and power, unto the Lord our God, while the four and twenty elders fall down and answer, Alleluia;"—to burn with their ardors;—to satiate the soul with their ecstacies;—to be with Christ;—to behold his glory;—to follow the Lamb whithersoever he goeth;—to look into his face;—to gaze upon his glorified form, and to think that every vein in that body bled for me;—to be ravished with his smiles;—to fall at his feet;—to cling there—to live there. . . . . My God! where is the world now? What is it worth? Yonder, yonder is a world for which the Christian Alexander may well weep—yonder it is all radiant with the gold and glowing with the sapphire! But this world—this world which so dazzles and intoxicates us—this clay world, with its clay honors, and clay pleasures, and clay riches—Ah! Lord, how little were eternal objects worthy of the strife, if no better than such a world. And how foolish are we, my dear hearers, is there a spark of reason in us, when we love this world; when we refuse to immolate this world; when we hesitate to gather all this world contains, and trample it in the dust, that we may spring upward and heavenward and grasp the undecaying glory, honor, and immortality set before us in the gospel.

Such is our argument; an argument convincing, and, as I said, of equal power in all ages and to all men. Wherever a preacher or a missionary goes — he may be a weak man, an unlearned man — but he goes armed with this, and by this he will conquer. Christ "lifted up" will be an argument to do what no reasoning, no philosophy can do — an argument high as heaven, and deep as hell, and against which no sophistry of earth, no subtlety of the Devil can avail. The proudest intellect will confess its conclusiveness; and the feeblest, that of the African and the untutored Burman, will rejoice in its majestic simplicity. This is our first article.

But, my brethren, (and I pass here to our second division,) my brethren and fathers, were it doing any thing, think you, to preach Christ crucified, if the cross were only an argument? Were it not utter ignorance of man, to suppose that any demonstration will disenchant him of the world? Why, the argument may be overwhelming, and the evidence establish a certainty — but what then? What is all this to one who will not listen to the argument, who will not weigh the evidence? What, in truth, my brethren, is the great difficulty we find in our hearers — and which the missionary, too, encounters in his? Is it to convince men who are awakened to eternal things? By no means; — that were easy. No, it is indifference, it is apathy. It is, that men are buried in the deep repose and lethargy of nature; that they are sepulchred in the senses. It is, that in the polite, we have to do with hearts turned into artificial frost-work; and in the sensual, with souls stupefied and imbruted; in short, that all are earth-struck — and that is worse than being moon-struck — that the care of the passions, the dissipations of pleasure, and the more fatal dissipations of business — its ceaseless urgencies and activities — engross the mind, and leave, as to eternity, only a heedlessness and listlessness as universal as they are strange and deplorable.

This is the grand difficulty. And, now, what expedient, what engine can be effectual for salvation which does not meet this? But what can meet it? What can rouse men from this fatal unconcern and callousness? The instrumentality, my brethren, to accomplish this work is still the same — it is the cross; the power is still in the same object, — the Saviour lifted up from the earth. It is idle to talk about what ought to influence us. The simple fact is, that preaching Christ crucified is God's ordinance to stir the souls of men, nor has it ever failed. Whatever the heedlessness of a man, there is in the cross an energy to rouse him, a power which ever has been, and ever will be acknowledged. This is the second proposition I advanced, and one which does not appear to me to require any proof. Why, look at history ; — I appeal to facts ; — I appeal to the thousands of all nations, ages, sexes, temperaments, and conditions, who have confessed this energy of the cross, and yielded to it. And if there be, in all this uncounted assembly, one who has never felt any thing while a bleeding Jesus has been lifted before him, then I know nothing of the human heart; let him stand up, — I wish to look at him; he is more or less than man.

Never felt any thing! but it is impossible, — I know better.

No, my brethren, hardened a man may be; he may have a heart of stone, of steel; he may glory in his obduracy; but if he has ever listened to that tale of love and sorrow, he has not been wholly unmoved. No, No, No, it cannot be! We have amongst us a class of people, who are always crying out — "No excitement, we do not want excitement in religion." Very well, let them get a preacher who knows nothing of Christ crucified in the heart, and says nothing of Christ crucified in the pulpit, and he will walk at their head, and lead them quietly and comfortably enough down to hell. The cross will excite. It is the most restless and resistless of agitators. No sooner was it erected, than all nature felt and confessed its instigations. The earth heaved, the veil of the temple was rent from the top to the bottom, it agitated the rocks, it shook the sheeted dead from their slumbers, and disturbed the sun himself. Nor hath it lost its power. I care not what the man is; let him be ever so desperate and wrapt in marble; let him be invulnerable to the most terrifying denunciations, and inaccesible to the most touching remonstrance; let vice fix her gorgon eye upon him, until he be petrified and frozen into flint;— I care not. He may be proof against all else; but when this tear-compelling story is unfolded, when there is mustered before him all the tempest which beat upon that sacred head, and all the love which welcomed that tempest for poor man — O, he will not, he cannot be proof against that!

True, he may bid away the holy feeling, he may quench it and perish. But he goes down, carrying with him the bitter recollection, that he had been there — in that world, that planet — where the cross was, and had been touched by it as by a wand. He may stifle the hallowed movement, but it will cost him a struggle, and, for the moment at least, the rock will be smitten, and the heart will gush, and the unbidden tear will tell that all is not yet quite lost.

No, brethren, the unparalleled phenomenon exhibited on Calvary, eighteen hundred years ago, can never die, can never grow old; and wheresoever that is proclaimed, there men's hearts will be shaken; the strings long silent will be swept by an unseen hand; the wells long sealed hermetically will be opened, and the waters stirred to their inmost depths. I know not why it was, that when the body of a dead man was let down into the cave, and touched the bones of the long buried prophet, it was quickened into life. But I do know, that whenever this truth descends into the bosom — the conscience may have been long dead, shrouded and entombed in adamant — yet its potency will revive at the contact, and the word, although sown in weakness, will be felt to be an active and powerful thing, instinct with vitality and vigor. Nor when I speak thus, when I affirm this so confidently, am I at all regarding the ability of the preacher, though that is important. Nor do I refer even to the invisible workings of the Spirit, though these, I am aware, are indispensable. I am well aware, my brethren, nor can we too constantly bear in mind, that it is the office of the Holy Ghost to apply the atonement. I know that, as in creation this glorious Agent brooded over the elements, and wrought out, from discord and darkness, light and harmony and loveliness, causing the shapeless mass to burst into effloresence and beauty, — so, now, it is his, to move plastically over the chaos of principles, affections, and hearts, disorganized and left in confusion and ruin by the shock of the fall, and to reduce them back, and refashion them to order and holiness, and thus become the author of the new creation. All this I know. But I allude not at present to this. The energy asserted by the text, and of which I speak, is that of the cross, and in the cross itself.

And, now, what if I were unable to account for this energy? What if I should just say, that there is an electric chain which binds our ruined race to the wonderful being who hangs there in our likeness? We are told that if two lutes, of the same form, and tuned exactly in unison, be in the same room, and one be struck into melody, the other, though untouched by mortal minstrelsy, will own a kindred sympathy, and give out soft and gentle murmurs. And what if I should only tell you that something like this takes place; — that when Jesus Christ assumed our form, and entered this world, and was smitten for us, there was a mystery in his pangs which should forever cause the sensibilities of human hearts to vibrate, and waken the play of feelings tender and unearthly? What if I should use the idea of an apostle, and say, that, in becoming man, Jesus Christ took not on him the *individual*, but the *nature;* and that — as by this assumption he finished an atonement sufficient for the whole world, and became in this sense " the Saviour of all men," and the sins of all thronged, and crowded, and gathered, and pressed, in crushing and excruciating weight, upon the sufferer — so, by the same union, there goes forth, — there is sent back and abroad and into men's souls, wherever a crucified Redeemer is preached among them, — an effluence, a sensation, a sympathy, thrilling and irresistible? What if I should only say this — and the Scriptures would bear me out — it were enough.

But, really, my brethren, all mystery apart, is it strange that the cross is invested with a power to rouse and shake the soul? Strange! is not the marvel this — not that men are moved — but that all are not instantly melted and subdued by it? Why, let men be only men, let them only have pulses that beat and hearts that throb, and this simple announcement, "*God so loved the world, that he gave his only begotten son, that whosoever believeth on him should not perish, but have everlasting life*" — O! the very thought is colossal, it is overmastering, and language droops under it — tell me, can this be received with coldness and indifference? is it supposable, is it possible? And, then, the amazing consummation — the Deed! the Deed! the Deed! the tragedy of which this earth was the theatre, while angels gazed confounded, and the hierarchies of heaven bent from their seats in silent astonishment, and Deity itself, I had almost said, must for once have been absorbed, for once have had all its universal regards and expatiations arrested, and fixed, and concentrated, — that deed — that spectacle — can that be viewed with apathy?

What! my brethren, that "the Word was made flesh" — that "the Ancient of days" was cradled as an infant — that He, "by whom and for whom all things were created," stooped to poverty and shame; — are *these* things to be heard and to have no influence? That, for us men and our salvation, "the brightness of the Father's glory," he who "thought it no robbery to be equal with God," emptied himself, and took upon him "the form of a servant," and terminoted upon a gibbet a life of pain, and tears, and blood, — O Jesus! IS THIS TRUE? Can I believe *this* and be unmoved? Can *this* fail to bow my soul, and wipe out every record from my heart, and live there alone, the one, single, all-controlling impression, stamped in to the very core, and moulding every fibre to itself? Who is surprised at what a distinguished missionary relates? He was sent among the Indians, and he preached to them with all his earnestness, of God, his power, his grandeur, and his glory; but they turned away and laughed at him. Why, they had heard far nobler sermons on these subjects than man could utter. They had sat down by day amid the wild pomp of their mountains, and the sublime silence of their forests; and at night had looked up at the pavement of unfading fire above their heads. They had listened to the rushing of the cataract, — "deep calling unto deep,"— and to the music of the tempest, and the cry of the hurricane. Before their eyes the lightning's fiery flood had rifted the sturdy oak; and hoarse and strong had thundered on beneath them the might of the earthquake. They had heard THESE preach, and they preached of God in tones which mocked the puny articulations of human eloquence. And now, that the white man should come to tell them that there is a God, and that this God is great, and powerful, and glorious . . . . they spurned at him in hardness and derision. Baffled in his first effort, the missionary changed his address, and proclaimed a crucified Jesus. He opened his Bible, and read to them those words " God so loved the world that he gave his only begotten Son that whosoever believeth in him should not perish but have everlasting life "—" God spared not his own Son but delivered him up for us all." Nor did he preach in vain now. The gaze of his audience was at once fastened. They were astonished at the doctrine, and their hearts were at once touched. As the speaker went on with "the faithful saying and worthy of all acceptation," as he led them from scene to scene of the Saviour's humiliation and sorrow,— from the manger to the garden, and from the garden to the judgment hall — smothered sobs and murmurs began to be heard; until at last, when he brought them to the cross, and showed them, nailed there, the abused and suffering Son of God, and said,—" All this for you,—these tears, these groans, this blood for you!"—the poor savages could refrain no longer; they had stood all else, but they could not stand this: they exclaimed " Is this true? Is this true?" and lifted up their voices and wept aloud.

 Sirs, sirs, men call me an enthusiast, but I ask you is not enthusiasm cold common sense here? "What a pity," cried the Roman, "that we have but one life for our country." Which of you but exclaims this night, what a pity we have not a thousand hearts for such a Saviour — a thousand hearts, and every one of them a holocaust, a whole burnt offering, a sacred conflagration of gratitude and devotion.

 Nor is it only the overcoming fact of the humiliation and

crucifixion of the Son of God that gives such power to the cross. From it what overwhelming truths flash out on a guilty world, as from a blazing, focal, radiating central-point. The cross! what an exhibition does it give of the value of the soul! The cross! what an admonition there of the miseries of the damned! Devouring flames, chains of darkness, howlings of despair, I need you not — the cross where Jesus bleeds to save us gives me a more terrific idea of hell than you can. The cross! what an awful lustre does it pour upon the justice, the holiness, and the severity of God! Above all, the love of God — how dazzlingly, with what surpassing brightness, does not that shine there — sending a heavenly effulgence all over this dark world, down even to the gates of hell! I ask again, can this cross be viewed with indifference? Is it strange that the cross has power to rouse and stir the heart? Is not this the wonder, not that men are shaken, but that all are not melted and mastered by the very first announcement of a crucified Redeemer; and that whenever and wherever this truth is proclaimed, the scenes of Pentecost are not renewed, and the place is not a Bochim, drenched with bursting tears rained thickly out of full hearts? A philosopher, and not of the worst school either, has declared "it is impossible to love God." For my part, when I look at the cross, I say how is it possible not to love God; not to call, with the Psalmist, upon heaven and earth, upon our souls and all within us, to love and praise Him; and, with Andrew Fuller, to find our hearts forever breaking out into unknown strains of love, and our lips — go where we will — still singing

"O for this love let rocks and hills
Their lasting silence break,
And all harmonious human tongues
The Saviour's praises speak?"

I ought now, my brethren, to enter upon our last article, and, having exhibited the cross as an argument and a motive, to present it in its most glorious aspect, as the wonder-working power of God in converting and saving the vilest. I am not ashamed, however, to confess that I have undertaken too much. Ashamed! if Paul, if Gabriel were in this pulpit, they would make the same confession. I have no ability to execute what I proposed, and were I foolish enough to make the attempt, a failure would not only be inevitable, but I should glory in it. "Young man," replied a great poet to one who asked him, "What is genius?"—"young man, if you have never felt it, I cannot tell you what it is." But if this be true of the inspirations of genius, with how much greater truth may I affirm, as to the transforming omnipotence of the cross, that those of you who know it not by experience, can never comprehend it by explanation. Say what I might, Christ crucified, while it is "unto them that are called, the power of God, and the wisdom of God," will be "to the Jews a stumbling block, and to the Greeks foolishness;" and, after all, you would only exclaim, "Ah, Lord God, doth he not speak parables?" Any terms I might use, although the very phraseology of the Bible, would be to the men of the world among you, only a mystical and unintelligible jargon. And to you, my brethren, what could I say, which you would not feel had been better left unsaid? I was much affected, not long since, in a distant city, by the words of an humble individual. We were receiving him into the church, and he was telling us, as well as he could, in his homely but strong language, of the change wrought in him. At length he stopped, and, looking at me with a countenance expressive of the deepest emotion, observed, "Sir, I cannot speak what I feel; God, sir, has not given a poor man like me the power to talk of this thing." My brethren, this is all I can say on our present article, God has not given a poor man like me the power to talk on this thing. It is this, my hearers, which makes the cross what it is — this, which gives it an efficacy imperial and peerless — this, that it is not only a demonstration to convince the mind, and a talisman to kindle the heart, but "the power of God" to the salvation of the soul. Here is the great thing, the grand attraction, the might, the majesty, the sweet though awful mystery of the cross. But here is just the thing that passeth man and angel. I say again, and the more I think the more I repeat it, what can mortal utterance do here? Where among you is the Christian who has not anticipated my remark, that this topic must be felt, and is matter for faith, not speculation.

That for a lost world there is but one remedy, and this a specific, we know. We know that where Christ crucified is not preached, nothing is done for eternity. Much there may be of sublimity and beauty in the orations of the pulpit; but if Christ crucified be not there — while the imagination may be entertained — all will be to the soul only the beauty of frost, and the sublimity of the desert. This we know. But how the cross exerts this power in conversion, who can explain? The emblem of the brazen serpent teaches us that the influence is inscrutable; and what can we say but this, that the cross is God's appointment to do this thing,— it is God's ordinance to do this thing. Look at Saul of Tarsus! What aileth him there at the gate of Damascus? What is this internal and spiritual revelation of a crucified Saviour, ("in me," as he says,) which in a moment transfixes that proud and haughty fire-soul, and beats him to the ground, and wrings from him the cry, "Lord, what wilt thou have me to do;" and, rivetting his gaze on a single object, sends him through the world exclaiming, "God forbid that I should glory save in the cross of our Lord Jesus Christ;"— who can tell what this is? Go to Corinth! What is this power at work in the church there, which, while the cross is lifted up, cleaves the bosom of that stranger who has come into the assembly, perhaps through curiosity, perhaps to scoff, and causes that unbelieving man to fall upon his face, awed, struck down by the manifestation to himself of the secrets of his heart, and there to worship, and adore, and, departing thence, to proclaim the presence of Jehovah in the congregation? Who can explain this? And who can say what is that mystery which, at a single look, can soften and disarm the most inveterate enmity; can unlock, as with a key — a spell, the soul, and untwist all the links which chain it in icy hardness, and break up all the springs and deep fountains of tenderness, and penitence, and love, and cause men to "look on him whom they have pierced and mourn as one mourneth for an only son, and be in bitterness as one who is in bitterness for his first-born?" What is all this? I know not. It is a subject, not for discussion, but adoration. My brethren, I know not; I only say, "not of the will of the flesh, nor of the will of man, but of God." I know not; I only know, (hosannas to God for this! O, cross, cross of my bleeding Lord, may I meditate on thee more, may I feel thee more, may I resolve to know nothing but thee,) I only know it is so. "Then he stood awhile, and looked, and wondered, for it seemed surprising that the sight of a cross should so affect him. He looked, therefore, and looked again, until the springs in his head sent the waters down his cheeks." Such is the simple, but beautiful language of Bunyan — language that finds an echo in many a heart here; and I have only to wave my hand thus, for hundreds in this house to stand up and tell, with starting tears, of this mystery, this unsearchable wonder of the cross. Nor only you. Thousands in other lands, thousands of the heathen, who were yesterday enveloped in guilt and wretchedness, are to-day telling of this power of the cross, and looking, and wondering, and looking again, until their swelling hearts run over, and the floods roll down their cheeks. Yes, O yes, thou wondrous cross! and might a sinner who cannot preach of thee, be permitted to testify, I too, O my God, ("my soul hath it still in remembrance and is humbled in me,") I too, unworthy as I am, could speak.

"In evil long I took delight,
 Unawed by shame or fear,
Till a new object struck my sight,
 And stopped my wild career.

I saw one hanging on a tree
 In agony and blood,
Who fixed his dying eyes on me
 As near his cross I stood.

Sure never till my latest breath
 Can I forget that look,
It seemed to charge me with his death,
 Though not a word he spoke.

My conscience felt and owned the guilt,
 And filled me with despair,
I saw my sins his blood had spilt,
 And helped to nail him there.

Alas, I knew not what I did,
 But now my tears are vain;
Where can my trembling soul be hid?
 For I the Lord have slain.

Another look he gave which said,
 I freely all forgive;
This blood is for thy ransom paid,
 I die that thou mayest live."

My Fathers, and Brethren, and Friends, I have finished, though all feebly, the discussion of the text. I am afraid I have detained you too long. I cannot help it, however, on such a theme as the cross of Jesus. In eternity, we shall wonder how we could ever have begun to talk of any thing else, or have ceased talking of this after we had begun. It rests now with ourselves not to allow the subject to be without fruit, but to derive from it the lessons it imparts. The words upon which we have been meditating are not isolated. They are selected from a passage which portrays as formidable indeed the engagement before us, the struggle to which as a body we are pledged and enlisted. "Now," says the Saviour, "is the judgment of this world." What a conflict! Wherever, then, superstition, and sin, and darkness reign, the gospel is to confront and assail them, and that, too, in a war of extermination. We wage with "the rulers of the darkness of this world" a contest glorious indeed, but how arduous! Let us gird ourselves with a courage worthy of such a cause; and wrestle, and strive, and strike, like men who feel within them celestial promptings, and in whose ears are ringing the acclamations of heaven, and the shout of the King himself, "the high calling of God in Christ Jesus." It was said of Julius Cæsar, "*Eodem animo scripsit quo bellavit*"—"He wrote with as much spirit as he fought." Let the converse of this be true as to us. Let us fight with as much spirit as we write and speak and pass resolutions, and what shall we not accomplish! Nor is the warfare a doubtful one. "Now," the Redeemer adds, shall the prince of this world be cast out." Where this gospel goes, Satan's throne is broken, his kingdom subverted, and a blow dealt which resounds throughout the borders of his dominions. How much has already been accomplished, and how swiftly, even while I speak, prophecy is leaping into fulfilment, you require not me to say. What hath not God already wrought! Beneath the stormy tides and agitated elements of passion, how, age after age, hath a strong and pure under-current been silently propelling the enterprise of heaven. What changes have not been already effected by the simple ministry of the truth — changes more astonishing than all the revolutions achieved by fleets and armies! And now, this day, every wave rolls and every wind wafts us the news of fresh and glorious conquests by our Emanuel "riding prosperously because of truth and meekness and righteousness." This is one lesson to be derived from our subject.

But, my brethren — while by the whole passage we are taught this lesson, while we are instructed there as to the combat to which we are championed, and hear there the cry to battle pealing out from the gospel of peace, to battle for truth, and man, and God, and hail there the certain triumph — let us fix our eyes intently upon the text as the cynosure of our hopes, and learn from that what is the only engine by which we can conquer, the only weapon which is "mighty through God to the pulling down of strong holds,"— I mean the cross — Christ lifted up from the earth to draw all men unto him. "Every battle of the warrior," says Isaiah, "is with confused noise, and garments rolled in blood; but this shall be with burning and fuel of fire." Only the silent, melting, subduing energy of the cross can succeed. Forget this,— employ man's wisdom,— and defeat awaits us, confusion will overwhelm us. But use this instrumentality, and before its almightiness Satan shall fall from heaven like lightning, and there can stand no resistance, there shall avail no enchantment of earth, no stratagem, no divination of hell, against Israel. " Let the heathen rage, and the kings of the earth set themselves, and the rulers take counsel together, against the Lord and against his anointed "— they "imagine a vain thing," if the cross be there. Let the banded might of numbers oppose — God is in the midst of us, we shall not be moved if the cross be there; "the Lord of hosts is with us, he will be exalted among the heathen, he will be exalted in the earth." In a word, let the night, which like a pall covers a nation, be ever so thick and palpable — let idolatry overshadow a people until it sweeps, with its dismal train, every star from out their sky — if the cross go there, its radiance will pierce the gloom, its beams will dissipate the darkness. This is another lesson taught by the subject. Do we not need it, my brethren? Has the preaching Christ crucified that prominence in our modern scheme of missionary operations, which it had in the system of the apostles? I ask, with humility, are we sufficiently imbued with this lesson?

And are we sufficiently mindful of another, and the last lesson I notice as to be gathered from our subject, and which more particularly regards ourselves. I allude to the necessity of our living always near the cross, and drinking deeply and perpetually its hallowing inspirations. Brethren, that Christians in these days are what, alas, most of us are — that the atonement affects us so feebly — is owing, not to that atonement's being now too common a topic, but to our contemplating it too little. How intense — still and soft — yet severely, sublimely intense, is the efficacy of the cross of Christ, where its entire, unmutilated influence is permitted. For my part, says the Apostle, "I am crucified by it to the world, and the world to me," — it "constrains me." O, let it crucify us; let it constrain us. The word "*constrain*" is, in the original, so powerfully energetical, so rich in expressiveness, that it is difficult to decide between several meanings, all equally just and beautiful. Nor am I going to decide. I choose rather to unite them all, and on them found my closing exhortation.

Does the term often signify "*transport?*" Let us adopt this meaning, and then let the cross transport us. Hear Paul, in a sort of ecstacy, crying out "If any man love not the Lord Jesus Christ, let him be anathema maranatha." Listen to one of the early Christians who says, "to me it seems much more bitter to offend Christ than to be tormented in hell;" and to another who declares, "I say the truth, if on one hand I saw the pains of hell, and on the other the horror of sinning against the love of Jesus, and I must be plunged in one, I would choose the pains of hell, — I could never sin against this love." My brethren, you are perhaps staggered at these exclamations; but these men spake just what they felt. They were transported, they were ravished, they were "beside themselves unto God." And what they felt we should feel; there are holy ecstacies of love which we should know. If the word signify "transport," then let the cross transport us.

But the terms mean also "*surround and urge on every side.*" Let us adopt this meaning, and then let the love of a crucified Saviour surround us. Let it be the circumambient atmosphere we breathe, and in which our souls are steeped; the all-penetrating, all-pervading, all-animating, all-inflaming motive. What motive like this to kindle our languid affections; much forgiven and yet but little love! My soul, can this be possible? What motive like this to deracinate the wretched selfishness of our nature; — why does he die? why, but that "they who live should live no more to themselves, but to him who gave himself for them?" Where such a motive to fortify us with holy endurance of hardness? Have the members any thing to do with roses, while the head is crowned with thorns? In short, what an incentive here to the noblest charity. "Ye know the grace of our Lord Jesus Christ, that though he was rich, yet for your sakes he became poor, that ye through his poverty might be made rich." Do ye know this grace my brethren? do ye study this grace? do ye feel this grace? Then you need nothing else to preach charity to you. Look at the cross! O ye that hear me this night, behold the man! behold how he loves you! there, there is a charity sermon for you! Ah, listen to it, listen to it. Give him love for love, charity for charity; sacrifice for sacrifice; heart for heart; give him every thing, for he gave more than every thing for you. Yes, if the word means "surround," let the love of Christ surround us; let it compass and press us on every side with a sweet but resistless violence.

Lastly, the import of the term may be, and literally is, "*Unite*." Let us adopt this meaning, and then let, O! let the love of Christ unite us. "Who," asks the apostle, "shall separate us from the love of God which is in Christ Jesus our Lord?" And I — I exclaim, with equal confidence, who, what, shall separate us from each other, united as we are by this love? What shall separate us? Shall persecution? No, that will only bind us closer. Shall the feuds by which in this world society is torn, and even members of the same family armed and exasperated against each other — sectional jealousies, and political rancor, and party malignity? No, the cross which lifted the Saviour from the earth, lifts us high above these petty tumults and distractions. What then? — what shall separate us? Internal strife, intestine dissension? God forbid. No, my brethren, I am persuaded better things of you. No, never, never, never; it cannot be. No, by our common toils and sufferings as Baptists; by the venerable men who sang together over the cradle of this convention — those whose reverend forms I still see lingering fondly here — and those who this night, it is no presumption to believe, are beholding us with ineffable concern even from their thrones in glory; by the blood which cements us, and the new commandment written in that blood; by the memory and love of him who hath bound us together with ties indissoluble and eternal, and who is now in our midst, shewing his wounds, his hands, his feet, his side, his head, and saying, "as I have loved you even so ought ye to love one another;" by all the glorious recollections of the past, and by all the more glorious anticipations of the future — this must not, will not, shall not, cannot be.

But my heart is too full. I must stop. My tears will not allow me to say many things I had wished to say. My feelings choke my utterance. Let me only repeat the Apostle's words — "The love of Christ constraineth us." Let me only renew the exhortation, Get nearer the cross. Live nearer the cross. Then no discord can interrupt our union, no troublesome birds of prey disconcert our sacrifice. "Now there stood by the cross of Jesus his mother, and his mother's sister, Mary the wife of Cleophas, and Mary Magdalene," — let us take our stand there too, and we shall never want zeal, we can never lack devotion to the Saviour, and love for each other. Nor is it long that we have to be here, and to do for Jesus. Where is Crawford? I seek in vain for his familiar face among you. Where is Knowles? It seems to me but yesterday that I was addressing many of you, and he was there — his countenance beaming with intelligence and affection. Where is he now? I look around, but I miss him to-night. And to-morrow, my Brothers and Fathers, where shall you and I be? To-morrow we, too, shall be missed. To-morrow the place that knows us shall know us no more. To-morrow we shall die, and the august throne shall be piled for judgment, and we ourselves be standing at the foot of the awful tribunal. Let us act in view of that hour. Let us listen to the voice which comes to each of us this night from heaven, " Be thou faithful unto death, and I will give thee a crown of life." My brethren, my very dear brethren, have we been faithful? Each of us can say, " I know whom I have believed, and that he will keep that which I have committed to him against that day." Can Jesus say, as to each of us, I know whom I have believed, and that he has been faithful to the trust which I have committed to him? O, let not the sin of perfidy rest longer upon us. Let not neglected duties and broken vows cry longer to heaven against us. Let not our works be longer " found unperfected before God."

> " Christians, view the day
> Of Retribution! Think how ye will bear
> From your Redeemer's lips the fearful words,
> ' Thy brother, perishing in his own blood,
> Thou saw'st. — Thy brother hungered, was athirst,
> Was naked, — and thou saw'st it. He was sick,
> Thou didst withhold the healing; was in prison
> To vice and ignorance — nor didst thou send
> To set him free.' Oh! ere that hour of doom,
> Whence there is no reprieve, brethren, awake
> From this dark dream.

> " The time of hope
> And of probation speeds on rapid wings
> Swift and returnless. What thou hast to do
> Do with thy might. Haste, lift aloud thy voice,
> And publish to the borders of the pit
> The Resurrection. . . . . Then, when the ransomed come
> With gladness unto Zion, thou shalt joy
> To hear the valleys and the hills break forth
> Before them into singing; thou shalt join
> The raptured strain, exulting that the Lord
> Jehovah, God omnipotent, doth reign
> O'er all the earth."

Even so, Amen. O God the Father, hasten that time! O Holy Ghost, inspire us with something worthy of the name of zeal in such a cause! O Glorious Shiloh, unto thee let "the gathering of the people be!" Let thy kingdom come! "For thine is the kingdom, and thine the greatness, and the power, and the glory, and the victory, and the majesty — all that is in the heaven and in the earth is thine — thine is the kingdom, O Lord, and thou art exalted as head over all — and blessed be thy holy name, and let the whole earth be filled with thy glory. Amen, and Amen."

THE GOSPEL ADAPTED TO THE WANTS OF THE WORLD.

BY

REV. NATHAN S. S. BEMAN, D. D.

His name shall endure for ever : his name shall be continued as long as the sun : and men shall be blessed in him : all nations shall call him blessed. — PSALM 72 : 17.

THIS divine song has a primary reference to the kingdom of Solomon, the son of David ; but was intended, at the same time, to typify the kingdom of Jesus Christ, David's more exalted son. With this single explanatory remark, I would leave the general structure of the Psalm, and the exposition of its various parts, to your own reflections. The passage to which I particularly invite your attention, asserts the extent and duration of the reign of Jesus Christ upon the earth, and presents a glowing picture of its prosperity and happiness. In relation to its extent, it is to embrace "all nations," and in duration, it "shall be continued as long as the sun." In other words, the kingdom of Jesus Christ — the Gospel kingdom — shall embrace all the nations of the earth, and endure, with undiminished power and glory, while the world itself shall stand. It is clearly asserted, too, that the happiness of the human family will be greatly increased under the predicted reign of the Son of God. "Men shall be blessed in him : all nations shall call him blessed."

Nothing can be more obvious than that this prediction asserts, that the religion of the Gospel will hereafter become, and will continue to be, the prevailing religion of our world. This fact is fully settled in the Bible. It was, for ages, the grand theme of the Old Testament prophets — and the truths which they committed, in strains of exalted poetry, to the sacred lyre, have been taken up and expounded with such clearness by their New Testament successors — by the Son of God and his apostles — that not a shadow of a doubt can rest upon their import. The same fact, that is, that Christianity will become the religion of the world, might be inferred, with equal certainty, from the admission, that God is its Author, that he had a grand design to accomplish by the Gospel, or that the Bible contains a revelation from heaven.

But, waving these considerations, there is another important truth, intimately associated with the universal spread of the Gospel, to which I would invite your attention on the present occasion. The truth to which I refer is this: that the religion of the Bible is adapted, in its nature, to become the exclusive religion of our world. This sentiment, it is apprehended, is more than intimated in the text. Jesus Christ, the appointed King of Zion, shall not only reign as long as the sun shall shine upon the earth, but " men shall be blessed in him: all nations shall call him blessed." The Gospel is adapted to man as such — to all men. It contemplates, not a specific class or order of men, but *man* in the large and generic sense. The Son of God has " received gifts for MEN." His empire embraces and secures the best interests of our fallen race. " Men shall be blessed in him." " All nations shall call him blessed." The Gospel is adapted, not to the Jew nor to the Gentile alone; not to the civilized nor to the barbarous exclusively — but to " all nations." And one nation after another, under the agencies which God has ordained, shall welcome the Gospel, as adapted to their common circumstances and their common wants, till an entire world of nations shall mingle their voices and send up the homage of their hearts in one universal song.

The single sentiment I shall attempt to illustrate is this: *The religion of the Bible is adapted, in its nature, to become the exclusive religion of our world.*

1. It is accommodated to every *stage of human society.*

I shall not here enter upon any nice speculations respecting the natural state of man, considered merely as an intellectual and social being; nor attempt to settle the question, whether that state is savage or civilized. The apostacy of our race occupies so early a page in the history of the world, that it may be difficult for us even to picture to ourselves, with any degree of certainty, what our condition would have been, as it regards social habits, intellectual progress, or the arts of cultivated life, had sin never marred this once lovely heritage of God. What is now called the state of nature — the wild and savage state, to which we may easily trace back

18*

the most refined and polished nations — would probably never have existed; and the more elevated conditions of society, which are now altogether adventitious, and which are superinduced by much care and culture, might have been perfectly natural to man. But these speculations apart, it is sufficient for my present purpose to refer you to the social condition of nations as it is, and remind you of the diversified forms of human society, which the world actually presents. These are not less marked and various than the geographical surface of different countries, or than personal form, the color of the skin, or the features of the human face.

A single glance at the world as it is, and this the intelligent eye has already taken, will save the speaker the necessity of entering into detail. We have on the surface of this globe a population almost infinitely diversified; the polished European, and his descendants not less elevated, in almost every land; the wild Arab, the wandering Tartar, the inert southern Asiatic, the bigoted Jew, the proud and self-confident Turk, the fierce cannibal of Australia, the debased Hottentot, the ignorant Greenlander, and the rude and savage tenant of our own native forests; — and these furnish but a mere specimen of the human race. Nations differ in almost every thing — in their modes of obtaining a livelihood, in civilization and intellectual culture, in moral habits and religious rites.

But the Gospel makes an appeal which men, in all these diversified national circumstances, are capable of feeling. This appeal they have felt. In the days of the apostles, the truth of God overleaped the frame-work of national caste, and evinced, in every land where its truths were announced, its power to save. And facts of the same character are interwoven with the whole history of modern missions. Such have been the triumphs of the Gospel in our day, that the foolishness of infidelity, which has loudly asserted that Christianity cannot be propagated among the nations who differ in their habits and religions from those who have long been under the influence of this system, has been rebuked and put to silence. The religion of the Bible is just such a scheme as is demanded, in order to accomplish the great objects which it proposes. As it is designed for a world, so it is suited to the exigencies of a world. It has a universality of purpose, and a universality of character, in order to carry out and perfect that purpose. It takes the world as it is, and goes about the work of making it better. It can reach men just where they are, notwithstanding their national peculiarities, and make them the friends of God and the heirs of heaven. It needs no pioneer. It asks for no herald to invoke other agencies to prepare the way for its coming and reception. It is itself the pioneer of Jehovah — the herald of the great King.

These things can be affirmed only of the Gospel. Were we to examine all the systems of ancient and modern philosophy which have proposed to make men wise and happy, and submit them to a critical analysis, we should perceive that they are all strongly tinged with the spirit of the age and nation in which they originated ; and were, at the same time, capable only of a limited application. Carry these systems across a few lines of latitude or longitude, and they become exotics in an ungenial clime, and perish of themselves. Protract their existence a single century, upon the very soil which gave them birth, and among the very people who originated and cherished their dogmas, and they become superannuated, and die of old age. The same is true of the religions of the world. They are all local and temporary — and well they may be, for they are dependent on circumstances for their very existence. It would be a thing next to impossible to bring the Turks and the Greenlanders to exchange religions ; and yet Turkey and Greenland may be made to feel the truth of God, and submit to its power. No system of false philosophy has ever been universal — no single form of paganism has established its dominion over the nations of the earth. But the Gospel is indigenous in every soil where it is planted. It is at home in every land. It accomplishes its own appropriate work wherever it goes, for God is in it.

I would not intimate in these remarks, that different states of society may not be more or less favorable to the propagation of the Gospel; nor deny that auxiliary agencies may be employed to unfold, diffuse, and enforce the truth of God ; and least of all would I affirm, that the Gospel will leave a nation as it finds it. Civilization and the useful arts of life, letters and refinement, in one word, all that can elevate man in the scale of being, promote his happiness, or adorn and beautify his social character, have never failed, other things being favorable, to follow in the footsteps of this revelation from heaven.

2. The Gospel is suited to the *common wants of man.*

This system was not contrived to relieve us from some factitious evils, nor to minister to our artificial wants; but it contemplates the world in its true light, and undertakes at once to mitigate, and ultimately to root out, all suffering from the kingdom of Christ.

And here we may see the difference between the Gospel and every antagonist and conflicting system. It is the difference between what is particular and what is general — between what is limited to individuals, and what is common to all men — between what is restricted to one country or one age, and what may be applied with equal propriety and practical effect to every country of the globe, or to every period from the beginning to the end of time. The Gospel overlooks, as unworthy of its high and heavenly aims, that which is circumstantial, local, and temporary; and selects, as the object of its benevolence, that which is essential, unlimited, and enduring. Among the pagans, many a deity has derived his existence from a mountain, stream, or forest. Altars and forms of worship have been called into being to avert some impending calamity, to stay the ravages of famine, to mitigate the rage of pestilence, or to turn aside the bloody scourge of war. The form and productions of a country, the customs of domestic and social life, the prevalence of certain types of disease, the peaceful or warlike habits of a people, and an endless catalogue of like circumstances, have not only shaped and modified, but have actually created systems of religious belief and practice.

But the Gospel is constructed upon another principle. It professes to supply what is most needful for man, upon a nobler and more magnificent scale. It never attempts, as most false religions do, to remove the trivial and incidental evils of life; to guard men against the disabilities which belong to their specific circumstances; nor to ward off disease or death by charms or talismanic power; but, regarding all these as light afflictions, which endure but for a moment, it settles down at once upon the common wants of men, as pilgrims on the earth and the heirs of eternity.

A few of the common wants of our dying world, for which the Gospel effectually provides, may very properly be enumerated in this place.

Man, in relation to all kinds of knowledge, is the subject of instruction; and in nothing does he more imperatively demand it than in religion. The lights of this world have become so dimmed, that he never clearly sees, nor fully performs his duties to God or his fellows, till a purer and brighter orb in heaven shines upon him. Sin has well nigh obliterated the perceptions of God and duty from the human mind. The world is perishing for the want of spiritual knowledge. This is seen and felt every where. Not a soul on earth can find the way to heaven, without the special interposition of God; and whether he communicates himself silently and mysteriously, in here and there a solitary case, without a written revelation, we are not informed, and it is a problem which we are not required to solve. But this we do know, for God has taught it, that the Bible is the grand source of religious instruction. The nations are in midnight without it. It is a darkness without the prospect of a dawn. It is deep, dense, central, visible; and not a star of promise has been seen in the heavens, as the harbinger of an opening day, by any telescope which nature or art has been able to construct. Without the Gospel, men are every where destitute of that knowledge necessary to the well-being of the soul; and with it, they have every thing which God himself deemed essential, when their salvation was the grand object to be accomplished. This fallen world needs an infallible guide, and that guide is to be found alone in a written revelation. No decrees of popes or councils can supply its place. No tradition, though it were to descend from heaven, and emanate from the throne of God, can become a substitute. The Jew, the Pagan, the Mohammedan, the Catholic, the Protestant, all need this volume. It is adapted to the common wants of a world; and the nation, whether refined or barbarous, that is destitute of it, is living without the sun.

But man needs not only an infallible instructor, but support under the nameless evils which sin has inflicted upon him. In every country under heaven, on every continent and every island of the sea, he is hardly less miserable than he is sinful. And yet the religion of the Saviour can mingle the ingredients of comfort in every bitter cup. Passing over a long list of ills which flesh is heir to, I would fix your attention on two to which all men are subject, in whatever state of society or condition of life, and for which the Gospel provides a perfect remedy. I refer to remorse of conscience and the sting of death. These are coëxtensive with the fallen race. Sin is an evil of so malignant a character, that it reveals itself in the present life — it is followed by a present retribution. Verily, there "is a God that judgeth in the earth." The poor pagan feels this, and hence his sacrifices and his self-inflicted tortures. It is on this principle that penance and pilgrimages belong to most systems of false religion. But the Gospel alone can calm the troubled spirit, pluck away the deep-seated anguish of the heart, and inspire that hope which prophesies of heaven. And not only are the great evils of life provided for by the religion of Christ, but death itself — that event every where dreaded in our world — that event which may, in itself, be considered the sum and concentration of all earthly ills — the primeval curse of God upon a world of rebels, may be divested of all its unloveliness, and disarmed of all its inflictions, and be converted into the richest blessing. The Christian victor's song is, "O death, where is thy sting? O grave, where is thy victory?"

3. The Gospel is adapted *to every order of mind.*

In this respect it differs from all human systems. Among the most distinguished ancient nations, they had one religion for the learned, and another for the illiterate. This was true in Greece, and probably, to some extent, in Rome. Their great men, and especially their sages and philosophers, gave little or no credit to the doctrines of polytheism admitted by the vulgar; but, on the other hand, approximated to something like a pure theism in their religious belief. I would not affirm that this was universal, possibly it was not even general; but, in many cases, it is an unquestioned fact. As to their systems of philosophy, they were too refined and subtle to be received by common minds. I do not say *understood*, for it may be fairly doubted whether they were understood by any. They were marked by intellectual caste; and this stamp had been put upon them intentionally, in order to protect the prerogatives of great minds, and to show the common mass of men that they had no right to think. Neither the system of the Stoics nor of the Epicureans could have become universal. They were limited by their very nature; the former to a certain order of mind, and the latter to a certain moral or physical temperament — and both of them entirely inapplicable, in all their parts and ramifications, to the society or population of any country. Were we to examine the speculations of any or every ancient philosopher, trace out the various systems, examine their origin, scrutinize their purposes or intentions, and follow their progress to their final results, we should arrive at this conclusion, that they were never designed for the world at large, and, being adapted to a particular order of intellect, their influence, whether good or bad, would be restricted to a small number of individuals, wherever their doctrines might be embraced.

By the side of these intellectual and moral schemes, contemplate the character of the Gospel in relation to the single feature of its adaptedness to every order of mind. While some religions are suited to the unlettered, and some to the cultivated, and while the same may be affirmed of certain systems of philosophy and morals, the Bible scheme is adapted to the intellect of every man. No elevation of mind can rise above the sublimity of its truths; no stretch of thought can go beyond the vast reach of its purpose; no analytic powers can detect a discordant element in its grand and complicated system. It teaches the great man, and makes him wiser and better. Time would fail me, were I to attempt to enumerate the men of mighty minds, the giants of the earth, who have towered above their fellows, as the oak above the saplings of the forest, who, at the same time, have acknowledged themselves indebted for their best lessons of instruction, to the Bible. Boyle, of whom it has been said, "To him we owe the secrets of fire, air, water, animals, vegetables, fossils, so that from his works may be deduced the whole system of natural knowledge," was in the habit of reading this letter from heaven upon his knees; and Newton, that child-like sage, investigated the wonders of revelation with an intensity not less excited and profound than that with which he scanned the starry heavens, or passed his measuring-line around the earth, or dropped his lead to its centre, or unbraided the complicated tissue of light.

Nor was this communication from God made for the instruction or entertainment of great minds alone, but is equally adapted to the humble and the unlettered. It is in revelation as in nature — sublimity and simplicity are always united. The same volume which furnishes the richest instructions to the sage, can be understood and enjoyed with as fine a relish by the husbandman who follows the plough, by the mechanic in his work-shop, or by the child in the Sabbath-school. What a vast variety, with respect to mental power and acquirement, may be found in the ranks of believers; and yet, gathered as they are from the four winds of heaven, they all entertain essentially the same views of the way of salvation, and have manifestly imbibed the same heavenly spirit. Indeed, I may add, what no one who has studied this subject can have overlooked, that the Gospel, being designed for a world as it is — a world in which the great majority of its inhabitants are ignorant and uninstructed, has been formed for the very purpose of meeting this case. It is a revelation to the benighted and the lowly. It teaches the sublimest truths in such a manner that babes may understand them, and inculcates the simplest with such a heavenly elevation and pathos, that minds of the largest compass and the profoundest thought are instructed and delighted.

4. The Gospel counteracts sin in *every possible condition*.

Sin is the source of all the other evils which prevail under the government of God; and the object of the coming Christ, and the introduction and spread of the Gospel, is the extermination of this great evil from our world. The Bible describes its nature, and tells us of its present and future consequences. It holds up, in the sun-light of eternal truth, its malignant features, and, for an illustration of its fruits, points us to a bleeding earth and a burning hell. The introduction of this evil into our world was the work of Satan; and "for this purpose the Son of God was manifested that he might destroy the works of the devil." No other system of morals or religion has made an attack upon sin as such. Some particular sins have been denounced, and to a certain extent, no doubt, counteracted by other influences; but it was reserved for the Gospel alone to proclaim war against every sin, great and small. It spares no man; it has no protecting shield for the transgressor. It has no mantle of charity to inwrap the sinner, and thus cover up his true character as the enemy of God. It lays the axe "at the root of the trees," and hews down the tall cedar as well as the withered bramble. It condemns the sinning monarch in terms as unsparing and uncompromising as it does the sinning beggar. For the city and country, for the refined and the ignoble, for Christian and for Pagan lands, there is but one law — " Without holiness no man shall see the Lord." It has no respect to age, station, learning, country, kindred, sex, family, or profession in life, but bears testimony against all who love and practice sin.

But the Gospel does something more than describe the nature of sin, and point out the present and future woes which hang around a wicked heart and life. It proposes a remedy. It would relieve our sinful and suffering world from its accumulated evils, by striking a death-blow at the very root of all the mischief. The Gospel is a scheme contrived of God, and revealed from heaven for the removal of sin. It undertakes to make men happy only by this process. It provides for the pardon of sin through the blood of the atonement; and by the instrumentality of truth, and the agency of the Spirit, subdues the affections to the love of God, and carries on in the heart of the penitent and believing sinner a work of progressive sanctification, which will be rendered perfect and triumphant in heaven. And unless this effect can be produced, of what use is any scheme of religion for such a world as this? A man may pass through a thousand changes, and till he pass from death to life, from sin to holiness, he wears his chains, and is on the way to execution. The great curse is still on him, and he must be miserable. Sin is uncancelled, and he cannot be happy. Of what avail are the stripes and lacerations which are self-inflicted by the poor pagan; or the austerities and penance of the Romanist; or the fine speculations of the unitarian or the deist on the beauty of virtue and the benevolence of God, while no radical change is effected in the moral character? Man is every where a sinner; and in all these human schemes and devices there is no provision for the removal of this fundamental evil. No system of religion, whatever name it may wear, whether Christian or pagan, can supply the moral demands of such a world as ours, unless it commence with sin. Spare this, and you ruin the world. Leave this unprovided for, and you shut for ever the gate of heaven against the human race. Omit this single item, and you open wide the door of perdition. Strike out from your scheme the provision for pardon and the power of sanctification, and you have a religion which can never become universal, and would be of no use were it to become universal, for it would bring no relief to a sinful world. But such is not the Gospel of the Son of God.

5. The Gospel is not dependent on any system of *human philosophy.*

The Bible teaches "as one having authority, and not as the scribes." In narrating facts, it records them as they are, and in their proper relations; in the revelation of doctrines, it presents them as fundamental truths which are to be accredited, and makes no explanations of the former, and enters into no reasonings respecting the latter. It discloses facts and principles of which all men, or the generality of men, were before ignorant, or in which, at least, they were but imperfectly instructed; and there it leaves them. And there these truths stand stereotyped for ever, without change of form or feature. The Gospel borrows nothing from the reigning philosophy, for it has nothing to decorate, that it may attract the eyes of men; nothing to render palatable by courting the popular taste; nothing to explain; nothing to reconcile. From the commencement to the close of its communications to our world, though these extend through more than fifteen centuries, and were furnished by a large number of sacred penmen, it never loses sight of one fixed purpose, and that is, to tell men what *truth* is. And when this is done, its work is finished. It never comments or philosophizes upon its own productions. Hence the Bible, like its Author, has a kind of ubiquity, and can live every where; and, like him, it has a perpetuity of existence, and is the same in every age. Systems of human philosophy may rise and fall and be forgotten, while Bible truth flows on in a steady and majestic stream, and not its surface is rippled by the change.

In the interpretation of revealed truth, and in the construction of human creeds and symbols, as well as in all the systems of false religion, the philosophy of the age, both intellectual and moral, and perhaps I might add in some cases, natural philosophy too, has exerted a very perceptible influence. This is what we might expect. If men construct a religion, it must be of course a human religion, and it will partake of human thoughts and qualities. Men cannot beget angels. We can hardly look upon one of these earthly productions without being able to detect its parentage, and to tell the age and country of its birth. The same is the case, to some extent, of all human symbols of the true religion. The creeds and commentaries of each particular age and nation embody much which belongs to that age and nation. Indeed, we cannot expect it should be otherwise; for they are the productions of men, and fathers generally live a second life in their children. But the Bible occupies an independent position. It is the production of God. It depends on no other system. It borrows nothing from any other. Other systems live, flourish, wane, and die; but this remains the same. It has already survived, amidst the changing theories and speculations of the world, almost six thousand years; and it is yet clad in all the freshness of its glory, as it was in the day when it was born in heaven, and sent down to the earth for our instruction. Time has not whitened its locks, or palsied its hand, or chilled its heart. Systems of philosophy and modes of interpretation, one after another, have gone down to the sepulchre, and are known only in their epitaph; but the Gospel lives, and is powerful to save. Other systems which are founded in error, will in like manner pass away; but the religion of the Bible will never cease to exist and act upon the world, till all that God has greatly purposed and kindly promised, shall be fully accomplished. Its truths may be tinged or obscured by a false philosophy, or by human speculations; but this effect is local and temporary. These things are no part of the system. The Bible remains the same; and, at another day, or in another country, all is restored. Clouds and mists may, in one hemisphere, or for a few days, cover the face of the sun and shut out the light, but the sun is not extinguished. He is always shining somewhere; and the clouds and mists of all human theories will by and by be dissipated, and he will break forth, and, in full-orbed radiance, shine every where, and fill the world with light.

6. The Gospel has no necessary connection with any form of *human government.*

The Bible acknowledges the right and sanctions the powers and prerogatives of civil government; but it does not prescribe any particular form. The most that is said on this subject in the New Testament, is rather incidental than direct; and is addressed principally to Christians, enjoining it upon them to be peaceful subjects of whatever government may happen to exist. The following are specimens: "Let every soul be subject unto the higher powers. For there is no power but of God: the powers that be, are ordained of God. Whosoever, therefore, resisteth the power, resisteth the ordinance of God; and they that resist, shall receive to themselves damnation." And again: "Render therefore to all their dues: tribute to whom tribute is due; custom to whom custom; fear to whom fear; honor to whom honor." It is also said, "Submit yourselves to every ordinance of man for the Lord's sake: whether it be to the king, as supreme; or unto governors, as unto them that are sent by him for the punishment of evil-doers, and for the praise of them that do well."

This language is accommodated to the existing governments of the apostolic age; but the spirit of these precepts may be applied, with equal propriety, to any and every form of civil and political institutions. Had the Gospel assumed any other ground than this, it would have been fatal to its prospects as designed for a universal religion. If any one form had been selected and approved, and others condemned, it would have converted the message of heaven into a political proclamation, and all nations, except those whose institutions might have received its approval, would have armed themselves against its approach. It would have been met and repelled with the same spirit with which men are accustomed to meet and repel invading fleets and armies.

That the Gospel is friendly to the rights of man and the liberties of the world, is a proposition too obvious to need proof. The influence of this system, wherever it is cordially received, is felt upon every great interest of society — upon the people and upon the government. It will show itself upon the legislation of a country — upon the character and the execution of its laws — and in various ways, and by pervading and controlling influences peculiar to itself, destroy oppression, and diffuse and protect equal rights among men. It makes good citizens and good rulers, without interfering directly either with the form or administration of government.

It was owing to this characteristic of the Gospel, that the first heralds of the cross gained access, with their message, to every country, notwithstanding the peculiar jealousies of the age respecting international communication; and though often accused of treason, they were never convicted of the charge. And it was on this principle that, without an attack upon any political institution, they introduced a train of moral causes which have greatly modified and well nigh revolutionized the governments of the civilized world. And it is on the same principle that modern missionaries might be permitted to go every where, and freely and fully proclaim their message, without any alarm on the part of existing governments. Indeed, this is the prevailing temper of the reigning powers of the earth at this moment. And in those cases where Christian missions are excluded by the laws of the land, their enactments are either founded on ignorance of the real objects of the enterprise, or, as is more generally the fact, are designed to protect some false system of religion, which has become publicly wedded to the state, and which, every one must know, would inevitably fall before the powers of the Gospel.

REMARKS. — 1. The religion of the Bible must be *true*.

It cannot be the product of the human mind. Its adaptation to the complicated circumstances — to the wants, the sins, and the miseries of the whole world, and that, too, through every period of its existence, is peculiar to itself, and has a parallel in no other system. This one property of the Gospel would require a greater compass of thought and stretch of ingenuity, a more intimate knowledge of facts, a clearer perception of causes and effects, and final results — of existing evils and their infallible remedies, than belong to the finite mind. You have only to compare the religion of the Bible with other systems, and you discern the difference between God's work and man's. The one undertakes only to provide for what is limited to time and place; the other, dispensing with ages and localities, takes a broad sweep, like the mind of its Author, and actually provides for what always exists, and is every where to be found.

There is not an individual religion of paganism among the nameless varieties that fill the world; not a speculation of ancient or modern philosophy; not a thought in the Vedas or Shaster of the Hindoos; not a disclosure in the Koran, the pretended revelation of Mohammed; not a system of error, or any part of a system, in any age or country, but might be the production of the human intellect and heart, and would ever be likely to be, in the same existing circumstances. But I ask, who but God could make the Bible? I speak now only of its adaptedness to the purpose for which it was intended. What eye but that which surveys the world at a glance, and beholds all nations, with their multifarious ills and complicated wants, as they are, and reads with intuitive certainty the moral pulsation of every heart, could see far enough, and wide enough, and deep enough, for such a work? What but the all-comprehensive mind could devise a religious system, humble in its grandeur and majestic in its simplicity, which should be equally applicable to men in every nation and every age; which has power to reclaim the heart and control the life; to disarm the world of its enmity against God; to restore the wanderer; raise the disconsolate; and light up a smile on the pale cheek of death? Surely, this is no common undertaking. There is but one Being who ever thought of doing it; and the volume that reveals this purpose has, written deeply and indelibly upon its sacred page, *the signature of God.*

2. The Gospel will finally *prevail*.

This might be inferred with great certainty from the fact, or the admission, that God is its Author. If He constructed the scheme, it was with some object in view; for some great and worthy purpose. The sins, and tears, and death-groans of our world had gone up to heaven, and God had fixed his heart on man's redemption. For this He formed the plan, sent his Son, accepted the sacrifice of his blood, and made, in his name, proclamation of pardon and peace to this great family of rebels. And shall not this plan go into full effect? Will the great Architect leave his noble edifice half finished? "God is not man, that he should lie; neither the son of man, that he should repent. Hath he said it, and shall he not do it? Or hath he spoken, and shall he not make it good?" Hear his own declaration; "The Lord hath made bare his holy arm in the eyes of all nations: and all the ends of the earth shall see the salvation of our God." His purpose is clearly expressed, and every jot and tittle shall be accomplished.

For the renovation of this world, we are not to forget that God has adopted a system of agencies suited to the object to be accomplished. The Gospel is not a dead letter, but "the power of God, and the wisdom of God." It embodies in itself the most effective moral influences which operate any where in the vast empire of God. It was contrived for a world in the ruins of sin, and it is the master-piece of Jehovah — the concentration of all that is wise and magnificent in heaven. It is just what the dying millions of our world need. It can reach and save them. Its appeals are such as human minds and hearts can comprehend and feel. It comes home to "the business and bosoms" of men, with a conviction and pathos with which no other system is armed. Every blow it strikes in our world, is felt upon some interest, and tells upon its final destiny. And, securing, as it does, in the hands of a faithful ministry and a praying church, the presence and power of the Spirit of God, it will go forth in its strength to the conquest of the world. And what shall stay the progress of that scheme of grace and restoration which God has constructed — which is adapted to man any where and every where — which has already gathered the first-fruits of the coming harvest — which has saved its millions in ages past — which is saving its tens of millions in the present age, and in reference to the faithful administration of which, by his devoted servants, Christ himself has said, "Lo, I am with you alway, even unto the end of the world?"

3. All who possess the Gospel should do all they can *to communicate it to others.*

This subject makes an appeal to Christians, which they must not, cannot resist. The Gospel, my brethren, has been committed to us;* and there is no aspect in which this matter can be viewed, which does not urge, in the tenderest and most powerful manner, our duty and our responsibility upon us. We have the very scheme of mercy which the world needs, and without which the world must perish. And this dearest gift of heaven was put into our hands, not that we should imprison or chain it, but that we should, to the very last stretch of power, give to it "the wings of the morning," and bid it fly to the uttermost parts of the earth. The wants of our dying world, the nature of the Gospel, the command of Heaven, the principle of benevolence, the pledge of success, the seal of God upon all past efforts, and the cheering aspect of this heaven-born enterprise of missions, all — *all* urge us to stand up like men upon whom the vows of God rest, to whom the eyes of perishing millions are directed, and whose hearts have taken hold on the interests of eternity, and then do as Christ and conscience would have us. God has opened wide the door of the world before us. The unevangelized millions of the earth feel, at this moment, more deeply than they ever felt, their need of the Gospel and its attending institutions, and its consequent moral, literary, social, and political blessings. And can we go back, or even stand still, when we contemplate what God has already permitted us to do, or has kindly done by us, in the work of making the world what he would have it? Let the American Board and American Christians look at things as they are, — at their eighty missionary stations, which appear as so many cultivated spots scattered here and there through the deep and dense wilderness of paganism — at their four hundred and seventy-eight foreign and native laborers, whose toils have already beautified these gardens of God — at their ten thousand eight hundred and ten reclaimed wanderers, who have taken shelter in the bosom of the church the last year — at their twenty-four boarding-schools, with their eight hundred and seven pupils — at their four hundred and fifteen free-schools, with their twenty-one thousand six hundred and six little inmates praying for instruction, — and then ask, shall this work cease? Shall another midnight succeed this dawning day? This is the time and this the place to settle this question. O, let us lift our streaming eyes and bleeding hearts to heaven, and, with a simple reliance on God, say this work must not cease. God bids us press onward.

We, my Christian friends, are engaged in an enterprise that honors God and blesses men! An enterprise in which the angels might wish to bear even an humble part — the progress of which is intensely engaged upon, by all the good on earth and all the perfected in glory, and the completion of which will fill the world with songs of blessedness, and heaven with shouts of endless triumph.

May God inspire us for this work, and take the glory to himself. AMEN AND AMEN.

THE MORAL ELEVATION OF THE CHURCH ESSENTIAL TO MISSIONARY SUCCESS.

BY

REV. GEORGE B. IDE.

O Zion, that bringest good tidings, get thee up in to the high mountain; O Jerusalem, that bringest good tidings, lift up thy voice with strength; lift it up, be not afraid; say unto the cities of Judah, Behold your God. — ISAIAH, 40: 9.

IN the commencement of this chapter, the prophet is instructed to comfort the depressed and sorrowing church of God, by a glowing prediction of the times of the Messiah, and of the blessings which should flow from his mission to our world. Borne forward by the divine spirit into coming ages, he beholds the precursor of Christ appearing in the wilderness of Judea, and hears, from its silent depths, the animating announcement, "Prepare ye the way of the Lord, make straight in the desert a highway for our God." He next proceeds to foretell the actual advent of the Redeemer, by declaring that "the glory of the Lord"— his glory as displayed in the person and work of his Son — should "be revealed;" and then, glancing his inspired vision rapidly onward to the period when the sublime destinies of the Gospel were to be consummated in its full and universal prevalence, exclaims, "All flesh shall see it together."

Having thus described the introduction of Christianity, and sketched, with a single comprehensive stroke, its ultimate triumphs, he passes from these bright unfoldings of prophecy, to urge upon the people of God the momentous obligation arising from their new and peculiarly favored circumstances. "O Zion, that bringest good tidings, get thee up into the high mountain; O Jerusalem, that bringest good tidings, lift up thy voice with strength; lift it up, be not afraid; say unto the cities of Judah, Behold your God." In their original application, these words had, doubtless, a specific reference to the apostles and immediate followers of our Lord. The devoted company of believers, which first gathered around the standard of his cross, then formed the spiritual Zion — the germ and nucleus of the future church; and to them was given the solemn commission of publishing, far and wide, the message of redeeming love. Beginning at Jerusalem, as the starting-point of their labors, they were to proclaim the doctrine of a crucified and risen Saviour, through every city and hamlet, in every lonely vale, and on every rocky hill of the chosen land. Nor was this the limit of their embassy. They were commanded to pass beyond the barriers of Jewish prejudice and restriction, and, going into all the world, to make known, wherever their steps could reach, or their voice could penetrate, "the unsearchable riches of Christ."

But while such was unquestionably the primary bearing of the passage before us, the appeal which it utters, viewed in its general design, addresses itself, with no less directness and urgency, to the disciples of Jesus in every age, and especially to those of the present day. The same Gospel, which brought life and salvation to the early Christians, and which they were every where to promulgate, as the only remedy for the sins and miseries of apostate man, has been imparted to ourselves, in all its renovating power, and with all its boundless wealth of consolation and mercy. Their privileges, their joys, their obligations are ours. The work, which, from the fewness of their hands and the brevity of their mortal course, they were able but partially to accomplish, has been transmitted, as a sacred and imperative charge, to us, who, in these far distant times, are called to inherit their hopes, and to share their responsibilities; while, through every rank of our consecrated hosts, there sounds as loudly and impressively as once it echoed along the brow of Olivet, the command of our ascended King, summoning us to the great enterprise of spreading the knowledge of his grace among all the millions of this revolted earth.

Regarding the text in this light, and following the order of its several parts, I propose to consider,

I. THE IMPORTANT TRUST COMMITTED TO THE CHURCH.

In entering upon this point, it may be proper to remark, that by the term church, as used in this connection, we do not intend any one society of professing Christians, organized on a particular model, and arrogantly claiming to be the *only* true church, the exclusive representatives of primitive faith, and the sole legatees of apostolical order and authority. We refer rather to the entire body of the renewed and pious in all lands, who, though bearing different names, and separated by distinctive lines, unite in maintaining the fundamental principles of the Gospel, and are animated by the spirit of their common Head. We think not, indeed, that the external forms of Christianity are unimportant; that no precise pattern of them has been revealed in Scripture; or that all the branches of God's ransomed family are equally pure in doctrine, and correct in their observance of the institutions which He has appointed. But we believe that, notwithstanding many errors and deficiencies, those of every denomination, who receive Christ as their divine and only Saviour, confidew holly in his atoning sacrifice, and manifest love to him and to his cause, are to be considered as members of his mystical body, partakers of his grace, and heirs of his glory. These constitute the church on earth — the spiritual Jerusalem, whose foundations were laid deep in the Redeemer's blood, and whose lively stones are all fashioned by his hand, and cemented by the golden bond of union with him.

Now, we learn from our text, that on the people thus chosen and sanctified, a vast responsibility has been imposed. It is that of carrying the Word of Life to a perishing world. This is clearly implied in the description given of Zion and Jerusalem as "bringing good tidings." The figurative language here employed, evidently represents the church as charged with the proclamation of the glorious intelligence, that a way has been opened for the recovery of our fallen race, through the obedience and death of the incarnate Mediator; and that, on the ground of his justifying merits, pardon, and peace, and the heritage of heaven are now freely offered to every believing penitent. And the fact that she is to circulate these tidings, is spoken of, not as a casual or incidental event in her history, but as her grand and paramount business — that which constitutes her office, and furnishes her appropriate designation. This is the great object of her existence and establishment. Other valuable purposes are, without doubt, designed to be effected through her instrumentality. But her special province, her characteristic vocation, is to bear the message of redemption to dying men. It is not her prerogative to invent a gospel; nor to change or modify, in the least particular, that which has been intrusted to her.

She is simply to communicate, pure and unmutilated, to all nations and in all languages, the teachings of that unerring record which has descended to her from the throne above, as alike the law of her faith, and the guide of her conduct. For this was the priceless boon of Revelation bestowed on her. God has not made her the depositary of his truth, in order that she should bury it in mystic recesses, or wrangle over it in profitless debate about questions of mere speculative orthodoxy; but that, with large and liberal measure, she might scatter it abroad, to enlighten and bless mankind. She is, indeed, to preserve the precious treasure incorrupt and stainless; yet, not that it may be kept carefully locked up in her inmost shrines, as ancient mysteries were guarded from eyes profane, but that, like the sun blazing on the forehead of the morning, it may pour its undimmed effulgence on the myriads that lie shrouded in darkness and wo. It is with this view that she has been selected as the receptacle of light from heaven—the radiating centre of moral influence—the reservoir, whence the waters of mercy, shed down from their celestial Fountain, are to flow out, in many a divergent stream, to purify the surrounding masses of unsanctified mind. In her hands is placed the lever that is to lift from the groaning earth the load of crime and sorrow, and raise its degraded population to holiness and joy. To her has been consigned that living Word, which, pregnant with ethereal energy, can quicken the dead in sin, and restore them to the image and service of their Maker. Thus furnished and endowed, she is to go forth into every clime—on the land and on the sea—through the whole extent of this outcast globe—calling upon its guilty inhabitants to "behold their God"—to look, in contrition and faith, to that Divine Redeemer, who, having expiated iniquity by his own blood, now sits enthroned at the right hand of the Father, to dispense the blessings which he has purchased. Her mission is to the human race; her tidings are the wonders of Calvary; her object, the moral emancipation of a world.

With the view now given of the peculiar sphere assigned to the church, *the testimony of Scripture closely corresponds*. The followers of Christ are represented as "the salt of the earth," placed amid its scenes of corruption and ruin, for the purpose of rescuing it from the grasp of spiritual death, and filling its entire expanse with the pervading power of truth, love and salvation. They are "the light of the world," shining, not with their own radiance, but with the beams reflected upon them from the Sun of Righteousness, and are intended to shed the splendors of heavenly day over the moral night which envelops so large a portion of mankind. They are likened to "a city set on a hill, that cannot be hid," but which, from its elevated position, towers up, conspicuous to every eye, the attraction and the goal of all hearts, inviting the wretched wanderers of earth to seek, within its grace-defended walls, a secure and blissful refuge from the pursuing sword of justice, and the gathering storm of divine wrath. And the Gospel, which they are required to disseminate, is compared, in its diffusive tendency, to leaven, which, though concealed and unregarded at first, gradually penetrates and informs the whole mass; thus showing the duty of Christians to labor for the evangelization of all men, and the efficacy and certain success of the instrument which they employ. But it is not by such metaphysical allusions alone, that this great obligation is inculcated. Our blessed Lord has pronounced upon it his own authoritative decision, in words so direct and explicit, that no sophistry can evade their force or question their import. He is the King of Zion, and the sovereign of conscience. His will is law; and, as a declaration of that will, he has said, "Go ye into all the world, and preach the Gospel to every creature." This command, originally given to his apostles, was addressed through them to the whole church in every successive age. That command has not been revoked. It is still the unrepealed and immutable statute of his kingdom. Nor will it ever be abated or superseded, until the farthest dwellers on the globe are subdued to his sway. This is his last and highest precept—the universal, ever binding enactment which he has left as the directory of his people, in all conditions, and for all time; and never can they prove unfaithful to it, without frustrating the chief end of their calling, and incurring the fearful guilt of treason to their Lord.

That to propagate the Gospel is the great duty of believers, is also evident from the *very nature and design of their religious profession.* The one is as inseparably connected with the other, as the fruit with the tree which produces it, or the stream with its parent source. What is it to be a Christian? What is the language of those who assume that hallowed name? They declare themselves to be influenced by the spirit of Christ, as a vital, controlling principle; to have an enlightened and ardent sympathy with the views, and aims, and feelings of him who left the realms of glory to save the lost, and laid down his life to restore an alienated world to God. And can they be indifferent to the conversion of that world; can they refuse to engage in efforts to promote it, without violating the express conditions of their discipleship? For what have they acknowledged their allegiance to the Saviour, and solemnly dedicated their all to his service? Is it simply that they may secure their own salvation, and pursue their solitary path to heaven, reckless of the multitudes whom they leave to travel on, unwarned, to perdition? Is it, that, having made a compromise with conscience by a public avowal of Christ, they may afterwards give themselves up to the unchecked indulgence of a secular spirit, accumulate riches, live in palaces, and lie on couches of ease, trembling at self-denials, while from the four winds there comes into their ears the cry of millions perishing in sin? O no; far, far different is the covenant by which they are bound. The very terms of their enlistment under the Christian banner, sacredly require them to strive with their utmost ability to carry that banner in triumph through every land; to plant it on every mountain top; to spread out its white folds beneath every sky,— the sign of peace and joy to a lost world. And if true to the name they bear, they will shrink from no sacrifice and from no exertion, to accomplish a result so glorious. Having tasted the preciousness of the Gospel, they will delight to lead others to the heavenly banquet. Themselves safe in Christ, it will be the absorbing desire of their hearts to guide the ruined children of earth to the same all-sufficient shelter. Nor will they regard this as the business merely of official men, of ministers, of missionaries, but as devolving, individually and collectively, on all the servants of God. For there is not in the Bible a plainer maxim, than that he who receives the Gospel, is bound to make that Gospel known. The very fact of its reception implies an obligation to diffuse it. Heaven is not farther removed from earth, than is true religion from every approach to selfishness. It is not an unsocial principle. It seeks not to bury itself in retirement, nor wastes its energies in idle contemplations and dreamy raptures, while the whitening fields, ripe for the harvest, summon it in vain to action. Such a religion, to all but its possessor, would be useless. Such a religion, like the flower that blooms in the desert, may give its fragrance to the barren air, and delight those unbodied spirits which survey the hidden feelings of men, but can shed no healing power over the race it was designed to influence and save. Like the gem which sparkles in the deep caves of ocean, or in the dark bosom of the mine, its lustre illumines no eye, and gladdens no heart. In opposition to this religion of indolence and seclusion, the piety which the Bible enjoins, is active, practical, diffusive; full of charity and good fruits; seeking out, like its great Exemplar, the abodes of destitution and sorrow; instructing the ignorant; lifting up the depressed; opening wide the gate of life to the perishing; pouring the beams of day on those who sit in the shadow of death; and going forth on its work of mercy, with an expansiveness of benevolence, that, overleaping the conventional barriers of country, and climate, and complexion, embraces, in its ample scope, the whole brotherhood of man. Such was the piety of the early Christians. Fired with a love for souls, allied to that which drew the Redeemer from the skies, they dispersed themselves abroad, proclaiming every where the message of salvation. Every convert was, in effect, a preacher of the faith of Christ. Every monument of the grace of God became an instrument of that grace for the conversion of others. Every light kindled up in the moral waste sent forth its radiance on the surrounding darkness. And from every point where a band of believers was gathered, the word of the Lord went out to the regions beyond it. O, had this ancient zeal but continued to animate the church, how different from what it now is would have been the aspect of our world! Long since, the victories of the cross would have encompassed the globe. And even now, were the spirit of primitive Christianity to return, what a new impulse would be given to the march of Emanuel's kingdom. Then, wherever spiritual night spreads its gloom, the messengers of truth would go forth in crowds, making the wilderness to rejoice, and the desert to blossom as the rose. Then would all the sons of Zion be holy unto the Lord; they would hold their possessions as sacred to Him; their pursuits would be arranged with reference to the advancement of his cause; and all their intercourse, connections, and employments, in the varied walks of civil and social life, would be so sanctified by religion, and thus rendered so subservient to its interests, that, in all directions, the Gospel would mightily prevail, and rapidly extend its conquests to the utmost limits of the earth. Let the

Christians of our day but act in simple accordance with the demands of their profession, and soon shall blest voices be heard in heaven, saying, "Now is come salvation, and the kingdom of our God."

The gratitude, moreover, which believers owe to Christ, binds them, by all its sweet and resistless claims, to publish on every shore the wondrous story of his love. No finite mind can compute the amount of their indebtedness to the Saviour. He has ransomed them, with the price of his own dreadful sufferings, from the chains of sin and the condemnation of hell, and brought them into the freedom and blessedness of the sons of God. Their present joys and their future glory, the privileges and comforts they now possess, the light of Revelation shining on their path, the consolations of the indwelling Spirit, and the immortal crowns reserved for them in heaven, are all the purchase of his life of sorrow and his death of ignominy. What return shall they render for benefits so precious, bestowed at such infinite cost? The only return which he seeks, apart from the submission of their own hearts to him, is that they should strive, earnestly and unremittingly, to extend his reign on earth. This world belongs to Christ. He has redeemed it; and he owns it. In virtue of his mediatorial office, he has become its rightful sovereign and proprietor. Its complete deliverance from the usurped dominion of Satan, and the subjugation of all its rebel provinces to his own peaceful sceptre, are promised to him as the reward of his atoning agony. And, in the fulfilment of this promise, "he shall see of the travail of his soul, and be satisfied." Must not, then, every demand of affection as well as of duty constrain those whom he has saved by his blood, to put forth their utmost endeavors to hasten a consummation so desirable? Can they withhold their instrumentality from a work, the accomplishment of which shall perfect his joy? Can they be willing that none of the seed which is to produce the harvest of his praise, shall be sown by their labors, and watered by their tears? And when the final triumphs of his truth shall place on his head the crown of the recovered nations, O, can they bear to reflect that their hands have added no jewel to that crown, and hung up no trophy of salvation in the temple of his glory?

The duty of the church to promulgate the Gospel is evinced, finally, by the fact, *that God has appointed no other channel for its diffusion.* The whole structure and design of the economy of grace, demonstrate the intention of its Author that the knowledge of it should be universally extended. And, as all power is his, he could have made whatever provision he saw fit, to secure this object. But he has adopted no miraculous or supernatural means, nor any means, except the instrumentality of his people, employed in the circulation of the preached and written word, and accompanied and rendered effectual by His Holy Spirit. Apart from this, there is not an agency in the universe whose office it is to publish redemption. No trumpet from the eternal throne proclaims it. No seraphic voices chant it from the sky. No angel messengers bear it on their wings. No Urim and Thummim flashes with its rays. No oracle announces it. No vision reveals it. No breeze murmurs it. No music of air, or earth, or sea, whispers, in its many-toned utterings, a syllable of the glorious theme. The vast temple of Nature, though rich in displays of God the Creator, has no manifestations of God the Redeemer. Nor is there in the human soul any moral intuition, which, without external aid, can teach it the message of the cross. The myriads of the unevangelized must remain forever ignorant of the salvation of Jesus, and perish in the blindness of heathenism, unless the news of his mercy be conveyed to them by the lips of its living heralds. This, the apostle Paul, in a series of emphatic and sublime interrogatories, has unanswerably decided. "How shall they believe in him of whom they have not heard? And how shall they hear without a preacher? And how shall they preach except they be sent?" The whole train of his argument conclusively shows, that, while those only shall be saved who call on the name of the Lord, and look in faith to his atonement, none will do this to whom the Gospel has not come through teachers delegated and sent by others. But there is no class of men, separate from the church, qualified to send forth the ambassadors of Christ, or prepared to sustain them in their labors. To her, and to her alone, has God intrusted the apparatus and the arrangements requisite for this purpose. On her he has conferred the authority to ordain and commission the ministers of his truth. To her keeping he has confided those inspired oracles which declare his will, and unfold the scheme of his grace. To her he has given holy zeal, and sanctified talent, and rivers of wealth, and countless hands and voices, and a key to all the treasures of Omnipotence, in the promise to hear her prayers, and prosper her efforts. And, to crown all, to energize all, he has appointed his blessed Spirit to be her perpetual guide and helper, imbuing her words with heavenly power, and rendering "the weapons of her warfare mighty through God, to the pulling down of strong holds." In view of these ample endowments, no one can doubt, that it is her chief and high vocation, to be Christ's witness to mankind; testifying, to all nations and tribes, the efficacy of his sacrifice; traversing, with eager step and weeping eye, this wide "valley of dry bones;" prophesying to its multitudinous dead; and bearing the uplifted cross through every island and continent, until its victorious ensign shall wave over a subject world.

Having thus shown the province of the church, I proceed to notice,

II. THE MORAL POSITION WHICH THE FULFILMENT OF HER SOLEMN TRUST REQUIRES HER TO OCCUPY.

This is set before us in the words, "Get thee up into the high mountain." The allusion is here to a herald, who, being charged with the announcement of important tidings, ascends some lofty eminence, in order that his voice may reach over a wider circuit. Under this image, Zion is exhorted to rise from her present depressed level, to that high and commanding ground, where her influence may be most powerfully felt, and her efforts attended with the largest success. It is, therefore, the *spiritual elevation* of the church which is exhibited as so essential to her efficiency.

1. This implies *that her views of divine truth must become much more clear and perfect.* One of the causes which now weaken and paralyze the church in her aggressions upon the empire of sin, is the corruptness of her doctrines. Though favored with that heaven-indited volume, in which is contained a complete revelation of the mind of God, the standard of faith, and the forms and delineations of all moral verities;— yet, owing to her partially sanctified state, and the perversity of the human understanding, she "sees through a glass darkly," and on many material points, utterly overlooks, or misconceives, the teaching of inspiration. Her beauty is consequently impaired by numerous heresies,—her peace disturbed by constant strife,—her primitive simplicity disfigured by human admixtures and distortions,—and that glorious unity, which her dying Lord supplicated for her, lost amid a thousand jarring sects, each pervaded by the very genius

of repulsion. Thus her strength, instead of being directed to the overthrow of Satan's kingdom, is expended in domestic feuds and endless controversies; while the world which she was appointed to enlighten and save, confirmed in its unbelief by her errors and divisions, is left to go down to death; and Heaven weeps and Hell exults over her suicidal discords, and the roar of her intestine war.

The extent to which this prevalence of unsound theology and unscriptural practice enfeebles the church, and disqualifies her for the work committed to her hands, will be evident, on the slightest reflection, to every candid mind. In the discharge of her momentous functions, it is her business to carry the message of the Gospel to all the families of men, enchained as they are in the fetters of delusion, imposture, and idolatry. But how can she do this successfully, when she herself disobeys that message? How can she bear the word of God triumphantly to the nations, when she misapprehends or corrupts that word, and even refuses to render, into the dialects of the heathen, the full and faithful import of its inspired originals? How can she hurl down the giant structure of formalism and Papal superstition, which overshadows the old world, and is beginning to cast its baleful gloom on this land of the pilgrims, when its very key-stone and main pillar is found in her own constitutions? O, would she but emerge from the mists of perversion and falsehood, into the pure atmosphere of the Bible, and, laying aside all human creeds and party watchwords, stand on the broad, shining platform of "the truth as it is in Jesus," how mighty would be her power, how brilliant the illumination which she would pour around her! Then would her voice be the voice of God. Then would her watchmen see eye to eye; and all her myriad children speak one language, and breathe one spirit. Then would her walls, planted on the Rock of Scripture, soar upward from their firm foundation, attracting the admiring gaze of mankind by their massive grandeur, their hamonious proportions, and their unearthly glory. Then would all her resources be combined, for the single object of advancing the Redeemer's cause; and, moving on, with unbroken front, under the great, central banner of "One Lord, one faith, one baptism," with what united and irresistible energy would she throw herself on the entrenchments of darkness!

2. The posture demanded of the church involves *a far*

higher elevation of Christian principle. The rules of conduct, which now govern a large majority of her members, are low and defective, and closely assimilated to the maxims of the irreligious. Multitudes, who have pronounced her vows, and received her ordinances, are idolatrously devoted to the vanities of time; grovelling in the dust and mire of this world of sense; and laboring, chiefly, to hoard up sordid treasure, or gain those fading honors which a breath bestows, and a breath can extinguish. Hence, the church is extensively secularized in her spirit and practice. In place of seeking only the glory of her exalted Head, and the promotion of his kingdom, imitating his example of self-denial and humility, and obeying his laws of purity and benevolence, — she is, in a great measure, living to herself, striving for temporal aggrandizement, courting the embrace of pride, and pomp, and fashion, and bowing herself down to the customs and manners of an ungodly generation. Forgetful of the injunction, to let her light so shine before men, that, seeing her good works, they may be constrained to glorify her Master, and acknowledge the lofty morality of his religion, she is solicitous rather to diminish its strictness, and square its requirements to the opinions and habitudes of society. She no longer bears that distinct and unequivocal testimony against wickedness, under all forms and in all places, which is one great end of her organization. How faintly she rebukes the rampant enormities of the age! While intemperance desolates the land, and profaneness insults the heavens, and licentiousness stalks abroad with unblushing brow, and the Sabbath of the Lord is desecrated and contemned, she utters scarce a note of remonstrance, or lifts a finger to stay the overflowing scourge. Nay, more; with some of the most atrocious systems of iniquity which the earth has ever seen, she is, throughout a large portion of her communion, directly identified. Not only does she forbear to reprove them, and drag forth their hideousness to the blaze of day, but exerts much of her talent and influence to give them patronage, and even attempts to wrest the statute-book of God, the exponent of all truth and righteousness, into their support and countenance.

Dishonored and polluted by such alliances with sin, how can she hope to evangelize the nations? With garments so defiled, can she exemplify to mankind the glorious beauty of the Gospel? Herself needing a new moral baptism, can she disciple the world to Christ? Can she extend over all the earth the victories of the Prince of Peace, bearing in one hand the emblem of salvation, and in the other the price of blood; break the chains of spiritual thraldom abroad, and rivet the fetters of her bondmen at home; or teach to the human race the law of universal love, while trampling on human rights, treading out the life from the immortal mind, and crushing, with iron heel, God's image in man? What marvel, if, when thus approached, the millions of the unconverted should wrap themselves up in their delusions, and prefer infidelity or paganism to a Christianity so stained and defaced? What marvel, that, in circumstances like these, dissension should agitate our Zion, and blasting and mildew descend upon her, filling all her borders with gloom; while an offended God draws back his hand, and commands his clouds to withhold their rain; and from our altars, and sanctuaries, and missionary fields, the angels of mercy are heard " gathering up their rustling wings," and saying, " Let us go hence ! " If the church would fully execute her mission, and become, what her Founder intended, the advocate and witness of his grace — the proclaimer of its cleansing power, and its living example — she must abandon all affinity with wrong in every shape, and ascend to the pure, cloudless, heaven-gilded summit of Christian consistency and rectitude, where she shall " have no fellowship with the unfruitful works of darkness;" but shine forth, "fair as the moon, clear as the sun, and terrible," to trangessors, " as an army with banners." Then will she receive the approving smiles of God, in the abundant communications of his Spirit; and be known and recognized of all men, as the great antagonist of unrighteousness, the moral regenerator of the world.

3. The elevation required of the church includes, also, *eminent personal holiness.* In addition to the want of high-toned principle, and the connection, direct or implied, with public evils, to which we have referred, there prevails, among the mass of Christian professors, a low standard of individual and practical piety. They entertain a very imperfect sense of their obligations to the Saviour, who has redeemed them, and called them to be partakers in the inheritance of his saints. Their religious exercises are marked by many deficiencies. Their repentance is superficial, their faith feeble and wavering, their zeal languid and fitful, their views of spiritual things obscure and distant, their hope of heaven a

vague desire, rather than a realizing certainty, and their love to Christ and to the souls of men, cold, speculative, and inconstant. Their entire character partakes largely of their former state of carnality and pollution. Their old tempers and passions yet rankle and tyrannize in their bosoms. The chains of lust, and avarice, and selfishness, but half broken, still hang clanking heavily around them. And while, for the shadows of this fugitive scene, the gains of commerce, the strifes and fluctuations of political parties, and the whole shifting panorama of earth's empty illusions, they are all alive and eager, they manifest but little concern, and make few and paltry endeavors, to promote the honor of Jehovah, and the recovery of our race to his rightful dominion. This absence of earnest and devoted consecration, on the part of believers, is a most fatal hindrance to the success of the Gospel. It chills and frustrates prayer, palsies the arm of exertion, dries up the stream of benevolence, shields the impenitent, as with triple steel, against conviction, and, closing the ear of God, arrests the descent of his all-conquering Spirit. Never will the church meet her solemn responsibilities, until her children, bursting asunder the shackles that bind them, and rising out of the slough of earthliness in which they are sunk, come up to that high measure of evangelical sanctification, which the voice of Scripture and the exigencies of a dying world alike demand of them. There is a moral omnipotence in holiness. Argument may be resisted. Persuasion and entreaty may be scorned. The thrilling appeals and monitions of the pulpit, set forth with all the vigor of logic, and in all the glow of eloquence, may be evaded or disregarded. But the exhibition of exalted piety has a might which nothing can withstand. It is truth embodied. It is the Gospel, burning in the hearts, beaming from the eyes, breathing from the lips, and preaching in the lives of its votaries. No sophistry can elude it. No conscience can ward it off. No bosom wears a mail that can brave the energy of its attack. It speaks in all languages, in all climes, and to all phases of our nature. It is universal — invincible; and, clad in immortal panoply, goes on from victory to victory. Let Zion, through all her departments, but reach this elevated point, and how rapid and triumphant would be her progress! With what overpowering demonstration would her tidings be attended! What numerous and ever-flowing channels would pour into her treasury the requisite means; and what hosts of her consecrated sons would stand forth, to publish on every shore the mandates of her King! And how richly would the showers of Divine influence be shed down, quickening into life the seed which she scatters, filling the desolate wastes with verdure and joy, and changing this blighted earth into the garden of the Lord!

4. Another characteristic of the position, to which the church is exhorted to ascend, *is near and intimate dependence on God*. In her present low standing-place, with the vapors of error and the fogs of worldliness floating all around her, her spiritual perceptions are clouded and distorted. The things of sense and time — the objects which are at hand and palpable — loom up in unreal magnitude; while those of the far heaven are hidden from her view, or appear in remote and shadowy outline. Hence, the great fact, that Jehovah alone is her Rock and her Defence, and his almighty Spirit the source of her advancement, is but dimly seen, and feebly apprehended. She may, indeed, cherish it as an article of her creed; yet, practically, it is unheeded and forgotten. Instead of reposing an undivided trust in the approbation and blessing of her enthroned Intercessor, she is too much inclined to rely on the splendor of intellect, the stores of learning, the numbers, and wealth, and temporal respectability which she can bring to her support. In some of her divisions, alliance is even sought with the civil arm, and princes, and potentates, and a mitred hierarchy, are regarded as her law-givers and protectors. O, how unlike is this to the conduct of the early disciples! They stood on " the high mountain," and saw the pomp of human power, and the gilded pageantry of crowns and sceptres, dwindle into a speck beneath them. How little did they estimate the glitter of riches, the halo of talents, the parade of titles, and the array of all earthly influence! The celestial realm, with its vast and absorbing realities, was close above them. The face of God, radiant with love, shone full upon their hearts, filling the whole field of their vision, and ravishing them with his ineffable perfections. Immersed in the divine effulgence, they lost sight of the world — of themselves — and God became " all in all " — the atmosphere in which they moved — their Element of Life, their Centre, and their Rest. They *felt* that to Him *only* must they look for succor; and that, without his presence, all the instrumentalities in the universe were vain

and worthless. They hung their hopes to the pillars of his throne; they laid their prayers at his very footstool; and He, honoring their confidence, prospered their labors, and made their names a wonder and a glory to all coming ages. O, could we, like them, win up to that sun-lit pinnacle, rising, pure and clear, above the smoke and din of this murky scene, where our access to the infinite grace of the Father and the Son should be full and free; where our communion with them should be obstructed by no intervening barrier; and where our faith, severed from all mortal reliances, and fixing its calm eye on the Omnipotent alone, should grasp with untrembling hand his immutable promises, what an amazing revolution would be wrought in our feelings and actions, and how victorious would be our assaults upon the strong holds of iniquity! Then would primitive fervor again animate the church, and apostolical strength gird her ministry, and ancient triumphs return to her banner, " God witnessing with " her in every land, and enduing his own word with energy from on high.

5. Another particular in which Zion needs to be elevated, is *in the grandeur and universality of her plans of benevolence.* The spectator, who occupies the mountain-top, has a much more extensive and commanding prospect, than he who dwells at its base. In like manner should the Christians of our day ascend into " the Mount of Vision," that they may survey the wide moral landscape, and take the dimensions of the whole mighty territory which they are summoned to invade and conquer. While remaining at a low point, we are apt to confine our aims and efforts within a narrow circle, and to think little of the far-spreading fields which distance, and interposing heights, shut out from our view. It is, therefore, necessary that we should attain a loftier post of observation, whence our eye may range over a broader compass, and where we may enlarge our calculations in proportion to the enterprise to be achieved. Planting our feet on the bright eminence which has been described, let us throw our glance over the immense regions that lie beneath, stretching away in illimitable perspective. A *world* is before us, with all its peopled continents, its crowding millions, its darkness and woe. Upon the whole boundless expanse, Guilt and Death, with raven wings, " sit brooding." Here, close at hand, we see our own favored country — where the free word of God, proscribed or trammelled in all other lands, has found its

refuge, and wrought its most signal results — sinking into the gulf of degeneracy; menaced with the fearful domination of "the man of sin;" sapped and convulsed by giant vices; its rulers, its politicians, and its insane population casting off the laws of Jehovah; while the church is at ease, her sentinels asleep, and the beacon-lights burning dimly on her towers. Yonder, we see Europe, the proud home of arts and civilization — one half of it shrouded in the blackness of Papal night, and the other, a solitary kingdom excepted, covered with the huge corpse of a dead Protestantism, and its monstrous emanation, a baptized Infidelity. And even in that single nation where vital Christianity still lives, we witness a concerted and vigorous attempt to pollute or destroy it, and substitute, in its room, the exploded mummeries of a darker age. On this side, we behold Africa — wronged, bleeding Africa — sitting in the dust, and mantled with one wide pall of barbarism. We see her vast interior thronged with savage hordes, scarce raised above the level of the brute, and given up to the most degrading idolatry. We see the slave-ship hovering on her coasts; and hear the clanking of her fetters, the shrieks of her children, the shouts of rapine and violence, echoing along her plundered shores. And there, far in the dim and ancient East — the hoary cradle of the world — we look on the unnumbered myriads of Asia, plunged in heathenism, a prey to debasing passions, strangers to hope, and hurrying blindly into the abyss. Every where, we perceive the presence and the power of that relentless enemy of God and man, whose throne is on the high places of the earth, and whose trophies are murdered souls. We see Romanism deluding its countless votaries; Paganism enthralling two-thirds of our species; and the fell imposture of Mohammed blasting the fairest portions of the globe, and even lifting its foul crescent above the hallowed scenes which the Redeemer trod. We see governments, laws, society, — both in lands benighted and civilized, — constructed on principles alien to the Gospel; and the spirit of ungodliness diffused through all ranks and classes of mankind; while the few, who cleave to the cause of truth and heaven, are, in comparison, but as the three bands of Gideon to the dense host of the Midianites, or as the lonely spots of verdure that gem an otherwise unbroken desert.

Such is the spectacle which, from the "high mountain," presents itself below and around us. The work which we are called to accomplish, is the moral renovation of this entire extent of sin and misery, its complete subjection to the authority of Christ, and its universal transformation into beauty and holiness. Not a corner of it is to be left unreclaimed; not a dark recess forgotten; not a remote isle of the sea unevangelized; not a wanderer of the wilderness unillumined; not a solitary child of Adam unblessed with the tidings of peace and pardon. Over all, the loveliness and purity of Eden are again to return. Over all, Christ is to reign, and to reign through the instrumentality of his people. Here, then, let us stand, and devise our plans, and form our resolves, with a vigor and a scope commensurate with the greatness of the undertaking which devolves upon us. To this all-viewing height, let the whole church come up, and estimate the task to be performed, the evils to be removed, the obstacles to be encountered, and lay out her schemes of effort with an amplitude that shall embrace the world. This brings us to consider,

III. THE SPIRIT WITH WHICH SHE SHOULD ENGAGE IN HER ARDUOUS MISSION.

"Lift up thy voice with strength; be not afraid." *Strength* and *courage*, then, are the qualities which she is to exhibit, in obeying the behest of her Lord.

1. She is required to devote to this work her *utmost energy*. All her endowments are to be concentrated upon it; all her resources called out in its behalf; all the means, and gifts, and piety of her members brought into requisition, and dedicated to the grand object of sending the word of life to the nations. The real strength of the church has never yet been developed. Sluggish and supine, she is ignorant of her own power. She little dreams what mighty exertions are within the compass of her ability. A few efforts, feeble and uncertain as those of a sleeping man, she has, indeed, made; and a small band of missionaries, scantily sustained, and slowly reinforced, has been despatched to heathen shores. But her contributions for this purpose have been only as a "drop in the bucket," to the overflowings of her abundance; and the men whom she has supplied are as nothing to that army of Christian heralds which she might and ought to have sent into all the earth. She has scarcely begun to feel her true responsibility, or to be in earnest in fulfilling its momentous demands. Her desires are stinted and weak; her expectations vague and meagre. Her immense revenues lie unem-

ployed, rusting in her coffers, or, squandered in selfish gratifications, corrode her graces, and become a poison and a snare. Hence, the conversion of the world lingers, and generation after generation descends into hell; while the church is idly reposing on her arms, or making slight and puny demonstrations against the march of the destroyer. O, were she to go forth in her collected might, furnished with all her numberless instrumentalities, surrounded and aided by all her sons and daughters — love for the world burning in every heart, prayer for the world ascending from every lip, bounty for the world dropping from every hand, the message of mercy to the world gushing from every tongue — with what wide-reaching strength would her voice be lifted up, and how like the trumpet of the archangel would her summons ring through all the dreary abodes of unbelief and idolatry!

2. She is to enter upon this work with *courage*. This implies *confidence* in her Almighty *leader*. It is Christ, " the captain of salvation," who marshals the church for the combat, and superintends all her movements. He is the Lord of Providence, the Sovereign Disposer of all human destinies. Above the storms and conflicts of time, the upheavings of society, and the mutations of empire, he sits serene, directing every event with unerring wisdom; and even overruling, for the final success of his truth, and the consummation of his glory, those which to mortal vision appear most adverse and disastrous. Arrayed in all the attributes of Divinity, he guides and supports his people, perceives every stratagem of the foe, foresees every peril, provides for every emergency. His cause can never fail; for " He must reign until he hath put all enemies under his feet." In reward of his abasement and sufferings, God has promised that the knowledge of his name shall fill the world as the waters the sea; and that he shall receive " the heathen for his inheritance, and the uttermost parts of the earth for his possession." This promise, made to him in the everlasting covenant, will infallibly be fulfilled. " All that the Father hath given him shall come to him." Every soul redeemed by his atonement, shall be conformed to his image, and set, as a polished jewel, in his eternal diadem. And it is in the general spread of the Gospel, that this grand result of his mediation is to be accomplished and displayed. With what unblenching courage, therefore, may his people go forward, assured that infinite power and faithfulness are pledged to their success, and that

every kingdom and nation shall yet bow to the glorified Emanuel!

The church is also to have *confidence* in the *tidings* which she proclaims. Her theme is the astonishing grace of God to sinful man, manifested in the gift of his only begotten Son to suffer and die. The cross, stained with the blood of incarnate Deity — the cross, in all its melting eloquence of love and sorrow, its mingled exhibitions of divine justice and tenderness, and its wondrous bearings on earth and heaven — is the weapon which she carries for the conquest of the world, — the balm which she brings to its stricken hearts — the elevator which she applies to its degradation and ruin. In the Gospel, when thus unfolded, there is a certain and irresistible efficacy. It is adapted to the nature of man, and meets all the tremendous exigencies in which he is involved. It comes home to his bosom, in all states of intellectual culture, at all times, and under all the forms of his social existence. No ignorance can misconceive, no darkness shut it out. It can neither be overcome, nor impeded. It springs elastic from every pressure. It rises imbued with new energy from defeat. It is a tide of influence ever deepening and widening, and hurrying forward with swifter current, and whose mighty waves, the strong embankments of prejudice, infidelity and error but cause to roll and swell the more; until, at length, all barriers give way, and it flows on, an ocean of glory, pure, boundless, and free. Such is the instrument on which, under God, the church relies; and, wielding this, is she not sure of ultimate triumph?

Finally, she is to be *undismayed by the number and power of her adversaries.* The human heart, everywhere intensely depraved; the worldliness and aversion to God which universally prevail; the general structure of civil politics; and the imposing systems of false religion — all backed and upheld by the legions of the pit — are combined in one vast phalanx of opposition against the progress of the Gospel. But this "great mountain," whose roots are in hell, and whose shadow covers the globe, "shall become a plain" before the tread of the advancing Redeemer; and the spiritual temple shall continue to ascend, until, the last stone having been laid in its place, amid the acclamations of the universe, shouting "grace, grace unto it," — it shall stand complete and perfect, the joy of earth, and the admiration of heaven. Every form of hostility to the grace and supremacy of God, every weapon which men or devils have devised for the overthrow of his cause, shall be broken and scattered by the finger of his Providence, and the breath of his Spirit; for He, whose counsels cannot be frustrated, hath decreed it. Discouraged, then, by no difficulties, appalled by no dangers, may the messengers of his word go forth, knowing that free and bright, as the orb of day when the cloud-rack has vanished, it is destined to traverse the circuit of the world, filling it with light, life, and salvation, and evoking from all its regenerated inhabitants the pure offering of love, and the glad incense of praise.

In the review of our subject, how blessed does the province of the church appear! How attractive and brilliant the sphere in which she is appointed to move! Jehovah might have ordained an angelic ministry for the promulgation of his mercy to men. And in such an office the loftiest seraph would rejoice. O, with what swift and exulting pinions would Gabriel cleave the sky, if commissioned to publish the everlasting Gospel to all that dwell on the earth! But, in condescending kindness, God has assigned this work to his people. He has made them the bearers of his grace — the distributers of the Bread of Life. He has commanded man to declare to his fellow-man, of every lineage and complexion, that all-sufficient Propitiation which has been offered for the human race.

Fathers and brethren! in what position do we stand, with respect to this delightful, this imperative duty? As members of the great Christian family, no small share of the world's evangelization devolves on us. Are we devoting to it our time and property, our strength and soul, the whole active energy of our ransomed nature? Are we occupying that high ground of religious consistency and personal holiness, which will best fit us for its successful prosecution? Only so far as we thus live, are we meeting the solemn claims of our profession. If indifferent and unfaithful here, we are but cumberers in the vineyard of the Lord — salt that has lost its savor — fountains whose waters are poisoned, and send forth disease instead of health. O, let us awake to the glory of Christ, and to the wants of the millions of our fellow-beings, enveloped in the shadow of death, and plunging, even while I speak, by thousands, into eternal despair. To all these perishing multitudes we are required to carry the "good tidings" of a Saviour. To this enterprise we are bound to consecrate every faculty and every endeavor, while life shall last. We may, indeed, pass to our final home ere the task be finished. But other hands will take it up, and conduct it forward to its completion. Be it ours to strive, that they may have nothing to do but to perfect what we have almost consummated, and to raise the shout of victory over the total destruction of a foe which we left routed and flying. We are urged, by every impressive and cogent motive, to arouse to action. Heaven, with its authoritative commands; earth, with its guilt and sorrows; and hell, with its quenchless fires, all invoke us to do what we can for the deliverance of our species. The predictions of Scripture, the developments of Providence, the aspects of the age, the success already granted to our incipient efforts, proclaim, with trumpet-tongue, that "the harvest of the earth is ripe;" and, from every surrounded point, there comes to us the thrilling mandate, "Thrust ye in the sickle, and reap," strengthened by the glorious incentive, "He that reapeth receiveth wages, and gathereth fruit unto life eternal."

Brethren, the drama of the world is hastening on to its crisis. Soon will the curtain be lifted, and disclose that new order of its moral creation, in which righteousness shall abundantly flourish, and perfect love, and purity, and joy, spread their balmy wings over our redeemed humanity. Then, and not till then, will the hour of rest arrive to the church. Then, and not till then, having accomplished her mission, she may repose from her toils; and, like some universal mother, gathering from the four winds her sinless and happy offspring, fold them in her arms, and nurse them at her bosom. Then will the ruins of the apostacy be repaired, and angel-lyres, and all human voices, unite to sound the anthem of a world recovered. And then will be realized, O how brightly! the entrancing vision of the poet, who, dwelling "fast by the oracle of God," drew from its sacred well his sweet and seraphic inspiration:

> "One song employs all nations, and all cry,
> Worthy the Lamb, for he was slain for us.
> The dwellers in the vales and on the rocks,
> Shout to each other, and the mountain tops
> From distant mountains catch the flying joy;
> Till, nation after nation taught the strain,
> Earth rolls the rapturous hosanna round."

THE BEARINGS OF MODERN COMMERCE ON THE PROGRESS OF MODERN MISSIONS.

BY

REV. JOHN S. STONE, D. D.

Surely the isles shall wait for me, and the ships of Tarshish first, to bring thy sons from far, their silver and their gold with them, unto the name of the Lord thy God, and to the Holy One of Israel, because he hath glorified thee. — ISAIAH 69 : 9.

THIS passage is from a most glowing prophetic description of the ultimately universal spread of the Gospel through our world. It is from a prophecy, which foreshows, not only that every *land* shall be subjected to Christ, but also that " the abundance of *the sea* shall be converted unto him." In this great work of winning the world, commerce, it seems, is to take a conspicuous part. While " the isles " wait for Christ, " the ships of Tarshish " are to be " first " in bringing the sons of Zion from far, with their silver and their gold as an offering unto " the name of the Lord their God," and as consecrated means in the hands of Him, who hath steadfastly purposed to " glorify the house of his glory."

Among all the means used in converting the human race to Christ, commerce, no doubt, is to be one of the most important. Three-fifths of the earth's surface are covered with waters ; while the remaining fifths lie in the shape of two vast continents, and of innumerable isles, — the abodes of men, and the depositories of those treasures which God has given for the use of men. Between these, the great deep is a broad highway ; and commerce, with her ships, the only system of intercommunication. Without commerce, neither science nor art, neither civilization nor religion, could spread beyond the boundaries of the land of their birth. All other agencies, not purely spiritual, are, when left to themselves, local. Commerce has the only created arm that can reach round the globe.

This, then, is the grand agent which God has prepared for himself, and which he purposes to use in the work of gathering in the nations to Christ, and in collecting the gold and silver, the redundant means, which that work demands. The connection of commerce with the spread of the Gospel, is, therefore, a thought full of interest. To its development, so far as the nature of the occasion, and the special object in view will admit, I now invite your attention. I restrict myself *to the bearings of modern commerce on the progress of modern missions;* and, even in this view, shall find more than can be adequately surveyed in the short time allotted to our examination.

I. By modern commerce, I mean that which has overspread the earth since the invention of the mariner's compass, and the consequent discovery, in 1492, of a new world, as distinguished from that ancient commerce, which, having no trusty guide, crept only along the shores, and explored only the inlets and interior waters of the old continent. This modern commerce is now the mightiest body of human power, that can be found in action on our world. From an unskilled infant, with little or nothing of experience, it has grown to a colossal giant, as dextrous in its skill as it is resistless in its power. In the discovery and application of steam, it has impressed into its service nearly all the agencies of nature; and it wields them with all the certainty of science, and with all the efficiency of experience. With this subtle power, it outstrips the wind upon the ocean, and almost copes in speed with the eagle on the land. With this viewless and resistless agent, it has opened the bowels of the earth, and penetrated the solitudes of the wilderness; and, in the results of agriculture, manufactures, and mining, has made ancient lands pay new tribute to the main, and new regions unlock their before hidden treasures to its grasp.

I spread the definition of modern commerce over these operations on *land*, not because the text has special reference to so broad a system, but because from the beginning the system has been actuated by one spirit; because the whole body of the great business world has but one soul; and because commerce in her *ships* is but the grand carrier for commerce on her *wheels*.

This, then, is the commerce of which I speak; that which has been growing up in the world for the last three hundred and fifty years. It is this, the bearings of which on modern missions, we are now to examine ; on *modern* missions, as distinguished from *ancient;* as springing up at the same time, and operating through the same period, with that commerce by which they have been affected.

This commerce, the word of God justifies us in believing, is at least a part of that which is to be instrumental in the divine work of evangelizing mankind, in bringing all her sons into the church of Christ, and in furnishing for the Lord the silver and the gold, the mere human means, which his enterprise of mercy requires. Has this commerce thus far done the work for which it has been raised up ? Has it yet been God's handmaid in gathering the nations to Christ, or in carrying to them that Gospel of salvation, which teaches man to love the Lord his God with all his heart, and his neighbor as himself; to recompense to no man evil for evil, but rather to overcome evil with good ; that Gospel, which is truth, and justice, and temperance—which is purity, and love, and peace, and which is intended to make earth like heaven, and man like God ? Has commerce yet taken her destined part in doing this her destined work ? For an answer, let us take as brief a survey as possible of her doings.

II. I begin by premising one thing. It is undoubtedly true, that modern commerce has been the occasion of a great extension of the arts of civilization, and of the blessings of true religion. Within the last half century especially, her ships have wafted the true missionary of the cross, with the true Gospel of Christ, and with the elements of true Christian civilization, to almost every part of the earth. And in almost numberless ways, through the channels which she has opened, almost numberless blessings have been spread over the world. Walls of separation have been broken down ; nations have been brought closer together ; and the bonds of one universal brotherhood have begun to be woven around the one great family of man. But, then, all this has been but an incident to the system, not its main object, nor yet its main result. It has not grown out of the spirit and tendency of commerce, but has come to pass in spite of that spirit and tendency. *Commerce* has spread these blessings, just as *war* has spread them. The object of war is not to civilize and Christianize, but to conquer and subdue. But, then, in its shock, refined nations sometimes mix with barbarous ; and thus, even though in *letters of blood*, teach them lessons of a thousand things, which before they never knew. So it has been with commerce. The blessings which she has carried, were not in her *heart*. They only followed unbidden in her *train*. They went, not *by* her, but *with* her, and often in *spite* of her. While, therefore, we must not be unmindful of the good of which she has been the occasion, this good must not be suffered to blind us to her real character, and to her own proper works. To proceed, then, in our proposed examination.

Unfortunately, modern commerce awoke at a time when Christianity had been sleeping for a thousand years in the growing, thickening darkness of a spiritual night; a night, which, as usual, grew darker and darker till the very break of day. Amongst the monstrous things engendered in that night of darkness, was the grand usurpation of the Papacy, which arrogated to itself the prerogative of Almighty God. "The Pope," to use the language of the historian Robertson, "as the vicar and representative of Jesus Christ, was supposed to have a right of dominion over all the kingdoms of the earth." Nor was this an unexercised right. For, immediately after the discovery of the new world, a mere "Italian priest boldly presumed to give away God's earth, as if he sat God's acknowledged vicegerent. Splitting this mighty planet into two imaginary halves, he handed one to the Spanish, and the other to the Portuguese monarch;"* thus pretending to convey to each a right to all the countries within their assigned limits which they might discover, not already occupied by any Christian nation. And who were the people to whom this monstrous grant was made? A part of the millions of that old world which for thousands of years had been growing more and more dense in population, more and more dense in superstition, more and more dense in the vices and diseases of old and corrupt institutions. Lust of power, and lust of gold, having fed to fatness on the men and the wealth of Europe and of Asia, stood eager for new victims and new gratification, when this great western world was thrown open by the hand of discovery to the knowledge of mankind. And what was the character of this freshly discovered world? It was *a paradise*, swarming with untold millions of simple inhabitants, beautiful, confiding and noble in their simplicity. It was a vast *storehouse*, full of the natural wealth of silver and gold, and of the natural beauties and luxuries of a most bountiful soil.

---

* Howitt's Colonization and Christianity, p. 21.

1. Awakening at such a period, in view of such a prize, and with such a training at home, modern commerce became in her very first movement, and has ever since continued, a *colonizing* spirit. Her ships have visited the new-discovered world, not to communicate, in exchange for honestly acquired wealth, knowledge and civilization, peace and love, but to pour in *colonies* of foreigners; to take possession of whole countries in the name of an arrogant and distant usurper; and, under pretence of planting the cross, and of spreading a religion of which they knew little but the name, to grasp at the whole incalculable mass of the treasures of the richest portion of the earth.

2. Under these circumstances, too, modern commerce soon became, and has ever since continued, a *war-waging* spirit. Having first, by cruel, exacting, and murderous measures, by deceit and treachery, roused the simple natives of the West Indies to resistance, it opened on them those baying mouths of death, its musketry and its cannon, and drove wars of extermination through their beautiful isles; wasting whole races before the deep-skilled prowess of tyrants, wearing the *Christian* name, and marching under the banner of the cross, the ensign of the prince of peace!

3. Nor is this all. Under the influences which reigned over its origin, modern commerce speedily became, and has ever since continued, a *slave-making* spirit. The hitherto gentle and unworked natives, doomed to bleed in war, to toil in the mines, and to sweat in the sugar factories of Hispaniola, vanished like the morning dew. Then was first conceived an idea, which has since been the parent of the deepest wrongs and miseries which this earth has ever suffered—the idea of filling the places made vacant by the vanishing of one race, with slaves, captured and dragged thither from another; the idea of making poor, sable Africa, the chained menial to do the work, and bear the frowns, and waste away under the reign of Christian avarice, indolence and tyranny.

4. And would to God there were nothing further on this catalogue of ills. But there is. The system which thus began its work, went on to do it with unaltered mind. Modern commerce early became, and has ever since continued, a corrupting spirit. What it could not wholly effect by treachery and war, exaction and oppression, it thoroughly accomplished by corruption. It corrupted the bodies and the minds of the once beautiful and healthy, the comparatively pure

and innocent aborigines of every land which it visited, by the systematic introduction and supply of intoxicating liquors, and by the reckless dissemination of the dark vices and deadly diseases of a misnamed civilization. In the former, it opened on them the burning waters of a river of death; and, in the latter, poured through the veins of both their bodies and their souls, the creeping poisons of a physical and a moral pestilence. Not content with deluging the most beautiful realms with those vices and diseases which are naturally communicated by the contact of depraved lust with unsuspecting innocence, it opened the very prisons and poor-houses of the old world, and vomited forth upon the new, colonies of the vile and the licentious, of the thieves and the assassins, with which the dark and corrupt bosom of so called Christian Europe teemed.

5. What was thus begun by the Spaniards in the West Indies, has been continued by every commercial nation in every portion of the aboriginal and pagan world, through the movements of an essentially colonizing, war-waging, slave-making, and corrupting commerce, whetting into fury its deep lust of gold, at the sight of boundless treasures not its own, and,—under the delusive idea of spreading a Christianity which it did not comprehend, and a civilization which it did not possess,—conquering, enslaving and wasting the fairest and the richest lands on earth.

6. Moreover, what was thus begun by commerce under the direction of Papal governments, was continued by commerce, under the direction of Protestant governments. Reformed in its main *doctrines*, Christianity did not become reformed in its entire *spirit*. The effects of a thousand years of error and corruption, could, with comparative ease be expunged from the creed of the church. But they had lingered deeply and long in the hearts of men. The Papal doctrine that "the heathen were given to believers as a possession," became protestantized; and the robber's principle, that "one outrage being committed, a second, or a series of outrages must be perpetrated to prevent punishment and secure the booty," has operated, if in a different way, yet quite as strongly, in the policy of the British East India Company, as it did in that of the Spanish conquest of Mexico. So far as the system of commercial aggrandizement is concerned, irrespectively, of course, of many individuals engaged in it, but one spirit has actuated the whole, from its conception to its present maturity,

under Papal and under Protestant auspices; and this spirit, in the words of a writer already quoted, has been "a fiery, rabid, quenchless lust of gold;" a passion, which, while it lives at home, is decently attired, and moderately restrained; but which, when it goes abroad, and stands in sight of the gold and the diamond mine, in sight of the rice-field and the cane-brake, in sight of the spicery and every other product of a prodigal earth, strips itself to nakedness, and, in its uncovered deformity, breaks every bond by which mankind are united, and, with unchecked rapine and violence, deceives, robs, oppresses and murders, without remorse; and, all this while, boasting of its civilization, and professing to bring to poor, benighted, barbarous heathen, a religion from heaven — the religion of the Gospel of peace and love, of truth and equity.

7. To give a history of all this would, of course, be impossible within the limits of a sermon. It would be to take you through the long horrors of those scenes, amidst which the Spaniards conquered, wasted and depopulated the beautiful West Indies, the mighty empire of Mexico, the dominions of the mysterious Incas of golden Peru, and the fair fields of wide-spreading, silvery Paraguay; — of those scenes, amidst which the Portuguese wrought the same enormities, throughout that land of the diamond mine, the broad Brazil, and on the rich isles and peninsulas of Eastern India; of those scenes, amidst which the Protestant Dutch became successors in the East to the realms and to the spirit of their Portuguese predecessors, and enacted, with deepening barbarity, the tragedy, which those predecessors had opened, among the peaceful and gentle Hindoos; of those scenes, amidst which the commerce of Britain,— humane, noble, Christian Britain,— introduced and carried forward its system of territorial acquisition, in Bengal and throughout all Hindostan, in New-Holland and through the myriad isles of the smiling Pacific, filling the most extensive and populous regions with some of the bloodiest and most devastating curses ever felt, poured out, too, by the hand of a people, who boast of being the most polished and Christianized on earth; of those scenes, amidst which the French run a shorter but scarcely less tragic race of competition with their commercial rivals, in Canada, Newfoundland, Nova Scotia, Madagascar, Mauritius, Guiana, some of the West India Islands, and parts of the East Indian and African Coasts; of those scenes, amidst which the Dutch and their

successors, the English, in South Africa, have proved themselves more barbarous, an hundred fold, than the so called barbarian Hottentots, Caffres and Bushmen, whom they have hunted, murdered, and exterminated; and finally, of those scenes nearer home, amidst which the combined and successive cruelties of the French, the English and the inhabitants of our own United States, have, for two hundred years, by treachery and the sword, by disseminated intemperance and disease, been weakening, wasting and blotting out the thousand tribes of one of the once finest races of men that God ever formed, — the aborigines of our own North America!

Think not that all this would be leading you through scenes of imagination, — the regions of mere poetry. Alas! they are regions too seriously, too sadly real; scenes, in which a sterner hand than that of imagination has been, and still is, doing its work! Sober history has written bloody facts all over her wide page, as the chronicler of the movements of modern commerce. Were I to give you the particulars of what I have exhibited merely in outline, you would only wonder at the feebleness of the sketch, and perhaps be thankful that a weak hand has not been able to torture you with a picture to the life, of what nations, professedly Christian, have been doing in the dark and distant realms of our world. It is sufficiently mournful to look over the page of ancient history, and read the acts of ancient heroes, conquerors, and enslavers of mankind; the Pharaohs and the Nebuchadnezzars, the Alexanders and the Cæsars of the East; — of their wars, their burnings, and their tortures; of their vices, their crimes, and their nameless abominations; — how they filled the earth with misery, and made mankind drunk with its bitter mixture! But it is more mournful, to look over that freshly written page, at which I have pointed. Modern commerce, during the three hundred and fifty years of her reign, has furnished for herself the materials of a darker, bloodier history, than that which has been written of the tyrants of the earth, during the whole four thousand years of ante-Christian barbarism! This commercial spirit has had a wider field on which to act, and more powerful enginery to put in action; and she has filled her field to fulness, and moved her enginery to the utmost of its power. The ancients conquered, but they did not exterminate; they enslaved, but they did not corrupt; they burned cities, but they did not annihilate races. The finishing up of the *extremes* of wickedness, barbarity, and pollution, seems to have been left for nations calling themselves civilized, boasting of their humanity, and professing to spread, or at least to believe, the religion of the Cross, the Gospel of the Prince of peace; — a religion of love and good-will, of truth and purity.

To show that the agents of modern commerce have not, even yet, done working up the dark picture of their atrocities, I need only refer you to what has just been passing in the East, in the efforts of British merchants to introduce and extend into all-populous China that awful curse, the opium trade. If missionaries, by the help of coasting vessels, attempt to introduce into that vast empire the Word of Life, men at home grow at once exceedingly conscientious, and cry out against the effort, as an interference with the religious institutions of the land. But they make no scruple in illicitly introducing there the drug of *death*, and that, in the face of the most solemnly proclaimed prohibitions of the emperor and his government. I do not suppose they would feel any special pleasure in murdering, outright, the three hundred millions of China; yet, for the sake of abstracting the immense wealth of the country, they would not hesitate to do what is worse, to besot both their bodies and their souls with a poison, which, in its work of human destruction, has few compeers, and still fewer superiors.

III. Let us now look at the effect of all this upon modern missions, upon the spread of the Gospel during the same three hundred and fifty years which we have been surveying.

When Commerce, with her newly-invented mariner's compass in her hand, went forth to the discovery of a new world, peopled with before unknown races of men, simple and guileless, generous and trusting — what a precious, what a glorious opportunity was presented, for carrying to them the blessings of real civilization, of useful knowledge, and of pure religion; and thus, for pouring the very soul of a heaven-descended Christianity into the minds, into the social state, and into the political and religious institutions of those, who looked up to the newly arrived with feelings of veneration, as to beings of a superior order! How was this opportunity improved? By holding out at first a wooden cross, as the symbol of an unexplained Gospel, and calling on the wondering multitudes to bow down and worship; and then, in their bowed down posture, loading them with every form and with every extreme of intolerable wrong. Instead of *christianiz-*

ing, the process *exterminated*. In the West Indies, the whole native population became speedily extinct ; the ten millions of that remarkable race, the noble Charibs, vanished like a morning mist before their oppressors. They bled in war ; they wasted away in the mines ; they toiled to death in the sugar-mills ; they were torn in pieces by trained squadrons of ferocious dogs ; and they pined and died in the dens and caves, whither they had fled from the foot of their civilized persecutors ; until, at length, their native lands held scarcely a remaining trace of their once beautiful forms. They had disappeared from the earth ; and, as their spirits vanished, they went, full of execrations upon the very name of that Christianity, which should have been the instrument of both their temporal and their eternal salvation.

In Mexico and Peru, history records that the Spanish sword drank the blood of forty millions of their sons. The whole Indian race in Newfoundland is extinct. Entire tribes in South Africa, and in North America, are no more ; while, in numerous lands and islands, great races of aboriginal and pagan men are wasting away to weakness and nothingness before the relentless approach of a power, bearing the ensign of life, but doing the work of death !

Where this power has not exterminated, it has wrought evils of a perhaps darker character. It has actually rendered the living savage *more* savage, and the living heathen *more* heathen than ever. It has made, not Christianity, — for of this little or nothing has been carried by the agents of this power, — but the name of Christianity, an offence and a loathing to the pagan world. Through all the realms of heathenism, it has made that name synonymous with hypocrisy and deceit, cunning and fraud, oppression and cruelty, avarice and extortion, pollution and crime. In this state of things, let the *true* missionary of the cross approach, and offer the genuine religion of the Gospel, as a light from heaven, and as the only means of purity and of salvation to benighted man ; and with what answer is he met ? " Go home, and convert your own countrymen ; cleanse your own seamen ; regenerate the agents of your death-dealing commerce, and thus show that your religion is the boasted blessing which you represent. Then come to us, and we will listen to your instructions, and examine the claims of the Gospel which you bring."

We hear often of *failures* in the foreign missionary work ; of the treasures of benevolence lavished in vain, and of the lives of the benevolent thrown away for nought. And these things, when they happen, are trumpeted abroad with a note of triumph, as though there were, even here at home, a spirit which exulted in the failures, and stood gloating at the prospect of utter defeat to the movements of Christianity. But whence these failures? From the inadequacy of the means employed? From the misdirection of Christian effort? From the indomitable character of savage and of pagan vices and superstitions? No, not from any *one*, or from all of these causes together. Proofs of this assertion will come in their proper place. But Christian missions fail, when they do fail, because they cannot penetrate where modern commerce has not been; because, as soon as the faithful missionary of the cross has begun to succeed in turning the miserable heathen from his idols, and in cleansing them from their pollutions, modern commerce, with its heart still lusting for gold, and fearful of losing its prey, rushes in, and, with its four great maces, war, slavery, intemperance, and disease, beats to the earth the work of heavenly benevolence, and knocks in head the new-born hopes of regenerated tribes!

A most remarkable instance of this interference is, at this moment, presented in the case of those numerous and beautiful islands in the Southern Pacific, which have been visited and blessed by the faithful missionaries of Christian England and America, and which may be considered as, in an encouraging sense, already civilized. These islands are spread in various directions from the great insular continent, New Holland, the seat of that monster evil, the penal colony of the British government, its Botany Bay, the vile home of its transported, convicted felons. By this fatal neighborhood, and the mischievous commerce of which it is the centre, all these triumphs of the Gospel amongst the islands are put in jeopardy. To use the language of a recent writer in England,* "All this springing civilization, this young Christianity, this scene of beauty and peace, are endangered. The founders of a new and happier state, the pioneers and artificers of civilization, stand aghast at the ruin that threatens their labors, that threatens the welfare, nay, the very existence, of the simple islanders, amongst whom they have wrought such miracles of love and order. And whence arises this danger? Whence comes this threatened ruin?"

---

* Howitt.

......" The savages of Europe, the most heartless and merciless race that ever inhabited the earth — a race, for the range and continuance of its atrocities, without a parallel in *this* world, and, it may be safely believed, in *any other*, — are busy in the South Sea Islands. A roving clan of sailors and runaway convicts have revived, once more, the crimes and character of the old buccaneers. They go from island to island, diffusing gin, debauchery, loathsome diseases, and murder, as freely as if they were the greatest blessings that Europe had to bestow. They are the restless and triumphant apostles of misery and destruction; and such are their achievements, that it is declared, unless government interpose some check to their progress, they will as completely annihilate the islanders, as the Charibs were annihilated in the West Indies."..... "What a shocking thing is this! that, when Christianity has been professed in Europe for eighteen hundred years, it is from Europe that the most dreadful corruption of morals, and the most dismal defiance of every sound principle, come! If Christianity, despised and counterfeited by its ancient professors, flies to some remote corner of the globe, and there unfolds to simple, admiring eyes her blessings and her charms, out from Europe rush hordes of lawless savages, to chase her thence, and level to the dust the dwellings, and the very being of her votaries." All this has been corroborated, by sober investigation, before members of that august body, the British parliament.

IV. But, let us turn to more cheering views. In this picture of darkness, *all* is not dark. Facts and reasonings, full of light, remain to be exhibited; and the Christian's spirit finds a blessed relief, in passing out from what is so shocking to moral sentiment, and in giving itself up to the contemplation of what is more congenial with Christian hope.

I remark, then, that—much as modern commerce has done to make the savage more savage and the heathen more heathen, to make the name of Christianity a loathing and that of civilization synonymous with a CURSE, — all this may be undone, and the aborigines and the pagan still reconciled to the Gospel, if governments, merchant companies, and trading men, will but learn justice, truth, and mercy in their dealings, and leave unobstructed Christianity to do her own proper work. Even the dismal *past* holds an ample store of facts, in proof of this position.

While the Spaniards and Portuguese, in Paraguay and

Brazil, were doing their dark work of conquest and of plunder, the Jesuit missionaries introduced themselves among the natives; and, though they carried with them a deeply corrupted Christianity, yet, carrying also, for once at least, the true spirit of love, and peace, and simple confidence in God, they wrought wonders of mercy among the untaught children of the new world. The Jesuit became the Indian's friend. Multitudes flocked to their teaching; and their numerous reductions, or settlements, became, amidst the wide moral waste around, scenes of smiling peace and beauty; blessed with the arts of life, and, so far as Christianity was understood, with the fruits of religion; — scenes, which might have continued smiling to this day, had not the greedy colonists, hungering for gold, and reluctant to lose their prey, poured in upon them with murderous fury, broke up their settlements, scattered the works of the missionaries to the winds, and made the memory of them like the fragments of a beautiful, but cruelly broken dream!

What was the effect, in this country, when Roger Williams and William Penn, — on whom, perhaps, too much praise was not bestowed, when they were called two of " the most perfect Christian statesmen that ever breathed," — throwing themselves in simple faith on the Providence of God, on the power of his Gospel, and on the truth and generosity of savage hearts, went forward to the settlement of their colonies in the spirit of honest purchase, good faith, and affectionate confidence? Did they meet with treachery, cruelty, incapacity for civilization, and a stubborn rejection of the Gospel? No. They were looked up to as godlike benefactors; they conciliated the confidence and affection of the aborigines; they won the fidelity of hearts, that never wavered from their faith; and they put in movement that work of civilization and of conversion to Christianity, which, had it not been, as in all other cases, broken up by the cupidity, cruelty, and faithlessness of neighbor colonists, professing their creed, but not exhibiting their spirit, would have left among us Christianized and ennobled specimens of a now vanished race; a race with whom we should have been proud to hold the alliances of a refined and elevated life.

What was the effect in South Africa, when, after Dutch and English barbarity had almost exterminated what we have been prone to consider the most degraded of human beings — the Hottentot race — a few of them, abandoning their own country to their oppressors, were allowed to choose a new spot in the wilderness, and there, almost without agricultural implements, to try, under the direction of the faithful, sympathizing Christian missionary, the experiment of taking care of themselves ; unaided, as they were, to furnish their families with sustenance, and to maintain their settlement against the incursions of the hostile savage from the wild ? What was the effect ? Why, in a few years' time, spent in digging roots with their fingers, fashioning rude implements of husbandry for themselves, and defending their households with little more than the good right arms which God had given them, they became a comparatively flourishing agricultural people, with schools, and a church, and temperance societies ; at peace, and in love among themselves, respected and joined in alliance by the once hostile Caffre, rejoicing in the bright hopes of the Gospel, and presenting a specimen of our nature which put to shame the character of those European oppressors, whose tender mercies had merely suffered them thus to conquer for themselves a name and a place among men !

And what has been the effect of more recent missionary effort among the untutored and once cannibal natives of the South Sea Islands ? It has been almost to bring back the age of miracles; and, — unless commerce, with her already begun trade in alcohol and disease, hatchets and murdering knives, should again succeed in arresting the triumphs of the Gospel, and in pouring darkness over the light of that new-born Christianity,—it *will* be to make those myriad isles smile as rejoicingly, under the full radiance of heavenly day, as they do amidst the beams of nature's sun, and the bounties of nature's God.

But perhaps the most signal instance of the triumphs of the Gospel, over all the obstacles which modern commerce has thrown in its way, has been exhibited among the Griquas of South Africa. These were a peculiar race, the offspring of European colonists and Hottentot women ; driven as outcasts from their guilty progenitors, and left, unportioned, to a wild, wandering, marauding life, till they became really the most wretched and filthy of the human race, " abandoned to witchcraft, drunkenness, licentiousness, and all the consequences which arise from the unchecked growth of such vices." But the missionary came. Patient and heavenly in his spirit, he followed them for five years in their wanderings, till, at length, they were "reduced to a settled and agricultural life;" "brought to live in the most perfect harmony" with those whom they had delighted to murder, and enabled to engage in a profitable and improving traffic with the colonists. Well, then, might the author who records this, exclaim, " Let our profound statesmen, who go on, from generation to generation, fighting and maintaining armies, ... look at this, and see how infinitely, simple men, with but one principle of action to guide them,— Christianity,— outdo them in their own profession! They are your missionaries, after all the boast and pride of statesmanship, who have ever yet hit upon the only true and sound policy, even in a worldly point of view; who, when profound statesmen have turned men into miserable and exasperated savages, are obliged to go and again turn them from savages to men; who, when these wise statesmen have spent their country's money by millions, and shed their fellow creatures' blood by oceans, and find only troubles, and frontier wars, and frightful, fire-blackened deserts growing around, go, and by a smile and a shake of the hand, restore peace, and replace these deserts with gardens and green fields, and hamlets of cheerful people."

No, Christian missions do not fail because the Gospel wants power to conquer, or because the missionary wants knowledge how to act, or because the pagan wants susceptibility to heavenly truth. These missions have often succeeded, in spite of all the vices and corruption of a most degraded condition; and, what is more, in spite of all the adverse influence which a destroying commerce has exerted, in opposition to their movements. And, if those who direct commerce would leave Christianity, unobstructed, to do her own proper work; if they would place truth, justice, and mercy, at the basis of their system,—these missions would generally succeed. The mistakes and indiscretions of here and there a movement, would hardly be felt amidst the onward impulses and vigorous actings of all-conquering Christianity. The success of missions, under all past discouragements, is an an hundred fold more than enough to justify all past expenditure, whether of money or of lives, and amply sufficient to sustain and encourage us under any future labors and sacrifices which the work may require. The spirit of the Gospel, — its spirit of love, peace, and purity, — is, when fairly presented, in action as well as in word, alluring to the poor unblessed savage and pagan. It is God's own power, fashioned for the very purpose of winning the hearts of his creatures. It is a calumny both upon Him, and upon the nature which he has given them, to suppose that the Indian and the heathen have not the sympathies and the wants of men, and that they would not see and acknowledge the heavenly origin of the Gospel, if they could once behold it in all its beauty and power, in the lives as well as in the words of those who call themselves Christians. There are, it is true, in the condition of the heathen, obstacles to the spread of the Gospel, almost inconceivable in their magnitude. Still, on examination, it will be found that the Gospel never has failed, and it may hence be inferred that it never will fail, in bringing the nations to Christ, except as its failure has been, or may be traced, directly or indirectly, to the shocking inconsistencies of those who boast its privileges. It spreads encouragingly even *against* these inconsistencies. What, then, will be its progress, when this obstacle shall be removed? Triumphant. Give it unobstructed way, or leave nothing but the obstacle of paganism itself, and it will be glorified. It will heave off from the whole unchristianized world the hatred and the scorn which our past impurities, falsehoods, and barbarities have excited, and make that world glad to receive the visits of love and of life from heaven, and from the ambassadors of heaven.

V. Is, then, this glorious possibility never to exist, save in the baseless visions of Christian hope? Not so, my hearers. Commerce has a different destiny before her. My text has yet to receive, at least in great part, its fulfilment. The isles have long waited for God's law, without fully receiving it, and the ships of Tarshish have been long gathering the silver and the gold of the earth, but not largely, to the Lord. God has glorified his Zion, in the conception of his purposes, but not yet in the full execution of those purposes. He has a work of wonder yet to perform before our eyes. This work is, *to convert modern commerce;* to sanctify it for Himself, and to make it his own great and glorious instrument in giving his law permanently to the isles, in gathering his sons to Christ from far distant realms, in bringing the silver and gold to the Lord, and in thus effecting fully the divine purpose of glorifying his church.

And this work, Christian brethren, will be done. We may not doubt its accomplishment. Why has that great colossal system of commerce, which we have surveyed, been suffered to grow up and attain its present maturity? In an age, when science with her discoveries, and art with her inventions, have brought almost all the powerful agents in nature into their service, and constructed machinery for working up nearly all the products of the earth, — nay, the very crust of the earth itself, — into some sort of fabric, or article for the use of man; in such an age, why have we seen this vast system of commerce arise and stand up, — the grand carrier for the human race? Stimulated by a thirst for gain, men have long since learned to build floating bridges across the ocean; and now they have learned to construct iron rivers across continents, that they may, with mightily accelerated movements, gather the riches of all lands and of all seas, and then, with keen intelligence of price current, distribute them through all channels and all markets. Commerce has thus become a Colossus, indeed; her feet resting on broad continent and on distant isle, her left hand holding a lighthouse for the world, and her right busy with all the moveable things of the earth. Why is this? Why has God suffered such a power to arise? That it may always stand to scourge his creatures, and, to the end of time, scatter misery and ruin through the world? Is it his purpose, that this power, moved by consummate skill, and sustained by ample means, shall permanently amass the wealth of the earth into the coffers of a few, while it leaves the innumerable many, poor, oppressed, broken in heart and hopeless of good? This were a solemn libel, both on his wisdom and on his goodness. No. This grand system has before it another destiny. Raised up under the sublime energies of mighty man, — mighty though sinful, — like man himself, it is to be *converted to God.* "The love of money" has heretofore been mainly serving itself. Hereafter it will be converted, and made to serve the Lord. Science and art have got ready, with their implements, to distribute all the products of the earth to her ever multiplying millions, The ways of distribution have been opened across sea and land. And now, over this whole body of agencies, God is to spread his own power, that it may do his own work, and scatter, — not curses, but blessings; — not death, but life. It is a body of agencies, which, when sanctified, will be wonderfully fitted to do his work; and that it is to be thus sanctified, furnishes the only explanation why it has been suffered to have origin and existence.

VI. I go further, brethren. This great work,— the conversion to God of modern commerce,— is now in progress; and the eye of Christian observation may easily discern and trace the steps which it is taking.

Why has modern commerce fallen mainly into the hands of two of the most Christian nations on earth; of two nations, most active in support of Christian missions; of two nations, which, in the irrepressibly enterprising and colonizing genius of their kindred races, command the world, and are fast spreading themselves over the world;— Great Britain and the United States? Why, but that God is beginning his work of converting this commerce to himself, and thus of bring over the earth the brightest day of glory that ever shone! Confirmatory of this view, there are other considerations.

The worst evils which commerce, in her unsanctified state, has disseminated, are war, slavery, intemperance and disease. Why, then, just as this commerce has reached to something like its maturity, and accumulated a power capable of moving the world, have we seen these two great Christian nations stirred and wrought up, internally, with deep, steadily growing and resistless efforts to disseminate the spirit and the principles of peace; to wipe out the blot of slavery from the earth; to quench the fires of all-devouring intemperance; and to wash clean from their pollutions those hitherto despised and neglected circumnavigators of the world,— our seamen? Had God designed the conversion of commerce, he could not, so far as we can perceive, have raised up a cluster of measures, more appropriate to his purpose than those, to the working of which, I have now pointed. What, then, must be our inference, when we see these measures really put in action, at the very time, and in the very places, where they are most needed; when we see mighty instrumentalities, embodying the common sentiment of the wise and good, pointed, like heaven's artillery, against the thickest host of the evils which modern commerce has bred, and pouring in upon that host a power, which is every year becoming more and more resistless? What, but that God is actually doing His great work; that He is turning this commerce to himself, and preparing to make her His handmaid, in carrying the blessings of salvation to all mankind?

Again; England is, questionless, empress over the august realm of moral sentiment in this world. Why, then, in her

Parliament, and among her people, has the strong spirit of investigation started up, with an eye that looks through the very soul of commercial abuses, and with an arm that makes that whole system of abuses tremble? Why has the voice of that spirit summoned into his presence native princes from Africa, officers of government, and missionary agents from the extremes of British colonization, and from them collected facts, which have at length torn off the veil from the Moloch of commercial avarice and lust of power, and poured in a terrible light upon the dark and deep and wide-spread wretchedness, into which that Moloch has so long been treading the aboriginal and pagan nations of the earth? Why, as the consequence, in the opening of the China trade, has an effort been made to cripple that mammoth monopoly, the East India Company, and thus to break the right arm of that power, which has been crushing and debasing the hundred millions of British India? Why, as a still further consequence, have we seen at least the shadowing forth of more humane counsels, in commercial and colonial policy, throughout British India, in South Africa, among the South Sea Islands, and wherever English colonies have been planted? And finally, why do we find, through the whole period which has been witnessing these ameliorations, an increasing number of individual merchants, both in England and in the United States, unassociated with chartered companies, and moved by the growing forces of Christian feeling in the world, among the noblest men that walk our earth — why do we find these men voluntarily espousing, in their commercial operations, the principles of Christian truth, justice, mercy and purity; forswearing the gains of unholy traffic; refusing to export death and corruption among the smiling paradises of the Pacific, and into those wide continental realms, within whose bosom God has hidden so much of the natural wealth of our planet? Why have all these cheering facts been thrown upon our observation? Is the spirit of investigation, in the British Parliament and among the British people, to be again put to sleep? Is the light, which that spirit has already elicited and thrown over the horrors of the past, to be once more darkened? And is commerce thus to revert again to her unwatched, unopposed career of oppression, extortion, corruption and ruin; and once more to walk securely forth upon her broad ways of death and desolation? Never! Opposition to the work of reformation will come, in all its shapes and with all its power; commercial gold and commercial intrigue will exhaust their resources for the defeat of that work, and thus tedious delays may be forced upon the cause of struggling, but reviving humanity. Yet all, at last, must prove in vain! An eye has been awakened, which cannot be put to sleep. A light has been struck up, which can never be darkened. Commerce, in the hands of Christian nations, can never go back and become what she has been. The awful discrepancy between our Christian boasts and professions and our unchristian practices and influences, has been made too appallingly apparent ever to be forgotten. Investigation will go forward; light will increase; the good effects of justice and mercy, peace and purity, as exhibited in particular cases, will become more and more apparent and influential; the empire of corrected moral sentiment will spread from England over Christendom, and, at length, the whole vast system of evil will be broken up; the work of the Lord will be accomplished; and commerce, converted, at last, to his purposes, will go forth over the world — the great, high-minister of his mercies to mankind!

VII. Look a moment, then, at the blessings of a sanctified commerce, even to the temporal lot of men.

The system, as it has operated in the past, depopulates. After gathering up what it can of the gold and other wealth of the lands which it has discovered, it leaves those lands a waste — peopled with a thin, imbruted and most miserable race; and then, having taken their riches home to the bosoms of once noble nations in the old world, deposits them there, to corrupt the heart, weaken the sinews, eat out the soul, and debase the whole spirit of those nations. Of this result, proofs are found wherever commerce has trod, whether in Asia, in Africa, or in America. The most conspicuous of these proofs, however, may be seen by looking over the wide and once happy pampas of South America, and over those degenerate nations of peninsular Europe, by whom that southern world was laid waste.

But the system, as it will work in the future, when it shall have been regenerated, will ennoble and enrich whomsoever it affects. Elevating knowledge and heavenly religion, the sentiments of a pure and peaceful, a just and a loving Gospel, will be exchanged, as well as articles of traffic, for the surplus wealth of golden, or of spicy lands. The hundreds of millions of aboriginal and of pagan man, will be raised out of their scorn and ignorance of the Gospel, into its light and its love, and, thus elevated, will take their stand among the regenerated tribes of the Lord's anointed king; and the honestly acquired treasures which shall have been gathered, while they leave still smiling and flourishing realms behind, will go, — not to canker in the heart, and corrupt the character of elder domains, not to lie heaped in the hands of a few, while the many pine in penury, — but to circulate among all, enrich all, and minister to the moral and intellectual elevation and improvement of all. Then the isles shall no longer wait in vain for God's law. The ships of Tarshish shall indeed bring his sons from far, their silver and their gold with them, unto the name of the Lord their God; and the Holy One of Israel shall be seen fully glorifying the house of his glory, the Zion that he loves.

VIII. This happy, this glorious period is coming upon the earth. Amidst the evil tidings, and the heaving convulsions of our own days, we still live in the light, which marks, by no faint traces, the dawning of that period. Blessed be God, we see its approach, and we labor amidst the influences which are accelerating its movement. It becomes us, therefore, seriously to inquire what, in view of all these things, is the duty of nominally Christian countries, especially of the professed church of Christ? On this point, however, though amazingly important, I am admonished to be brief.

What, then, is the state of the whole case before us? Simply this. Nominally Christian nations have, by the iniquitous operations of their commercial system, plundered, debased and wasted the aboriginal and heathen races of our earth. Multitudes of the lordly estates and the lordly mansions, which spread forth their beauties and glitter in their ornaments, on English soil and under English skies, and vast amounts of the funds, which are continually coming over to this country from England and from Holland, for investment in our productive stocks and public works, are but parts of the immense wealth, which has been most unrighteously drawn from robbed, despoiled, depopulated India, and those numerous other lands, on which, for centuries past, modern commerce has been doing her dark deeds, till she has made their inhabitants loathe the very names of Christianity and civilization, as synonymous with all that is, deceitful, impure and relentless. Such being the plain, unvarnished state of facts, it is now but the simple dictate of common justice, that we, the whole mass surnamed Christian, should repent of our works, cleanse our hearts from avarice and worldliness, take our unjustly acquired gold in our hands, go on our knees before the wronged and ruined heathen, confess to them our numberless and immeasurable sins; and then, in our charities and labors above measure, give them a long and living example of the real justice, purity and love of that Gospel, which we have taught them to disbelieve and to scorn; seek, by ages of self-humiliation and social equity, to efface the sense of those injuries which we have inflicted, and thus carry them some small, though late remuneration, for the giant extortions, and the long-lived sufferings, in which those injuries have consisted. We have heaped on them the curses, we should now go and carry them the blessings, of civilization.

In this great work of Christian repentance and Christian justice, the church should take a special part. Heretofore, colonization has been in the hands of the agents of commerce. Hereafter the church ought to colonize. Not merely in the person of here and there a self-devoted missionary, but in the whole hosts of her best blood and her best hearts, she should put herself into the ships, and gather the silver and the gold — not to gratify the lusts of pleasure and of power, but to consecrate them to the service of the Lord — and should place, wherever the isles or the continents are waiting for the law, companies of Christ's faithful servants, to teach, by precept and by example, the living way to happiness and heaven. Even the church has had, indirectly, her share in the treasures which have been wrung from the poor heathen. The church, therefore, should help to pay them back, in something better than gold — in the treasures of life eternal. To effect this, she should be busy at home as well as abroad. She should labor and pray for the spread of temperance, that our land may be no longer a fountain, sending forth burning waters to consume the savage and the idolater. She should throw herself into the seamen's cause, that they may soon cease to carry disease and death into the lands which they visit. And she should make herself heard, — however silently, yet powerfully, — in the ear of governments, that they may become ashamed of the atrocities, which, for three hundred and fifty years, they have been perpetrating; and, in the counsels of true, universal peace and freedom, learn henceforth to deal justly and mercifully with mankind.

The obligations of the church to missionary labor — to be, at one and at all times, and wherever a place for labor may be found, whether at home or abroad, a missionary body — these obligations I have ever deemed among the simplest deductions from the spirit and the principles of her faith, and from the bearings of the civilized on the uncivilized portions of our race.

If Paul felt himself "a debtor both to the Greeks and to the barbarians," what, I pray, has the church now become to the whole unchristianized world? A debtor indeed; involved in a debt, which she will never have done paying till the last of an unconverted race shall, under her leading, have come home to God. When we call on her members for their silver and their gold, — ay, for their whole bodies and souls, — we do not call on them for *charity*; we call on them to aid in the payment of a *simple debt;* a debt which we most righteously owe; a debt, which, until it is paid, will leave us, as a body, under the burthens of uncleansed, unannealed guilt. The effect of Christian colonization has been to exterminate whole races of men, to put to the sword unnumbered millions of other races, and to set the whole surviving world of heathenism in just hate of the vast mis-named mass of Christian men. And now, unless the church, which has had so large a share in these evils, or their gains, arise, and give back to the mighty, injured tribes, a recompense in the true peace and blessings of the Gospel, how can God suffer her members to live on his earth? To me it seems that the particular church, which will not engage in sending the Gospel to the heathen, has the doom of God's decree, written in the eternal records of his ways, against it, that it shall perish! The denomination, which perseveringly holds back from this work of *debt-paying*, must be cast out. It cannot live. Its very spirit, and the measures which that spirit dictates, will, even at home, shut it out from quickening, life-sustaining influences. It will die. It will become a reservoir for the refuse of a once covetous world; and then, with that world, it will perish.

Brethren, I have not time to refer, in conclusion, to the particular movements of our own denomination — to the extending missionary operations and prospects of this Zion of our affections. On this point, I can merely refer you to our current missionary publications. I cannot close, however, without the addition of one further thought, in connection with the great topic which has been reviewed.

Probably, in the survey through which the colonizing measures of the last three centuries have been made to pass, the question has suggested itself to the attentive mind, how came the fearfully covetous, extortionate and oppressive spirit, which this survey has aimed to expose — how came it in the bosom of the church of Christ? Did he breathe it there; or is his Gospel its parent? No. It came from old, covetous, persecuting heathenism itself. Avarice is the natural growth of the human heart. But, avarice, coupled with so much of false philosophy, with so much of false morals in the maxims of trade, and with so much of ingenious and relentless cruelty, as we have seen in action, though all, in one sense, the growth of our sinful nature, yet needed peculiar circumstances for the fostering of its growth. Those circumstances it did not find, under the Gospel, even during the reign of Papal darkness. That is, the spirit did not *originate* in that reign. Popery received it from heathenism, at the time when the latter, after having persecuted genuine Christianity into consideration and into prosperity, seemed disposed, under the auspices of the first Constantine, to turn and pour itself, *en masse*, into the church; and when, consequently, Christianity began to change into a kind of baptized paganism, and Christian doctrine to be mixed up with the falsehoods of pagan philosophy. Yes, the spirit which we have exposed came from the heart of ancient heathenism. It is the fruit of that old form of rebellion against God, which took its shape in the abominations of idolatry. Read the first chapter of Romans, and you will find its pedigree. "Because men did not like to retain God in their knowledge, God gave them over to a reprobate mind," and to all the awful consequences of their sin. For four thousand years, that reprobate mind, bowing down to idols in the offering of an unclean worship, possessed and ruled the bodies of men with almost undivided sway. When Christ came to dispossess it, it resisted, in an awful struggle, during which, it almost wrested back from Messiah his early conquests. And even when he made a sort of second advent, at the Protestant reformation, so strong was the hold which this spirit of evil had upon men, that it was carried down even into the bosom of the reformed church. There it has ever since been at work. Shielded by its old code of false morals, and combining itself with the intense energies begotten amidst the light of the reformation, and thus becoming a mightier engine of mischief than ever, it has acted back, with tremendous effect, on the very seat of its ancient parentage, on the realms of old and wide-spread heathenism. Thus God has made pristine rebellion chastise itself; and, from our hands, most terrible has the chastisement proved. Heathenism, at first, sought to destroy true Christianity. At last, through the channel of a corrupt Christianity — a Christianity which it had itself corrupted — it has almost literally destroyed itself!

And now, what is to be the end of the matter? This. God's purposes seem ripening into accomplishment. The system of horrors, which, under the auspices of commerce, has reigned since 1492, appears to be breaking up. The Christian world is waking to a view of the criminal part which it has had in the guilt of a long series of centuries, and the whole church of Christ is doing, or preparing to do, her great work of repentance and of justice, before those whom she has wronged. This work, however slow at present, she will, by God's grace, carry on to completion. And then, as a sharp sickle, fitted for the hand of the Lord, she will sweep over the whitened field, reap the harvest of a willing world, and bring home great glory to that God of salvation, who alone doeth wondrous things.

MESSIAH'S THRONE.

BY
REV. JOHN M. MASON, D. D.

But unto the Son, he saith, Thy Throne, O God, is forever and ever. — HEBREWS, 1: 8.

In the all-important argument which occupies this epistle, Paul assumes, — what the believing Hebrews had already professed, — that Jesus of Nazareth is the true Messiah. To prepare them for the consequences of their own principle — a principle involving nothing less than the abolition of their law, the subversion of their State, the ruin of their city, the final extinction of their carnal hopes — he leads them to the doctrine of their Redeemer's person, in order to explain the nature of his offices, to evince the value of his spiritual salvation, and to show, in both, the accomplishment of their economy, which was "now ready to vanish away." Under no apprehension of betraying the unwary into idolatrous homage, by giving to the Lord Jesus greater glory than is "due unto his name," the apostle sets out with ascribing to him excellence and attributes which belong to no creature. Creatures of most elevated rank are introduced; but it is to display, by contrast, the pre-eminence of him who is "the brightness of the Father's glory, and the express image of his person." Angels are great in might and in dignity; but "unto them hath he not put in subjection the world to come. Unto which of them said he, at any time, Thou art my son?" To which of them, "Sit thou at my right hand?" He saith, they are spirits, "ministering spirits, sent forth to minister unto them who are the heirs of salvation." "But unto the Son," — in a style which annihilates competition and comparison, — "unto the Son he saith, thy throne, O God, is forever and ever."

Brethren, if the majesty of Jesus is the subject which the Holy Ghost selected for the encouragement and consolation of his people, when he was shaking the earth and the heavens, and diffusing his Gospel among the nations, can it be otherwise than suitable and precious to us on this occasion? Shall it not expand our views, and warm our hearts, and nerve our arm, in our efforts to exalt his fame? Let me implore, then, the aid of your prayers; but, far more importunately, the aids of his own Spirit, while I speak of the things which concern the King: those great things contained in the text — his personal glory, his sovereign rule.

1. His *personal glory* shines forth in the name by which he is revealed; a name above every name, THY *throne* — O God! To the single eye, nothing can be more evident, in the *first* place, than that the Holy Ghost here asserts the *essential deity* of our Lord Jesus Christ. Of his enemies, whom he will make his footstool, some have, indeed, controverted this position, and endeavored to blot out the text from the catalogue of his witnesses. Instead of *thy throne, O God*, they would compel us, by a perversion of phraseology, of figure and of sense, to read, "God is thy throne;" converting the great and dreadful God into a symbol of authority in one of his own creatures. The Scriptures, it seems, may utter contradictions or impiety, but the divinity of the Son they shall not attest. The crown, however, which "flourishes on his head," is not to be torn away; nor the anchor of our hope to be wrested from us, by the rude hand of licentious criticism.

I cannot find, in the lively oracles, a single distinctive mark of deity, which is not applied, without reserve or limitation, to the only begotten Son. "All things whatsoever the Father hath, are HIS." Who is that mysterious Word, that was "in the *beginning*, with God?" Who is the "Alpha and Omega, the beginning and the ending, the first and the last, the Almighty?" Who is he that "knows what is in man," because he searches the deep and dark recesses of the heart? Who is the Omnipresent, that has promised, "Wherever two or three are gathered together in my name, there am I in the midst of them?" the light of whose countenance is, at the same moment, the joy of heaven and the salvation of earth? who is encircled by the seraphim on high, and "walks in the midst of the golden candlesticks?" who is in this assembly? in all the assemblies of his people? in every worshipping family? in every closet of prayer? in every holy heart? "Whose hands have stretched out the heavens and laid the foundations of the earth?" Who hath replenished them with inhabitants, and garnished them with beauty, having created all things that are in both, "visible and invisible, whether they be thrones, or dominions, or principalities, or powers?" By whom do all things consist? Who is "the Governor among the nations," having "on his vesture and on his thigh a name written, *King of Kings and Lord of Lords?*" Whom is it the Father's will that "all men should honor even as they honor himself?" Whom has he commanded his angels to worship? whom to obey? Before whom do the devils tremble? Who is qualified to redeem millions of sinners from the wrath to come, and preserve them, by his grace, to his everlasting kingdom? Who raiseth the dead, having life in himself, to quicken whom he will, so that, at his voice, all who are in their graves shall come forth; — and death and hell surrender their numerous and forgotten captives? Who shall weigh, in the balance of judgment, the destinies of angels and men? dispose of the thrones of paradise? and bestow eternal life? Shall I submit to the decision of reason? Shall I ask a response from heaven? Shall I summon the devils from their chains of darkness? The response from heaven sounds in my ears; reason approves, and the devils confess — This, O Christians, is none other than the GREAT GOD our SAVIOUR!

Indeed, the doctrine of our Lord's divinity is not, as a *fact*, more interesting to our faith, than, as a *principle*, it is essential to our hope. If he were not *the true God*, he could not be *eternal life*. When, pressed down by guilt and languishing for happiness, I look around for a deliverer such as my conscience and my heart and the word of God assure me I need, insult not my agony, by directing me to a creature — to a man, a mere man like myself! A creature! a man! My Redeemer owns my *person*. My immortal spirit is his *property*. When I come to die, I must commit it into his hands. My soul! my infinitely precious soul committed to a mere man! become the property of a mere man! I would not, thus, intrust my *body*, to the highest angel who burns in the temple above. It is only the *Father of spirits*, that can have *property* in spirits, and be their refuge in the hour of transition from the present to the approaching world. In short, my brethren, the divinity of Jesus is, in the system of grace, the sun to which all its parts are subordinate, and all their stations refer — which binds them in sacred concord, and imparts to them their radiance, and life, and vigor. Take from it this central luminary, and the glory is departed — its holy harmonies are broken — the elements rush to chaos — the light of salvation is extinguished forever!

But it is not the deity of the Son, simply considered, to which the text confines our attention. We are, in the *second* place, to contemplate it as subsisting in a personal union with the human nature. Long before the epistle was written, had he "by himself purged our sins, and sat down at the right hand of the Majesty on high. It is, therefore, as " God manifested in the flesh;" as my own brother, while he is "the express image of the Father's person;" as the Mediator of the new covenant, that he is seated on the throne. Of this throne, to which the pretensions of a creature were mad and blasphemous, the majesty is, indeed, maintained by his divine power; but the foundation is laid in his mediatorial character. I need not prove to this audience, that all his gracious offices and all his redeeming work, originated in the love and the election of his Father. Obedient to that will, which fully accorded with his own, he came down from heaven; tabernacled in our clay; was "a man of sorrows and acquainted with grief;" submitted to the contradictions of sinners, the temptations of the old serpent, and the wrath of an avenging God. In the merit of his obedience, which threw a lustre round the divine law; and in the atonement of his death by which " he offered himself a sacrifice without spot unto God," — repairing the injuries of man's rebellion, expiating sin through the blood of his cross, and conciliating its pardon with infinite purity and unalterable truth; — summarily, in his performing those conditions, on which was suspended all God's mercy to man and all man's enjoyment of God, in these stupendous works of righteousness, are we to look for the cause of his present glory. " He humbled himself and became obedient unto death, even the death of the cross; wherefore, God also hath highly exalted him, and given him a name which is above every name; that at the name of Jesus every knee should bow, of things in heaven and things in earth, and things under the earth; and that every tongue should confess that Jesus Christ is Lord, to the glory of God the Father." *Exalted* thus, "to be a Prince and a Saviour," he fills heaven with his beauty, and obtains from its blest inhabitants the purest and most reverential praise. *Worthy,* cry the mingled voices of his angels and his redeemed, " worthy is the Lamb that was slain, to receive power, and riches, and wisdom, and strength, and honor, and glory, and blessing." *Worthy,* again cry his redeemed, in a song which belongs not to the angels, but in which, with holy ecstasy, we will join, "worthy art thou, for thou wast slain, and hast redeemed us to God by thy blood."

Delightful, brethren, transcendantly delightful, were it to dwell upon this theme. But we must refrain; and, having taken a transient glance at our Redeemer's personal glory, let us turn to the

II. View which the text exhibits — the view of his *sovereign rule* —— Thy THRONE, *O God, is forever and ever.* The mediatorial kingdom of Christ Jesus, directed and upheld by his divinity, is now the object of our contemplation. To advance Jehovah's glory in the salvation of men, is the purpose of its erection. Though earth is the scene, and human life the limit, of those great operations by which they are interested in its mercies, and prepared for its consummation; its principles, its provisions, its issues, are eternal. When it rises up before us in all its grandeur of design, collecting and conducting to the heavens of God millions of immortals, in comparison with the least of whom the destruction of the material universe were a thing of nought, whatever the carnal mind calls vast and magnificent shrinks away into nothing.

But it is not so much the nature of Messiah's kingdom on which I am to insist, as its *stability*, its *administration*, and the *prospects* which they open to the *church of God*.

Messiah's throne is not one of those airy fabrics which are reared by vanity and overthrown by time; — it is fixed of old; it is stable and cannot be shaken, for

1. It is the throne of GOD. He who sitteth on it, is the Omnipotent. Universal being is in his hand. Revolution, force, fear, as applied to his kingdom, are words without meaning. Rise up in rebellion, if thou hast courage. Associate with thee the whole mass of infernal power. Begin with the ruin of whatever is fair and good in this little globe — pass from hence to pluck the sun out of his place — and roll the volume of desolation through the starry world — What hast thou done unto him? It is the puny menace of a worm against him whose frown is perdition. *He that sitteth in the heavens shall laugh.*

2. With the stability which Messiah's Godhead communicates to his throne, let us connect the stability resulting from his Father's covenant. His throne is founded not merely in strength, but in right. God hath laid the government upon the shoulder of his holy child Jesus, and set him upon Mount

Zion as his king forever. He has promised, and sworn, to build up his throne to all generations; to make it endure as the days of heaven; to beat down his foes before his face, and plague them that hate him. But my faithfulness, adds he, and my mercy shall be with him, and in my name shall his horn be exalted. Hath he said it, and will he not do it? Hath he spoken it, and shall it not come to pass? Whatever disappointments rebuke the visionary projects of men, or the more crafty schemes of Satan, "the counsel of the Lord, — that shall stand." The blood of sprinkling, which sealed all the promises made to Messiah, and binds down his Father's faithfulness to their accomplishment, witnesses continually in the heavenly sanctuary. "He must," therefore, "reign till he have put all his enemies under his feet." And although the dispensation of his authority shall, upon this event, be changed, and he shall deliver it up, in its present form, to the Father, he shall still remain, in his substantial glory, *a priest upon his throne*, to be the eternal bond of our union, and the eternal medium of our fellowship with the living God.

Seeing that the throne of our King is as immovable as it is exalted, let us with joy draw water out of that well of salvation which is opened to us in the *administration* of his kingdom. Here we must consider *its general characters*, and the *means* by which it operates.

The general characters which I shall illustrate, are the following:

1. *Mystery.* — He is the unsearchable God, and his government must be like himself. *Facts* concerning both, he has graciously revealed. These we must admit upon the credit of his own testimony; with these we must satisfy our wishes, and limit our inquiry. To intrude into those things which he hath not seen, because God has not disclosed them, whether they relate to his arrangements for this world or the next, is the arrogance of one vainly puffed up by his fleshly mind. There are secrets in our Lord's procedure which he will not explain to us in this life, and which may not, perhaps, be explained in the life to come. We cannot tell how he makes evil the minister of good; how he combines physical and moral agencies of different kind and order, in the production of blessings. We cannot so much as conjecture what bearings the system of redemption, in every part of its process, may have upon the relations of the universe; nor even what may be all the connections of providence in the occurrences of

this moment, or of the last. " Such knowledge is too wonderful for us: it is high, we cannot attain it." Our Sovereign's " way is in the sea, and his path in the deep waters; and his footsteps are not known." When, therefore, we are surrounded with difficulty, when we cannot unriddle his conduct in particular dispensations, we must remember that he is God; that we are to walk by faith; and to trust him as implicity when we are in the valley of the shadow of death, as when his candle shines upon our heads. We must remember, that it is not for us to be admitted into the cabinet of the King of kings; that creatures constituted as we are, could not sustain the view of his unveiled agency; that it would confound, and scatter, and annihilate our little intellects. As often, then, as he retires from our observation, blending goodness with majesty, let us lay our hands upon our mouths, and worship. This stateliness of our King can afford us no just ground of uneasiness. On the contrary, it contributes to our tranquillity. For we know,

2. That if his administration is mysterious, it is also *wise*. " Great is our Lord, and of great power; his understanding is infinite." That infinite understanding watches over, and arranges, and directs all the affairs of his church and of the world. *We* are perplexed at every step; embarrassed by opposition; lost in confusion; fretted by disappointment; and ready to conclude, in our haste, that all things are against our own good and our Master's honor. But this is our infirmity; it is the dictate of impatience and indiscretion. We forget the " years of the right hand of the Most High." We are slow of heart in learning a lesson which shall soothe our spirits at the expense of our pride. We turn away from the consolation to be derived from believing, that, though we know not the connections and results of holy providence, our Lord Jesus knows them perfectly. With him there is no irregularity, no chance, no conjecture. Disposed before his eye in the most luminous and exquisite order, the whole series of events occupies the very place and crisis where it is most effectually to subserve the purposes of his love. Not a moment of time is wasted, nor a fragment of action misapplied. What he does, we do not indeed know at present; but, as far as we shall be permitted to know hereafter, we shall see that his most inscrutable procedure was guided by consummate wisdom; that our choice was often as foolish, as our petulance was provoking; that the success of our own wishes would have been our most painful

chastisement, would have diminished our happiness, and detracted from his praise. Let us study, therefore, brethren, to subject our ignorance to his knowledge; instead of prescribing, to obey; instead of questioning, to believe; to perform our part without that despondency which betrays a fear that our Lord may neglect his, and tacitly accuses him of a less concern than we feel for the glory of his own name. Let us not shrink from this duty, as imposing too rigorous a condition upon our obedience, for a

3. Character of Messiah's administration is *righteousness*. "The sceptre of his kingdom is a right sceptre." If "clouds and darkness are round about him, righteousness and judgment are the habitation of his throne." In the times of old, his redeemed "wandered in the wilderness in a solitary way; but, nevertheless, he led them forth by the right way, that they might go to a city of habitation." He loves his church and the members of it too tenderly to lay upon them any burdens, or expose them to any trials, which are not indispensable to their good. It is right for them to "go through fire and through water," that he may "bring them out into a wealthy place" — right to "endure chastening," that "they may be partakers of his holiness" — right to "have the sentence of death in themselves," that they may "trust in the living God, and that his strength may be perfect in their weakness." It is right that he should "endure with much long suffering the vessels of wrath fitted to destruction;" that he should permit "iniquity to abound, the love of many to wax cold," and the dangers of his church to accumulate, till the interposition of his arm be necessary and decisive. In the day of final retribution, not one mouth shall be opened to complain of injustice. It will be seen that "the Judge of all the earth has done right; that the works of his hands have been verity and judgment," and done, every one of them, in "truth and uprightness." Let us, then, think not only respectfully but reverently of his dispensations, repress the voice of murmur, and rebuke the spirit of discontent; wait, in faith and patience, till he become his own interpreter, when "the heavens shall declare his righteousness, and all the people see his glory."

You will anticipate me in enumerating the *means* which Messiah employs in the administration of his kingdom.

1. The *gospel*, of which himself, as an all-sufficient and condescending Saviour, is the great and affecting theme. Derided by the world, it is, nevertheless, effectual to the salvation

of them who believe. "We preach Christ crucified to the Jews a stumbling-block, and to the Greeks foolishness; but to them who are called, both Jews and Greeks, Christ the power of God, and the wisdom of God." The doctrine of the cross connected with evangelical ordinances — the ministry of reconciliation; the holy sabbath; the sacraments of his covenant; briefly, the whole system of instituted worship, is the "rod of the Redeemer's strength," by which he subdues sinners to himself; rules even in the midst of his enemies; exercises his glorious authority in his church, and exhibits a visible proof, to men and angels, that he is King in Zion.

2. The efficient means to which the Gospel owes its success, and the name of Jesus its praise, is the *agency of the Holy Ghost*. Christianity is *the ministration of the Spirit*. All real and sanctifying knowledge of the truth and love of God is from his inspiration. It was the last and best promise which the Saviour made to his afflicted disciples at the moment of parting, "I will send the COMFORTER, the Spirit of truth; he shall glorify me, for he shall take of mine and shall show it unto you." It is he who "convinces the world of sin, of righteousness, and of judgment" — who infuses resistless vigor into means otherwise weak and useless. "For the weapons of our warfare are not carnal, but mighty through God," — God the spirit, — " to the pulling down of strong holds." Without his benediction, the ministry of an archangel would never "convert one sinner from the error of his way." But when he descends, with his life-giving influence, from God out of heaven, then "foolish things of the world confound the wise; and weak things of the world confound the things which are mighty; and base things of the world, and things which are despised, yea, and things which are not, bring to nought things which are." It is this ministration of the Spirit which renders the preaching of the gospel to "men dead in trespasses and sins" a *reasonable* service. When I am set down in the *valley of vision*, and view the bones, *very many and very dry*, and am desired to try the effect of my own ability in recalling them to life, I will fold my hands and stand mute in astonishment and despair. But when the Lord God commands me to speak in HIS name, my closed lips shall be opened; when he calls upon "the breath from the four winds to breathe upon the slain that they may live," I will prophesy without fear — "O ye dry bones, hear the word of the Lord," and, obedient to his voice, they "shall come together, bone to his bone;

shall be covered with sinews and flesh;" shall receive new life, and "stand upon their feet, an exceeding great army." In this manner, from the graves of nature and the dry bones of natural men, does the Holy Spirit recruit the *armies of the living God*, and make them, collectively and individually, "a name, and a praise, and a glory, to the Captain of their salvation."

3. Among the instruments which the Lord Jesus employs in the administration of his government, are *the resources of the physical and moral world*. Supreme in heaven and in earth, "upholding all things by the word of his power," the universe is his magazine of means. Nothing which acts or exists, is exempted from promoting in its own place the purposes of his kingdom. Beings rational and irrational, animate and inanimate; the heavens above and the earth below; the obedience of sanctified, and the disobedience of unsanctified men; all holy spirits; all damned spirits; in one word, every agency, every element, every atom, are but the ministers of his will, and concur in the execution of his designs. And this he will demonstrate, to the confusion of his enemies and the joy of his people, in that "great and terrible day" when he "shall sit upon the throne of his glory, and dispense ultimate judgment to the quick and the dead.

Upon these hills of holiness, — the stability of Messiah's throne, and the perfect administration of his kingdom, — let us take our station, and survey the prospects which rise up before the church of God. When I look upon the magnificent scene, I cannot repress the salutation, "Hail thou that art highly favored!" She has the prospect of preservation, of increase, and of triumph.

1. The prospect of *preservation*.

The long existence of the Christian church would be pronounced, upon common principles of reasoning, impossible. She finds in every man a natural and inveterate enemy. To encounter and overcome the unanimous hostility of the world, she boasts no political stratagem, no disciplined legions, no outward coercion of any kind. Yet her expectation is, that she shall live forever. To mock this hope, and blot out her memorial from under heaven, the most furious efforts of fanaticism, the most ingenious arts of statesmen, the concentrated strength of empires, have been frequently and perseveringly applied. The blood of her sons and her daughters has streamed like water; the smoke of the scaffold and the stake, where they won the crown of martyrdom in the cause of Jesus, has ascended in thick volumes to the skies. The tribes of persecution have sported over her woes, and erected monuments, as they imagined, of her perpetual ruin. But where are her tyrants, and where their empires? The tyrants have long since gone to their own place; their names have descended upon the roll of infamy; their empires have passed, like shadows over the rock — they have successively disappeared, and left not a trace behind!

But what became of the church? She rose from her ashes, fresh in beauty and in might. Celestial glory beamed around her; she dashed down the monumental marble of her foes, and they who hated her fled before her. She has celebrated the funeral of kings and kingdoms that plotted her destruction; and, with the inscriptions of their pride, has transmitted to posterity the record of their shame. How shall this phenomenon be explained? We are, at the present moment, witnesses of the fact; but who can unfold the mystery? This blessed book, the book of truth and life, has made our wonder to cease. THE LORD HER GOD IN THE MIDST OF HER IS MIGHTY. His presence is a fountain of health, and his protection a *wall of fire*. He has betrothed her, in eternal covnant, to himself. Her living Head, in whom she lives, is above, and his quickening Spirit shall never depart from her. Armed with divine virtue, his gospel, secret, silent, unobserved, enters the hearts of men and sets up an everlasting kingdom. It eludes all the vigilance, and baffles all the power, of the adversary. Bars and bolts and dungeons are no obstacle to its approach. Bonds and tortures and death cannot extinguish its influence. Let no man's heart tremble, then, because of fear. Let no man despair, in these days of rebuke and blasphemy, of the Christian cause. The ark is launched, indeed, upon the floods; the tempest sweeps along the deep; the billows break over her on every side. But Jehovah-Jesus has promised to conduct her in safety to the haven of peace. She cannot be lost, unless the pilot perish. Why then do the heathen rage, and the people *imagine a vain thing*? Hear, O Zion, the word of thy God, and rejoice for the consolation. "No weapon that is formed against thee shall prosper, and every tongue that shall rise against thee in judgment thou shalt condemn. This is the heritage of the servants of the Lord, and their righteousness is of me, saith the Lord."

Mere preservation, however, though a most comfortable, is not the only hope of the church; she has

2. The prospect of *increase*.

Increase — from an effectual blessing upon the means of grace in places where they are already enjoyed; for thus saith the Lord, "I will pour water upon him that is thirsty, and floods upon the dry ground; I will pour my Spirit upon thy seed, and my blessing upon thine offspring; and they shall spring up as among the grass, as willows by the watercourses."

Increase — from the diffusion of evangelical truth through pagan lands. "For behold, the darkness shall cover the earth, and gross darkness the people; but the Lord shall arise upon thee, and his glory shall be seen upon thee. And the Gentiles shall come to thy light, and the kings to the brightness of thy rising. Lift up thine eyes round about and see: all they gather themselves together, they come to thee: thy sons shall come from far, and thy daughters shall be nursed at thy side. Then thou shalt see, and flow together, and thine heart shall fear, and be enlarged; because the abundance of the sea shall be converted unto thee, the forces of the Gentiles shall come unto thee."

Increase — from the recovery of the rejected Jews to the faith and privileges of God's dear children. "Blindness in part has happened unto Israel" — they have been cut off, for their unbelief, from the olive-tree. Age has followed age, and they remain to this hour, spread over the face of the earth, a fearful and affecting testimony to the truth of God's word. They are without their sanctuary, without their Messiah, without the hope of their believing ancestors. But it shall not be always thus. They are still "beloved for the Father's sake." When the "fullness of the Gentiles shall come in," they too shall be gathered. They shall discover, in our Jesus, the marks of the promised Messiah; and, with tenderness proportioned to their former insensibility, shall cling to his cross. Grafted again into their own olive-tree, "all Israel shall be saved." It was "through their fall that salvation came unto us Gentiles." And, "if the casting away of them be the reconciling of the world, what shall the receiving of them be, but life from the dead?" What ecstasy, my brethren! the Gentile and the Jew taking "sweet counsel together, and going to the house of God in company!" the path of the swift messenger of grace marked, in every direction, by the "fullness of the blessing of the gospel of Christ" — a nation born at once — the children of Zion exclaiming, "The place is too strait for me: give place to me that I may dwell." The knowledge of Jehovah overspreading the earth, as the waters cover the sea; and all flesh enjoying the salvation of God!

This faith ushers in a

3. Prospect of the church — the prospect of *triumph*.

Though often desolate, and "afflicted, tossed with tempest and not comforted," the Lord her God will then make her an eternal excellency, and repay her sorrows with triumph —

Triumph — in complete victory over the enemies who sought her hurt. "The nation and kingdom," saith the Lord, "that will not serve thee shall perish; yea those nations shall be utterly wasted. — The sons also of them that afflicted thee shall come bending unto thee; and all they that despised thee shall bow themselves down at the soles of thy feet; and they shall call thee the city of the Lord, the Zion of the Holy One of Israel." That great enemy of her purity and her peace, who shed the blood of her saints and her prophets, the "MAN OF SIN who has exalted himself above all that is called God," shall appear, in the whole horror of his doom, as the "son of perdition, whom the Lord shall consume with the spirit of his mouth, and shall destroy with the brightness of his coming." The terrible but joyous event shall be announced by an angel from heaven, "crying mightily with a strong voice, Babylon the great is fallen, is fallen!" "ALLELUIA!" shall be the response of the church universal; "Salvation, and glory, and honor, and power, unto the Lord our God; for true and righteous are his judgments; for he hath judged the great whore which did corrupt the earth with her fornication, and hath avenged the blood of his servants at her hand!" Then too, "the accuser of the brethren — that old serpent which is the devil," shall be cast down, "and bound a thousand years that he shall deceive the nations no more." — This will introduce the church's

Triumph — in the prevalence of righteousness and peace throughout the world. "Her people shall be all righteous." The voice of the blasphemer shall no longer insult her ear. Iniquity, as ashamed, shall stop its mouth, and hide its head. "All her officers shall be peace, and all her exactors, righteousness." The kings of the earth, bringing their glory and honor unto her, shall accomplish the gracious promise. "The mountains shall bring peace to the people, and the little hills by righteousness." Her prince, whose throne is forever and ever, "shall judge among the nations, and shall rebuke many people; and they shall beat their swords into ploughshares, and their spears into pruning hooks: nation shall not lift up sword against nation, neither shall they learn war any more!" Every man shall meet, in every other man, a brother without dissimulation. Fear and the sword shall be far away; "they shall sit every man under his vine, and under his fig-tree, and none shall make them afraid." For thus saith the Lord, "Violence shall no more be heard in thy land, wasting nor destruction within thy borders; but thou shalt call thy walls, Salvation, and thy gates, Praise."

Triumph — in the presence of God, in the communion of his love, and the signal manifestation of his glory. "Behold, the tabernacle of God shall be with men, and he will dwell with them, and they shall be his people, and God himself shall be with them, and be their God." Then shall be seen "the holy Jerusalem descending out of heaven from God, which shall have no need of the sun, neither of the moon, to shine in it; for the glory of God shall lighten it, and the Lamb shall be the light thereof. And the nations of them which are saved shall walk in the light of it, — and they shall bring the glory and honor of the nations unto it; and there shall in no wise enter into it any thing that defileth, neither whatsoever worketh abomination, or maketh a lie: but they which are written in the Lamb's book of life."

Such, according to the sure word of prophecy, will be the triumphs of Christianity; and to this issue all Scriptural efforts to evangelize the heathen contribute their share. That mind is profane, indeed, which repels the sentiment of awe; and hard is the heart which feels no bland emotion. But let us pause. — You exult, perhaps, in the view of that happiness which is reserved for the human race; you long for its arrival; and are eager, in your place, to help on the gracious work. It is well. But are there no heathen in this assembly? Are there none who, in the midst of their zeal for foreign missions, forget their own souls; nor consider that they themselves *neglect the great salvation?* Remember, my brethren, that a man may be active in measures which shall subserve the conversion of others, and yet perish in his own iniquity. That very Gospel which you desire to send to the heathen, must be the Gospel of *your* salvation; it must turn "you from darkness to light, from the power of Satan unto God;" it must make "you meet for the inheritance of the saints," or it shall fearfully aggravate your condemnation at last. You pray, "Thy kingdom come." But is the "kingdom of God within you?" Is the Lord Jesus "in you, the hope of glory?" Be not deceived. The *name* of Christian will not save you. Better had it been for you "not to have known the way of righteousness"—better to have been the most idolatrous pagan—better, infinitely better, not to have been born, than to die strangers to the pardon of the Redeemer's blood, and the sanctifying virtue of his Spirit. From his throne on high he calls; calls, my brethren, to you; "Look unto me, and be ye saved, for I am God, and there is none else. Seek ye the Lord while he may be found; call ye upon him while he is near; let the wicked forsake his way, and the unrighteous man his thoughts, and let him return unto the Lord, and he will have mercy upon him; and to our God, for he will abundantly pardon."

On the other hand, such as have "fled for refuge to lay hold on the hope set before them," are commanded to be "joyful in their King." He reigns, O believer, for thee. The stability of his throne is thy safety. The administration of his government is for thy good; and the precious pledge that he "will perfect that which concerneth thee." In all thy troubles and in all thy joy, "commit thy way unto him." He will guard the sacred deposit. Fear not that thou shalt lack any good thing fear not that thou shalt be forsaken—fear not that thou shalt fall beneath the arm of the oppressor. "He went through the fires of the pit to *save* thee; and he will stake all the glories of his crown to *keep* thee." Sing, then, thou beloved, "Behold, God is my salvation; I will trust, and not be afraid; for the Lord Jehovah is my strength and my song; he also is become my salvation."

And if we have "tasted that he is gracious;" if we look back with horror and transport upon the wretchedness and the wrath which we have escaped; with what anxiety shall we not hasten to the aid of our fellow-men, who are "sitting in the region and shadow of death." What zeal will be too ardent, what labor too persevering, what sacrifice too costly, if, by any means, we may tell them of Jesus, and the resurrection, and the life eternal! Who shall be daunted by difficulties, or deterred by discouragement? If but one pagan should be brought, savingly, by your instrumentality, to the knowledge of God and the kingdom of heaven, will you not, my brethren, have an ample recompense? Is there here a man who would give up all for lost, because some favorite hope has been disappointed? or who regrets the worldly substance which he has expended on so divine an enterprise? Shame on thy coward spirit and thine avaricious heart! Do the holy Scriptures, does the experience of ages, does the nature of things, justify the expectation, that we shall carry war into the central regions of delusion and crime, without opposition, without trial? Show me a plan which encounters not fierce resistance from the prince of darkness and his allies in the human heart, and I will show you a plan which never came from the inspiration of God. If missionary effort suffer occasional embarrassment; if impressions on the heathen be less speedy, and powerful, and extensive, than fond wishes have anticipated; if particular parts of the great system of operation be, at times, disconcerted; if any of the ministers of grace fall a sacrifice to the violence of those whom they go to bless in the name of the Lord; — these are events which ought to exercise our faith and patience; to wean us from self-sufficiency; to teach us where our strength lies, and where our dependence must be fixed; but not to enfeeble hope, nor relax diligence. Let us not " despise the day of small things." Let us not overlook, as unimportant matter, the *very existence* of that missionary spirit, which has already awakened Christians in different countries from their long and dishonorable slumbers, and bids fair to produce, in due season, a general movement of the church upon earth. Let us not, for one instant, harbor the ungracious thought, that the prayers, and tears, and wrestlings of those who " make mention of the Lord," form no link in that vast chain of events by which he " will establish, and will make Jerusalem a praise in the earth." That dispensation which of all others is most repulsive to *flesh and blood*, — the violent death of faithful missionaries, — should animate Christians with new resolution. " Precious in the sight of the Lord is the death of his saints." The cry of martyred blood ascends the heavens; it enters into " the ears of the Lord of Sabaoth." It will give him no rest, till he rain down righteousness upon the land where it has been shed, and which it has sealed, as a future conquest, for him who " in his majesty rides prosperously because of truth, and meekness, and righteousness."

For the world, indeed, and perhaps for the church, many calamities and trials are in store, before the glory of the Lord shall be so revealed that all flesh shall see it together. " I will shake all nations," is the divine declaration, " and the desire of all nations shall come. The vials of wrath which are now running, and others which remain to be poured out, must be exhausted. The supper of the great God must be prepared, and his *strange work* have its course. Yet the missionary cause must ultimately succeed. It is the cause of God, and *shall* prevail. The days, O brethren, roll rapidly on, when the shout of the isles shall swell the thunder of the continent; when the Thames and the Danube, when the Tiber and the Rhine, shall call upon Euphrates, the Ganges, and the Nile; and the loud concert shall be joined by the Hudson, the Mississippi, and the Amazon, singing with one heart and one voice, Alleluia! Salvation! The Lord God omnipotent reigneth!

Comfort one another with this faith, and with these words:

Now, "Blessed be the Lord God, the God of Israel, who only doeth wondrous things. And blessed be his glorious name forever: LET THE WHOLE EARTH BE FILLED WITH HIS GLORY! Amen, and Amen!"

MISSIONARY POWER.

BY

REV. BARON STOW.

Tarry ye in the city of Jerusalem, until ye be endued with power from on high.
LUKE 24: 49.

GREAT enterprises require strong men. The missionary enterprise is by far the greatest in which human agency was ever employed, and, for its effective execution, demands the strongest men which the churches can furnish.

It was upon this principle, I suppose, that the Saviour, when about to ascend, gave to his disciples that extraordinary direction, "Tarry ye in Jerusalem, until ye be endued with power from on high." He had already appointed them as his missionaries, and charged them to preach "repentance and remission of sins in his name, among all nations, beginning at Jerusalem." But the undertaking was one of immense magnitude, environed with appalling difficulties, and involving peculiar personal hazards; and he well knew that, notwithstanding all the instruction which they had received, and all the discipline to which they had been subjected, and all the examples which they had witnessed in himself, as the faultless model of missionary excellence, they were but imperfectly qualified for the arduous labors and weighty responsibilities, which the service would impose.

They needed the ability to speak the languages of the people whom they might visit; and this, if they should proceed immediately to their work, must be miraculously supplied. They were to commend to an infidel world a system of religion, whose claims to credibility must be established by some extraordinary manifestations of its divine origin; and they needed the power of working such wonders, as should carry conviction to the most incredulous, that their message was no fable, their apostleship no imposture. Besides, they needed a large increase of intellectual and moral strength, such as should qualify them for any exigency. They needed clearer and more comprehensive views of that scheme of redemption, whose mysteries they were to unfold to the ignorant nations. They needed to have the narrow, selfish prejudices of their remaining Judaism entirely removed; and their hearts expanded by a benevolence that should encompass the world; and their whole moral natures more deeply impregnated with the spirit of their mission — the spirit of him who came, "not to be ministered unto, but to minister, and to give his life a ransom for many." They needed a faith, that should embrace all the promises; a boldness, that should fearlessly encounter any opposition; a courage, that should be terrified by no danger; a fortitude, that should quietly endure any suffering; a wisdom, sufficient for any emergency; a love, that should make them inexpressibly tender, and melt before them a pathway through the ice and the iron of human depravity.

All this the Saviour knew and appreciated; and, with a prudence in which kindness and wisdom were richly blended, he directed them to remain where they were, until the requisite qualifications should be imparted. He was about to take his place upon the Mediator's throne; and one of his first acts, after receiving the joyous welcome of the heavenly choir, who had long been rehearsing for the occasion, and were then waiting in mid heaven for his triumphant arrival, would be the fulfilment of the glorious promise — the sending of that Spirit, which should work in them every needed transformation, and clothe them with the required energies.

They obeyed his command, and, ten days afterwards, while engaged in social devotion — the very employment which Heaven loves especially to sanction — the promised Influence descended, and enveloped them, and penetrated them, and wrought such changes, as that each of them became at once a man of strength, "thoroughly furnished unto all good works." Emerging from this baptism, they were conscious of the transition through which they had passed; and, "strengthened with might," they went forth to their work, assaulting the strongest defences of sin, grappling with Satan's veteran phalanxes, and winning for their prince a thousand bloodless victories.

How soon, and how surely, did the nations feel and confess the power of these evangelical giants! Divinely illuminated, supported, protected, they said what no others could say, they did what no others could do, they endured what no others could endure; and, passing from province to province, we hear them ever and anon exclaiming, "Thanks be unto God, who always causeth us to triumph in Christ, and maketh manifest the savor of his knowledge by us, in every place."

The Romans, in the days of their national vigor, constructed magnificent roads, commencing all at the Forum, and extending to the frontiers of the empire, thus making every portion of the realm accessible to their arts and their arms. These disciples of Jesus, who, "out of weakness were made strong," proceeding all from the cross, as the point of departure, cut each his way right onward, through the domains of sin, to the outermost limit of the known world; and then, with the columns of converts which lined these radii — the right of each column resting upon Calvary — they swept the intermediate segments of the circle; and thus was executed, as has never since been done, the behest of the ascending Saviour, "Go ye into all the world, and preach the Gospel to every creature."

Salutary, indeed, was the transformation which every where appeared in the track of these moral conquerors. Not more surely can the eye, from the summit of the pyramid, trace the meanderings of Egypt's river, by its line of velvet verdure, through the brown and sterile desert, than the observer of apostolic movements could discover the progress, from week to week, of these mighty ones, by the improvement, — moral, intellectual, political, and physical, — which was uniformly the result of their labors, and which denoted, unequivocally, the accompaniment of a superhuman influence. No candid one has ever doubted that they were strong men.

At no time since the apostolic period, has the Head of the Church considered it as necessary to qualify his missionary servants for their work, by the intervention of miracles; and with some of the elements of power, which he then deemed to be requisite, he very soon dispensed, giving no intimation that they would ever again be required or conferred. But the necessity that the missionary to the heathen should be a strong man, is by no means suspended. The command just quoted, for the disciples to wait until endued with power from on high, I take to be an explicit recognition of the principle, that the enterprise requires agents of more than ordinary ability; and though, as a specific injunction, it pertained to the few who were personally addressed, yet, in its spirit, I suppose, it inculcates a lesson suited to all their successors.

The term *power*, when applied to men, even to missionaries, you will of course understand me as using in a subordinate and qualified sense, differing widely from the acceptation in which we employ it, with respect to their Almighty Ally, the Holy Spirit. We use it, as denoting those qualities which adapt them to the accomplishment of the proposed end; constituting them — not the mere instruments — a term which ought never to be applied, in such a connection, to moral beings — but the qualified agents, through whose voluntary and well-directed efforts, God may gather into one his chosen who are scattered abroad. There is such a thing as special adaptation to usefulness in the missionary work, and this adaptation we denominate Power.

The Saviour was pleased to increase the ability of the few missionaries whom he had selected, rather than to multiply their number; and thus he established for us the principle, not only that this class of laborers should be well qualified men, but also, that, while "the laborers are few," we render an important service, by enlarging their qualifications for their appointed and peculiar work. If, by any means, the ability of a missionary candidate to be useful can be doubled, then, by doubling his ability, we do essentially the same as to call into the field an additional laborer. If we increase his power ten-fold, then we render him ten times as capable of effect, without any addition to the expense of his support. Who of us has not seen this practically demonstrated — an individual, with faculties and affections all thoroughly trained, moving through the world with a consecrated momentum, which fifty others, destitute of his qualifications, could never equal?

It would be but common-place, if I were to consider the elements of this desirable power under the bi-fold classification of Intellectual and Moral; and yet, to manufacture any other distinction, or adopt any other names, would be sheer affectation. Let these, then, be the simple designations of the two kinds of ability, which, united in suitable proportions, constitute MISSIONARY POWER.

I. INTELLECTUAL POWER.

This department includes a number of important particulars.

1. *Native talent.* This I mention first, for it is fundamental. Without it, you cannot, by any process, make a strong man. Neither education nor grace supplies constitutional defects. A man may have the requisite piety, and he may have been favored with the best facilities for extended intellectual culture, and yet not possess the kind or measure of native talent appropriate to a work so formidable as the evangelizing of a world that lieth in the wicked one. The missionary should have a mind that is originally vigorous and well balanced, with no faculty unduly protuberant, and no one greatly depressed — a mind susceptible of harmonious and well proportioned development — a mind naturally strong, and capable of being made, by judicious training, a hundred fold stronger. The churches contain multitudes of good men, whose moral feelings and principles can be trusted, and whose desire to be useful is worthy of all commendation, but whose intellectual natures are so cast and constructed, as that by no training can they be qualified to make much impression upon their race. The men we need for effective service among the heathen, are not those whom nature has modeled upon a small scale — men of puny minds, whose predestination is intellectual dwarfishness and imbecility; — but men whose mental structure includes no weak timbers — men whose inward architecture partakes largely of the sturdy and magnificent Doric — men who, by the simple majesty of their native qualities, would anywhere command the respect of the multitude. There are fields in which men of slender capacity may labor, and not without effect; but those fields are at home. To send such men to convert the pagan world, is more than inexpedient.

2. *Practical good sense.* Every one is acquainted with ministers of talent, intelligence, and piety, whose influence is feeble, and who can never accomplish much for Zion, because of a deficiency of that indefinable, and yet invaluable quality, denominated common sense — an element of character that is not quite as common as its name imports. In the estimation of all men, — Jew and Gentile, ignorant and learned, — nothing is a substitute for it, or can make amends for its absence. Where it is wanting, respect and confidence are wanting, and the man's influence is almost a nullity. But

where it exists, in happy combination with other qualities, it is always an element of power, rendering its possessor considerate and discreet, not only in selecting his mode, but in applying his means, of usefulness. No where is this quality so important as in the missionary, and especially the missionary pioneer, whose least indiscretion might jeopard interests of the greatest magnitude.

Experience has taught some lessons upon this subject, which it is undesirable should be repeated, and the question, — " Has he good sense ? " — is sure to be propounded, respecting every candidate for missionary service. And they who know the most of the peculiar character of that service, having been the longest on the high places of the field, and become the most deeply interested in the success of the enterprise, are pressing this question the most closely, and insisting upon an unqualified and unequivocal answer. Has he good sense? — practical wisdom ? Is he careful, circumspect, judicious ? Is he one whose footsteps may safely be trodden by his successors, and whose influence none may have occasion to deplore? The man who discards prudence as a superfluity, or discretion as an incumbrance, even under the pretext of being guided by the Spirit, is tolerable no where; in the missionary field he is a nuisance, from which the heathen may well pray, " Good Lord, deliver us ! "

3. *Extensive Knowledge.* Lord Verulam said, and so, parrot-like, have said a million others, that " Knowledge is power." Trite as may be the expression, yet how just is the sentiment. It is as true in morals as in physics, in religion as in philosophy, in the missionary of the cross as in the artisan, the civil engineer or the statesman. The possessor of truth can exercise a species of sovereignty, that approaches nearer than any other in resemblance to the divine. Not only is he stronger than any other man, but stronger than many others who have it not, for he can accomplish things to which they are inadequate. He has the true Archimedean lever, with which the world is heaved.

The great object of the Christian missionary is such, in a a variety of aspects, as that the unintelligent are not suited to its accomplishment. We prescribe not the measure of his necessary knowledge, nor how, nor where, it must be acquired ; but we hesitate not to say, that, other things being equal, the more copious his intellectual acquirements, the greater is his ability to do good. It is a singular fact, that the most learned apostle was the one whose history fills the largest space in the evangelical record, and whose productions a careful Providence has preserved, for the benefit of subsequent generations. In all the circle of the missionary Anakim, he was the Saul, — head and shoulders above the most prominent of his comrades. His intellectual power was the greatest, his influence the most extensively felt, his impression upon society the deepest and the longest perpetuated. The world has seen but one Paul; and, in selecting him as a model missionary, and giving him such extraordinary success, and transmitting to us so largely and minutely his instructive history, the great Superintendent of missions has authorized the conclusion, that the missionary enterprise demands strong men.

That a man may have power over the minds of others, for useful purposes, he must be well acquainted with his own mind, its structure, functions, capacity, susceptibilities, and projectile force. "Know thyself," is an injunction of both divine and human wisdom, which no religious teacher can with impunity disobey, but which is preëminently important to him who assumes the high responsibilities of a missionary to the heathen. Whatever else he may know, if he be ignorant of himself, he will perpetrate many mistakes, and be the victim of a thousand mortifications. The lightest penalty which he will have to pay, will be the humiliating necessity of witnessing his own inefficiency. Self-knowledge is power.

He must also be thoroughly acquainted with mind in general, and especially with the mind which he is to instruct and elevate. If supremacy over matter requires knowledge of matter's constitution and laws, so is knowledge of the human mind indispensable to supremacy over mind. He who would control it, must know it, and know it not only in its anatomy, but also in its physiology; and this knowledge, derived from patient observation and careful analysis, is always an element of intellectual power. The Great Teacher had a perfect acquaintance with mind, and when he preached, "his word was with power." "He knew what was in man," and therefore could address others' thoughts, as we address their words, so that the concession was extorted from unexpected sources, "Never man spake like this man." Knowledge of human nature is power.

Nor is it less important that the missionary should be intimately familiar with the instruments of his service, which are nothing less and nothing else, than the truths of divine revelation. He has a specified message to the guilty and perishing, and with that message he must be well acquainted; not only with its cardinal doctrines, and more important precepts, but with its secondary principles and requirements, its implications and influences, its extensions and limitations. The ability to ring a hundred changes upon a few consecrated phrases and favorite illustrations, is an inferior attainment. There must be that familiarity with the Gospel, which is obtained only by personal investigation, and which will enable him to exhibit truth in detail; for it is by descending from generals to particulars, rather than by ascending from particulars to generals, that the human mind is best affected, so as to be impressible and persuasible. The power of the Saviour, as a preacher, resided very much in his happy facility at analysis, developing and spreading out truths in their individuality, rather than in their relations and dependencies. It was when he *opened* the Scriptures, and not when he classified and put them under the screws of systematic divinity, that the hearts of his hearers burned within them. Knowledge of the Gospel is power.

4. *Correct Discipline.* This is but the result of all right education. Hence, Plato, when asked what he meant by education, replied by the single word, "discipline." And a greater than Plato, an intellectual Goliath of our own age and country, has justly said, that "a man is not educated, until he has the ability to summon, in an emergency, all his mental powers into vigorous exercise, to effect a given object." In the author of this sentiment we have an illustration of the meaning of the word *discipline,* as denoting an element of intellectual power. He has acquired the mastery of his own mind, and thus attained to a supremacy, next to sovereign, over the minds of others. "The greatest of all warriors," he adds, "who went to the siege of Troy, had not the preeminence because he possessed superlative strength, and carried the largest bow, but because self-discipline had taught him to wield it." A man of one idea, who can apply it to a hundred uses, is wiser and more efficient in practical life, than he whose head is a warehouse of knowledge, of which he knows not how to avail himself for any useful purpose.

If I were solicited to mention an individual, in whom resided the intellectual power that is desirable in the Christian missionary, I could furnish from the annals of missions no better specimen than the apostle Paul. He possessed native talent, common sense, extensive knowledge, and correct discipline; and, in all these respects, he was especially adapted to the work assigned him. He could suit his temper, his manner, and his labor, to all varieties of mind, and address all classes, with a fitness, and propriety, and energy, that made them feel and confess his superiority. Often was he called to grapple with men of might, who, in disputation, had never known defeat, and who looked upon him, as the champion of Gath looked upon the shepherd of Judah. But such was his power, as that he never retired from the conflict other than a victor. His arguments swept through their hollow sophistries, like cannon shot among egg-shells.

We shall not be required to send a very large number of men to the heathen. The conversion of the Pagan, and Mohammedan, and nominally Christian world, is to be effected mainly through the labor of native preachers. But such as we must depute, should be strong men; for only such can accomplish what, in the incipient stages of the enterprise, is indispensable to future and enlarged success. The primary work, including the translation of the Scriptures, the formation of model churches, the commencement of trains of far-reaching influence, and the imparting of correct, permanent impressions, is indeed most difficult, and involves responsibilities of the weightiest character. For such a service, the ablest men are needed. The Saviour acted on this conviction, and therefore endued his missionary pioneers with special power, that they might commence the work with vigor, and clear away the most formidable obstacles, and set the whole machinery in energetic operation; well assured, that afterwards the enterprise could advance with an agency of ordinary ability.

II. MORAL POWER.

By moral power, I understand the possession of those moral qualities, which enable a man to influence the moral feelings and moral conduct of other men. With this the missionary to the heathen needs to be largely supplied; for upon this, immensely more than upon intellectual ability, will his useful efficiency depend. The elements of this kind of power are so numerous, that I must limit myself to a selection.

1. *Personal holiness.* It is to be taken for granted, that he who proposes to enter this service is a Christian; that he has

for himself, and furnishes to others, the most satisfactory evidence of a spiritual union with the Saviour. If serious doubts exist upon this point, whether in his own mind or in the minds of such as he would benefit, his ability will be essentially crippled. No man needs, so much as he, to be relieved from the fettering embarrassment of unassured hope. Let him, therefore, settle this matter as the antecedent of every other inquiry, and thus save, for the good of the heathen and the glory of Christ, the time which would otherwise be given to the frequent reconsideration of the primary question, "Am I a Christian?" He will have enough to do to watch against temptation, and keep himself in the love of God, and so endure unto the end, without the necessity of inspecting often and minutely the validity of his original experience.

But simple conversion, however clearly ascertained as a fact, does not necessarily invest an individual with moral power. *Eminent piety* is essential to *eminent usefulness* in the work of missions; and this necessity grows out of the nature of the enterprise. Consequently, we find that those who have been the most distinguished for deep, consistent piety, have ordinarily been the most efficient laborers. Need I mention more than the names of Brainerd, Schwartz, Martyn, Boardman? These men were preëminently spiritual. They walked with God, were filled with his Spirit, dwelt upon the sides of eternity, and thought, felt, spake, and acted with reference to that day which shall conclude time, and commence the everlasting awards of heaven and hell. Thus breathing a heavenly atmosphere, and imbued with a heavenly unction, their deportment and spirit, as well as their teachings, combined to render them powerful, commanding for them the respect of the vilest, and giving them influence over minds, which none of inferior holiness could ever have moved. Their piety set them off so far, in holy separation, from an ungodly world, as that they occupied in morals the true Archimedean *position* — the πού στω — from which their whole ability could be most advantageously applied.

Holiness is power; for it gives unity, symmetry, and compactness to character, combining in one harmonious, well-proportioned whole, the excellences which insure for their possessor the confidence of mankind, however degraded or unprincipled. It gives purity and elevation to the motives, direction and energy to the active powers, robustness and elasticity to the moral constitution. It makes the life consistent, and carries to every beholder the conviction of undissembled sincerity, and, by the consciousness which it begets, that the heart and the life are in full sympathy with the calling, imparts to the mind a power of projection that renders influence far-reaching and effective. "Which of you convinceth me of sin?" was the challenge of the holy Saviour. His energy was debilitated by no consciousness of discrepancy between his life and his doctrine.

Holiness is power; for, by softening and subduing one's own soul, it softens and subdues the souls of others. Opening the deep fountains of sensibility, it sends forth a stream of tender influence, before which the heart of adamant yields and becomes as unresisting as the mellowest of substances.

Such is the godliness needed by the missionary — a piety distinguished for substance rather than show, for steadiness and uniformity rather than impulse and excitement; not like the Geysers of Iceland, heated by volcanic fires, and discharging in periodical jets the waters that scald and excoriate, but like the living stream, deriving its supplies from an exhaustless reservoir, pouring forth a noiseless and equable current, and diffusing, wherever it meanders, the richest and loveliest productiveness. The piety needed, is that which brings the soul within the circle that encloses heaven's favorites, and, by giving near access to the throne, and familiar intimacy with him that sitteth thereon, best qualifies for the work of intercession. Our heavenly Advocate is a prevalent Pleader, because he is "*Jesus Christ*, THE RIGHTEOUS;" for within the veil, as every where else, holy character is power; and he who resembles Him the most perfectly in moral qualities, will ever be the most effective in his pleadings at the footstool of the great Hearer of prayer. Like Jacob, he will have "power with God," for "the effectual fervent prayer of *the righteous man* availeth much."

The holy missionary is a powerful missionary. In his intercourse with men, in his intercourse with God, his power is felt and acknowledged, and eternity only can develop the extent and the beneficence of its results.

2. *Entire devotedness to the work.* It is but little, comparatively, that a man can accomplish in any department, during the short life that is allotted to him upon earth. But, ordinarily, he is the most effective who consecrates himself to one pursuit, and faithfully identifies with it his whole temporal ex-

istence, and his entire ability. The work of the Christian missionary is surely large enough and important enough to justify the exclusive application of his time and energies. So the first missionaries viewed the subject; and such was the entireness of their consecration to their grand enterprise, as that each of them could say, and say it uncontradicted, " *This* ONE *thing I do.*" Ask them, ask their successors in every age who have trodden most closely in their steps, the secret of their success, and, while they refer you to the Holy Spirit, as the primary cause, they will tell you that, secondarily, their efficiency is attributable to the singleness of their aim, the unity of their purpose, the complete devotedness of their lives to their great object, counting every thing else, compared with the salvation of the heathen, " one grand impertinence."

He who understands the nature of the human mind, knows that its full energies are never put forth unless its object be single as well as great. He who comprehends the legitimate object of the Christian missionary, is aware that it deserves and must have his undivided attention, and the intense application of all his powers. He who is familiar with the history of the enterprise, needs not to be told that those who have effected the greatest good in their own age, and whose impression upon posterity has been the deepest, were distinguished for the simplicity and entireness with which they gave themselves to the duties of their vocation. And of the fifteen hundred evangelical missionaries now in the field, who are affording the most conclusive proofs of useful efficiency? Are they not the men who, with the proper qualifications, are confining themselves to their appropriate work?

Am I mistaken, then, in specifying this devotedness as an element of power? It gives concentration to talents which would otherwise be scattered and wasted, and which now produce effect, upon the simple principle that combination is strength. Rays of knowledge are thus collected into a focus, and made to illuminate and burn. The faculties and affections all move in one direction, for the production of a single result; and, moving together in obedience to one common impulse, they acquire a momentum that is not easily resisted; and, digging a channel for themselves, they leave permanent traces, by which coming generations may know that some agent of extraordinary power has been there.

3. *Deep sympathy with the object.* In every department of practical life, success is dependent, not merely upon acquaint-

ance with the theory of one's business, but also upon the spirit with which the service is undertaken and prosecuted. There must be *interest* as well as understanding, *heart* as well as head, *feeling* as well as action. If your employment be agricultural, or mercantile, or mechanical, or political, or literary, or scientific, your spirit must correspond with the nature of the object, and so deeply sympathize with it, as that you and your object shall seem to be joined by a living union, one and inseparable.

In every vocation it is indeed necessary that we should distinctly perceive *what* is to be done, and *how* it is to be effectuated. "Wisdom is profitable to direct." But it is quite as essential that we should have warm sympathy with the end to which our efforts are to be directed. What is it that often renders some one person more effective than a hundred others in modern enterprises of moral reform? Is it extraordinary genius? Is it profound erudition? We have seen the strong men of all the learned professions stand up in the high places, and lecture with ability upon particular vices, and with most eloquent pleadings call upon wrong-doers to repent, and we have seen them expend their intellectual energies without effect. They reclaimed not, for they reached not, the wretched victims of imbruted appetite. They lacked this element of moral power — the sympathy that embraces the guilty and degraded. We have seen others enter the service, in whom this quality was the presiding spirit. Charged with pity for the miserable outcast, and yearning with tenderest solicitude for his recovery, they descend to his low level, and exhibit in his welfare an affectionate interest, and thus secure his confidence, until the sympathy becomes reciprocal, and the elevation mutual; as the humane sailor goes down for his drowning ship-mate, and feels after him in the mud and seaweed, until he finds him, and then, seizing each other with the death-grasp, they come up together.

This sympathy was one of the elements of the Saviour's moral power. He came to seek and to save the lost; and, understanding perfectly the philosophy of reform, he descended, and placed himself alongside of the lowliest of the race, and showed himself to be really what he was reproachfully styled, "a friend of publicans and sinners." And it was by means of this condescension, and this tender interest in their welfare, that he had such power over the multitude. "The common people heard him gladly."

Who are the men that accomplish the most for Zion's enlargement? Who but they whose souls are interpenetrated with the spirit of their enterprise — they in whose bosoms sympathy with man's recovery and eternal life is an all-absorbing, all-controlling passion? You see them at their work, and feel assured that they are not performing a heartless service. They labor not coldly or mechanically, but are in devout earnest, with all the soul alive, thrillingly sensitive to every thing that bears upon their object, and intent upon the salvation of as many as possible. Read the published sermons of Whitefield, and you see not there the secret of his wonderful efficiency. From the depth of his moral nature, there gushed a spirit of which language was never the medium — a spirit which not even he could transfer to the written or the printed page — a spirit which he threw, like net-work, over and around an audience, holding them as by enchantment, whilst he employed every faculty and affection in communicating to their hearts the benevolent pulsations of his own.

Yes, my brother, there is such a thing as a transfusion of that moral influence with which the holy man is endued by the grace of God. His sympathy with heaven connects him with the upper Reservoir of spiritual blessings; his sympathy with man connects him with the souls that fill the circle of his influence; and this double sympathy becomes a consecrated channel for the conveyance of the richest boon of heaven to the perishing of earth. We may not know how it was that the body of the dead man, when it touched the bones of the long buried prophet, revived and stood up animated, resuming life's functions and life's duties. But we do know, more than theoretically, that dead souls are quickened by a heavenly influence, of which Christian sympathy is the medium. Elisha sent his staff to be laid upon the face of the deceased child of the Shunamite, but the expedient failed. He must go and stretch *himself* upon the cold, pulseless frame, — eyes to eyes, mouth to mouth, hands to hands, — and then the flesh of the lad waxed warm, and the prophet delivered him alive to his mother.

The missionary who would be efficient, must have a sympathy as close and all-embracing. His object must be to save the souls of the people to whom he is sent, and, to accomplish this, he must throw around them his warm affections, and bring his living heart into contact with their dead hearts, and keep it there until they are resuscitated by the power of the Holy

Spirit, which worketh in him and through him mightily. In this way millions of the deadest of all beings, the dead in trespasses and sins, have been made alive.

4. *Strong faith.* Upon this principle, as an element of moral influence, the Saviour, when teaching his missionaries, constantly insisted; and he availed himself of every fitting occasion to summon it into lively exercise. If opportunity offered for the relief of suffering by miracle, he proposed to them the inquiry, "Believe ye that I am able to do this?" When his disciples, foiled in their attempt to expel a demon, asked him to explain the cause of their failure, he promptly replied, "Because of your unbelief." And how strongly did he assure them of the wonders which they might accomplish, if they only had "faith as a grain of mustard seed." The smallest conceivable quantity would increase their power; and every addition to their stock of faith, would be so much added to their moral resources, until the feeble should become as David, and David be endued with superhuman energy. Was it the language of hyperbole, or of sober truth, when Jesus said, "All things are possible to him that believeth?" And when he so frequently said to his candidates for missionary appointment, "According to your faith be it unto you," what did he intend them to understand, but that the amount of their faith should be the measure of their success?

Every man is endowed by his Creator, with a certain amount of physical ability, a portion of which is available on all occasions that may require it, while the remainder is intended only for special exigencies. When circumstances demand, he can draw upon this reserved fund, and thus accomplish what would otherwise be impracticable. Let his house take fire, and he will lift and bear away burdens with a facility that astonishes himself.

Much of the mind's energy lies retired, as reserved capital, to be employed only in extraordinary emergencies. Faith is the principle that has access to this private fund, and whose draft upon it is never dishonored; and, therefore, faith increases the *available*, if not the *actual*, power of the soul. He who believes a thing can be done, is generally the man to do it, for he is under the influence of a principle that calls forth the latent ability, and enables him to achieve results, which, without faith, would be impracticable. In all the camp of Saul, there was not a veteran who could safely have encountered the champion of Philistia, for not a man of the host had faith in God sufficient to brace up his courage and nerve his right arm for the conflict. Such faith was found only in the youthful shepherd; and as he believed, so he proceeded. His confidence lifted him above the fear of peril that made the sternest warriors quake, and called forth all his inward energies to one sublime effort; and the headless trunk of his antagonist soon lay stretched in the valley which had rung with his boastings.

Sacred history is, to a large extent, a record of the achievements of faith. In the eleventh chapter of the Epistle to the Hebrews, we have a summary and graphic sketch of the cases mentioned in the inspired narratives, which no one can read without the conviction that the writer regarded faith as an element of power. He understood perfectly well that incredulity benumbs and paralyzes the soul, cutting its very sinews, and laying it prostrate, helpless, strengthless. He also knew, by what he had seen and felt, that faith gives to the mind nerve, elasticity, steadiness, and right onward force. "This is the victory that overcometh the world, even your faith."

There is something in the confidence that we do not stand alone, but are befriended and succored by another and mightier, that gives determination and vigor to the soul. A Puritan writer has quaintly said, that, "If a man meet a dog alone, the dog is fearful, though ever so fierce by nature; but if the dog have his master with him, he will out upon that man from whom he fled before." And hence he reasons, that if lower natures, when backed by higher, increase in courage and energy, certainly man, backed by Omnipotence, is a kind of omnipotent creature. A timid child, in company with his father, so long as he feels the warm pressure of the paternal hand, will walk unanxious by night through pathless forests, or on the beetling precipice. So the servant of God, with simple reliance upon a promising Father, will fearlessly press his way through difficulties and dangers the most appalling. Though called to walk through the valley across which death has thrown his gloomiest shadow, he triumphantly says, "I will fear no evil, for thou art with me."

In the world's transactions, faith is important to efficiency. Weaken it, and you enfeeble the springs of secular enterprise. Destroy it, and you unnerve the community. Quite as indispensable is it in the cause of missions, which is pre-eminently a "work of faith," and of faith of the highest order. What could the first preachers of Christianity have accomplished without it? What but confidence in their Master's promise and presence could have given them such heroic boldness, such indomitable courage, such unfaltering perseverance, such power of endurance? Sustained by it, they did and suffered what impostors never could have done and suffered. They were "men that hazarded their lives for the name of the Lord Jesus," and the assurance, ever fresh in their recollection, " Lo, I am with you alway, even unto the end," was their unfailing support. They believed that the world could be and would be converted to Christ, and this faith rendered them bold and energetic as agents in the difficult service. They made no experiments. They proceeded not upon probabilities, but upon certainties; and confidence in the promises made them strong, so that "with great power gave they witness," and thrones trembled, and idols tumbled, and truth and holiness were welcomed by a subjugated world.

When faith is really brought into action, the magnitude of an obstacle, even were it increased a hundred fold, is a matter of little moment. "Difficulties heaped upon difficulties can never rise to the level of the promise of God;" and, formidable as they may appear, the power of faith brings in the divine sufficiency, and we overcome them with ready facility. "In the history of the heroes of this world," says Dr. Merle D'Aubigné, — " of such men as Charles XII., or Napoleon, — there is always a critical moment which shapes their career and insures their future glory; it is that in which a consciousness of their own strength is suddenly imparted to them. And a moment not less decisive than this, though stamped with an impress *altogether different,* is to be found in the life of every heroic servant of God; — it is that moment in which he first recognizes his absolute helplessness and nothingness: then it is that the strength of God is communicated to him from on high." * There is a link which connects the impotence of the creature with the omnipotence of Jehovah, so that the creature is encouraged to attempt the greatest things, while conscious of personal inability to do the least things. A weak faith lays hold of a strong Christ; and, lying low and looking high, the believer declares, "when I am weak, then am I strong." Thus allied to the mighty,

---

* Hist. of the Reformation, Vol. ii. p. 327.

he is endued with power; and he can meet unmoved the shock of any trial; for, as Leighton well says, "The firmest thing in this lower world is a believing soul;" and he can execute any service, however difficult, for his faith enables him to feel and say, "I can do all things through Christ, who strengtheneth me." What can interfere with the efficiency of him who goes forth to publish salvation, obeying his Saviour's command, trusting his Saviour's promise, favored with his Saviour's presence? Intimidated by no opposition, discouraged by no perplexities, he presses forward to the achievement of his purpose, winning a revolted world to Christ by the attractions of the cross.

5. *An affectionate spirit.* Need I multiply proofs that love is power? What is the efficiency of God's moral government, but the efficiency of love? Wherein consists the energy of the cross, if not in the matchless love which it develops? What is a Christian but a living witness to the all-subduing efficacy of love, overcoming, as it has, the spirit of rebellion, reconciling the alienated heart, reforming the wayward conduct, and giving to the soul a heavenward tendency? And what is the song of the redeemed in glory, but a grateful recognition of their indebtedness to One who loved them, and proved the strength of his love by giving himself for them, and washing them in his blood — the blood of Love?

Love is the grand distinctive quality of the Christian system, and especially of its ministry, which is eminently the "ministry of reconciliation." And this is the quality which, above all others, should pervade the tone of the ministry both at home and abroad. The cause of truth may be weakened by a false manifestation of its spirit, as well as by an inaccurate exhibition of its principles. The temper of the ministry is quite as important as its matter; and a primitive missionary assures us, in his own case, that if he were to "speak with the tongues of men and of angels," yet without love, his message would be destitute of music, — harsh, dissonant, and repulsive. The heathen sophists insisted upon kindness in an orator as indispensable to success; and one of them illustrates the sentiment by reference to the fabulous stories of Amphion and Orpheus, the moral of which, he thinks, teaches the extraordinary power of the tender and the affectionate over insensible and unyielding hearts. Homer introduces his hoary Nestor pleading in the most gentle, insinuating strain, and thus prevailing where threats and steel were ineffectual. We find it true in civilized lands, and it is quite as true of the barbarous and savage, that men do not open their hearts to the preacher, unless the tone of his instructions, and his whole manner have impressed them with the conviction that he sincerely regards their best interests. The spirit of depravity rouses itself to resist and resent whatever is harsh and denunciatory.

"Leviathan is not so tamed."

But where love is the presiding spirit — love, that sympathizes, on the one hand, with the cross of Christ, and, on the other, with man's degradation and doom, there is power that disarms prejudice, conciliates affection, and conquers the heart. We wonder not at the success of the apostle Paul, when we read that he ceased not to warn the people "night and day with tears." We are not surprised at the efficiency of another man of God who seldom addressed sinners without an overflow of tender emotion, and whom we hear saying, "You blame me for weeping, but how can I help it, when you will not weep for yourselves, though your immortal souls are upon the verge of destruction, and for aught you know you are hearing your last sermon, and may never have another opportunity to have Christ offered to you." It has been said of another, that, when warning the impenitent of their danger, and inviting them to the gracious Saviour, he was often so overcome by the gush of his feelings as to be unable to proceed — a testimony far more creditable than any applause for originality, taste or genius. "I have not wept but once these forty years," said a veteran military officer, "and that was when I heard Jesse Bushyhead, the Cherokee preacher, address his countrymen from the parable of the prodigal son, the tears flowing faster than he could wipe them away." Love is the key to the human soul, and he who takes it with him, may go to any part of the world, and gain access to hearts, and open the most secret doors, and walk unforbidden through every chamber of the moral nature. When the infuriated Seminoles attacked a settlement, butchering, scalping, burning, whom did they spare — whom but a family which they recognized as the friends of the red man, residing there in the self-denying spirit and practice of Christian missionaries?

LOVE IS POWER; for it renders the servant of God gentle, tender, earnest, persuasive. His manner is winning, and his spirit melting. The smile of heaven plays upon his features, and the tones and inflexions of his voice approach nearer to the angelic than the human. More than gratuitous would it be in him to assure his hearers that he loves them, and desires their salvation. The fountain of tears unsealed and gushing, the quivering lip, the tremulous voice, the heaving bosom, are proofs which the stupidest pagan would interpret more easily than a thousand professions and protestations. It may sometimes be necessary for him to declare most awful and terrific truths, but he does it with holy tenderness, mingling no wrath of his own with the wrath of God. The meek, the gentle Redeemer foretold, with all plainness, the doom of the wicked, and pronounced wo! wo! wo! until he could utter it no longer, and his pent-up compassions then burst forth like a flood — "O Jerusalem! Jerusalem!" Powerful, irresistible is he who is baptized into the affectionate spirit of Jesus. His words, bathed in his heart's sensibility, soften whatever they touch, and souls, hard and cold as the Alpine glacier, melt under their influence like snow in a summer sun.

Such, brethren, are some of the elements of that power with which it is desirable the Christian missionary should be endued. The whole of these combined, in due proportion, make up a strong character, which wants little else than a physical frame of corresponding strength, to complete the sum of missionary excellence. Happy for the heathen, happy for the interests of Christianity, when the missionary field shall be supplied with laborers who possess the intellectual and moral power required by so grand an enterprise. Some such are already there, and in the character of their labors, and the measure of their efficiency, we perceive not only occasion for devout gratitude to God, but the most valid reasons for the prayer from the church universal — Lord, multiply them a thousand fold.

THE END.

Other Solid Ground Titles

THE COMMUNICANT'S COMPANION by *Matthew Henry*
THE SECRET OF COMMUNION WITH GOD by *Matthew Henry*
THE MOTHER AT HOME by *John S.C. Abbott*
LECTURES ON THE ACTS OF THE APOSTLES *by John Dick*
THE FORGOTTEN HEROES OF LIBERTY by *J.T. Headley*
LET THE CANNON BLAZE AWAY by *Joseph P. Thompson*
THE STILL HOUR: *Communion with God in Prayer* by *Austin Phelps*
COLLECTED WORKS of James Henley Thornwell (4 vols.)
CALVINISM IN HISTORY *by Nathaniel S. McFetridge*
OPENING SCRIPTURE: *Hermeneutical Manual* by *Patrick Fairbairn*
THE ASSURANCE OF FAITH *by Louis Berkhof*
THE PASTOR IN THE SICK ROOM *by John D. Wells*
THE BUNYAN OF BROOKLYN: *Life & Sermons of I.S. Spencer*
THE NATIONAL PREACHER: *Sermons from 2nd Great Awakening*
FIRST THINGS: *First Lessons God Taught Mankind* Gardiner Spring
BIBLICAL & THEOLOGICAL STUDIES *by 1912 Faculty of Princeton*
THE POWER OF GOD UNTO SALVATION *by B.B. Warfield*
THE LORD OF GLORY *by B.B. Warfield*
A GENTLEMAN & A SCHOLAR: **Memoir of J.P. Boyce** *by J. Broadus*
SERMONS TO THE NATURAL MAN *by W.G.T. Shedd*
SERMONS TO THE SPIRITUAL MAN *by W.G.T. Shedd*
HOMILETICS AND PASTORAL THEOLOGY *by W.G.T. Shedd*
A PASTOR'S SKETCHES 1 & 2 *by Ichabod S. Spencer*
THE PREACHER AND HIS MODELS *by James Stalker*
IMAGO CHRISTI: *The Example of Jesus Christ* by *James Stalker*
LECTURES ON THE HISTORY OF PREACHING *by J. A. Broadus*
THE SHORTER CATECHISM ILLUSTRATED *by John Whitecross*
THE CHURCH MEMBER'S GUIDE *by John Angell James*
THE SUNDAY SCHOOL TEACHER'S GUIDE *by John A. James*
CHRIST IN SONG: *Hymns of Immanuel from All Ages* by *Philip Schaff*
DEVOTIONAL LIFE OF THE S.S. TEACHER *by J.R. Miller*

Call us Toll Free at 1-877-666-9469
Send us an e-mail at sgcb@charter.net
Visit us on line at solid-ground-books.com
Uncovering Buried Treasure to the Glory of God

www.ingramcontent.com/pod-product-compliance
Lightning Source LLC
Chambersburg PA
CBHW020350170426
43200CB00005B/117